LIVING INSIDE OUT

LIVING INSIDE OUT

HOW AND WHY THE HEART DEFINES THE CHRISTIAN

IMITATING THE APOSTLES, PROPHETS, AND THE FAITHFUL
THROUGH THE AGES

GERALD A. HAYNES

XULON PRESS

Xulon Press Elite
2301 Lucien Way #415
Maitland, FL 32751
407.339.4217
www.xulonpress.com

© 2023 by Gerald A. Haynes

Edited by: Stephen Gannon

All rights reserved solely by the author. The author guarantees all contents are original and do not infringe upon the legal rights of any other person or work. No part of this book may be reproduced in any form without the permission of the author.

Due to the changing nature of the Internet, if there are any web addresses, links, or URLs included in this manuscript, these may have been altered and may no longer be accessible. The views and opinions shared in this book belong solely to the author and do not necessarily reflect those of the publisher. The publisher therefore disclaims responsibility for the views or opinions expressed within the work.

Unless otherwise indicated, Scripture quotations taken from the New American Standard Bible (NASB). Copyright © 1960, 1962, 1963, 1968, 1971, 1972, 1973, 1975, 1977, 1995 by The Lockman Foundation. Used by permission. All rights reserved.

Paperback ISBN-13: 978-1-66286-987-7
Hard Cover ISBN-13: 978-1-66286-988-4
Ebook ISBN-13: 978-1-66286-989-1

ABSTRACT

God is concerned about spirituality, while humans are concerned with tools, techniques, and resources to perfect Spirituality. God has chosen Spirituality as His tool, technique, and resource to perfect mankind. This book provides valuable insights into understanding spirituality from God's perspective. This is important because spirituality begins internally and proceeds externally—it begins from the heart.

Many Christians are distracted and consumed by outward activities, ministries, and techniques, so much so that true Spirituality is neglected—it is buried in the chaos of doing. Many Christians are exhausted, defeated, feeling that they never measure up and aching for a reality they know exists but seems just out of reach, and sometimes . . . hopelessly elusive. When Christians lose hope, they despair of life—precisely the opposite of what God has intended.

Despite the past 2,000 years of cultural diversity, denominational differences, and varying understandings of spirituality, there remains a remarkable consensus regarding the essentials of the Christian life. Though particular activities characterize the faithful they are inadequate to define them. It is the new heart characterized by love, humility, holiness/obedience, and faith produced by the indwelling Holy spirit which defines spirituality. External disciplines or devotion to Scripture, Prayer,

Living Inside Out

Fellowship and Communion/worship are visible marks, which in turn, nourish the internals. The external activities are inter-related and characterize the church over different periods. The internals of the heart are not only interrelated but in fact, interdependent.

The book can be divided into two Sections. Section 1 examines the relationship between Love, Humility, Holiness, and Faith. Section 2 explores the exercise of these internal qualities through prayer, devotion to the scriptures, fellowship, and The Lords Supper or Communion as rooted in the Passover. Each subject is examined in the context of Biblical theology, and Church History. In some chapters multiple historical periods or individuals are contrasted while in others a particular individual predominates. The result is a manual of spirituality suitable for all Christians with footnotes and resources for Pastors and teachers.

Preface - Acknowledgments

Christian Spirituality is intangible, yet we are constantly looking for someone to make it tangible—to put recognizable handles on it—to show us the way. Paul wrote to the Philippians enjoining them to imitate his life and those who walked according to his example or pattern (Phil 3:17). He wrote the same to the Corinthians: "Be imitators of me" twice in the same book (1Cor 4:16, 11:1), and sent Timothy to remind them of his ways in Christ, "as I teach everywhere in every place" (4:17). Paul's claim was not to perfection but direction. He wrote, "Not that I have attained ...but I press on" (Phil 3:12-14); "Be followers of me as I am of Christ" (1Cor11:1). So where are the models today?

This work has come about in part as the result of my own quest for models of true spirituality and my desire to follow in their footsteps. Herschel Martindale, now with the Lord, was "one who walked according to the pattern" Phil 3:17. Herschel challenged me along with a group of university students to list fifty key topics in the scriptures we might use in disciple-making. When we returned to compare our results, he instructed us to mix and match—then cut the list to twenty-five. Finally, he encouraged us to choose the ten most important topics from our lists. Every list was unique, but as you might expect, there were many similarities.

Living Inside Out

I kept my lists—the fifty, the twenty-five, and the ten. I noted that some key topics were internal, they referred to that which we ARE as Christians. Other key topics were external and related to that which we DO as believers. It was clear to me that these internal and external topics were interrelated. I quickly realized that these were not simply topics for study, but priorities for life. I later discovered these internals and externals have characterized the leaders and movements of spiritual renewal and reform over the centuries.

Early in my journey the subjects seemed complex, but now, though I see the complexity of their interrelated operation, I also see a profound simplicity at their core: at the heart of spirituality is—the heart. We are not merely imitators of Christ, but children of God, new creations, given clean hearts, born of the Spirit, those transformed by the renewing of our minds. The scriptures illustrate the process in metaphors and in history; but at the heart of Spirituality, is always the heart. We are changed yet changing. At times though, the process seems to be going backwards—we stumble, we fail, we despair of life only to discover anew the grace of God.

It was with these thoughts in my mind, that early in my Christian life, I was gripped with the story of a promising young man. Moses, born in the most powerful nation in the world, educated in the court of kings, groomed for leadership only to lose it all in a moment. In an action to protect an innocent victim, he assumed would be appreciated, he was suddenly alienated from his people, his power, his wealth, and his dreams—set aside to serve God. Friends, those knock-down life experiences happen to us all.

At forty years of age, Moses found himself caring for sheep in the desert, probably wondering how he could have been so wrong and what he could have been had he chosen differently? Moses came upon a "wondrous sight": a bush that burned yet was not consumed. One cannot help but ask, "Did he see in the bush a power he had not seen in his own life?" He had burned in zeal for what he thought was right—what he thought was God's will but had burned out in a moment and amounted only to a heap of ashes.

Now here was a bush which burned yet was not consumed, "a wondrous sight." Then suddenly out of the midst of the bush God spoke! "Take off your shoes for the place you are standing is holy ground." It was holy because God was there. The bush could burn yet not be consumed because God was there, not because it was any different than any other bush. God in its midst made it a "wondrous sight."

Any old bush would have done, and so it is with men. When God is in them, they become amazing sights. The Lord spoke and commissioned Moses to deliver his people and lead them to the Promised Land....Oh yes, and He promised him, "I will be with you." And that made all the difference. Before Moses had gone in his own strength; now he would go in the strength of the Lord.

Certain specific characteristics about the heart of Moses are recorded in scriptures. They are the same characteristics we observe in all those who "catch fire" so to speak. It is obvious that we cannot produce these characteristics any more than Moses could, or, for that matter, more than the bush could cause itself to burn without being consumed. They are all results of God's indwelling power. He fills empty vessels; He gives life to dry bones; and He saves those who call on Him. Our greatest work is to recognize His priorities and look to Him to produce in us that wondrous sight which constitutes the Glory of the living God shining out from his people. It is the looking, the confident expectation, the faith, the longing after Him which characterizes the one heart God seeks.

I have seen hundreds of "earthen vessels" who have revealed the glory of God, some of whom deserve special thanks: first, Billie and Marilyn Parker, who opened their home and their hearts, their wallets, their cars, and refrigerator, their mornings, and sometimes their very late evenings, to me and countless other students like me, who discovered Jesus in their lives. I thank God for men like Darrell Valdois, a Navigator who rose early enough, not for a few months but for five years to pick me up, lead a 6:30 AM Bible study for a small group of young men, provide doughnuts, get us to school on time, and then take us mountain climbing on the weekends.

There have been men like Ron Bennett, Larry Shaw, Jim Wright, and Alex Strauch who spent years counseling and teaching me. I am thankful for men like Jim and Bill McCotter and Herschel Martindale, who modeled and instilled the vision of the Great Commission. Special thanks to the entire congregation of Princeton Bible Church who loved and encouraged me over 20 years of ministry. I am thankful too to all those friends and co-workers in the kingdom who delight to contribute behind the scenes, for example, long-time friends like Bill Hollis who assisted with graphics and Steve Gannon, a troubled teen I met in high school who gave his life to Christ and whom God eventually placed as the Southern California Regional Manager of EMF Broadcasting (K-LOVE and Air1 radio). It was Steve who edited this final work of "Living Inside Out" as it appears today.

A second group of teachers deserve special thanks for giving me the tools to pursue these studies and produce this

Preface - Acknowledgments

work: Dr. Tim Crawford, Dr. Tim Laniak, Dr. Mike Palmer, Dr. Bob Mayer, and especially Dr. Garth Rosell who has made Church History such a delightful and enriching part of my life. Without your help and encouragement this work could never have achieved the breadth it has taken.

Lastly and most importantly, this work would not exist without the tireless sacrifice and encouragement of my wife Cathy and my mother Georgene. As my wife has often observed, my mother has always believed in me. Similarly, my wife Cathy has been an enduring example of service and personal discipline. My wife first encouraged me to pursue post graduate studies and not only transcribed, but edited the original doctoral thesis, supplying countless references, missing page numbers, misplaced punctuation, ad infinitum. I cannot say it better than the proverb, "A virtuous woman who can find, her treasure is far above rubies... the heart of her husband safely trusts in her."

Dedicated to the one I love, my wife Cathy—a true
Proverbs 31 woman.

Life is like a box of chocolates...it's what's on the inside that
a person loves or hates! Make sure the "inside" is what you
desire for your spiritual walk.

TABLE OF CONTENTS

Chapter 1   Introduction, Internals And Externals 1

SECTION I

Chapter 2   Defining Love, The Most Important Thing . . . 21

Chapter 3   Discovering Humility, Prerequisite For

Guidance 45

Chapter 4   Discerning Holiness, Obedience 63

Chapter 5   Delivering Faith, The Mystery 85

SECTION I

Chapter 6   The Apostle's Doctrine, The Word Of God . . .115

Chapter 7   Fellowship, Partnership With

God And Man 136

Chapter 8   Communion, Sharing In Life And Death . . 154

Chapter 9   Prayer, Communication With God 184

Chapter 10 Living Inside Out, Conclusion 212

CHAPTER 1

INTRODUCTION, INTERNALS AND EXTERNALS

As Christians, we are more than the sum of our parts, ...and much more than the sum of our activities. Life is more than what we do. While spirituality may be intangible to us, we are constantly looking for living examples. The need for models of spirituality has plagued the Church since its birth. Jesus commanded his disciples to make disciples, baptizing them and teaching them to do all that he commanded, ...and His very last command was—to make disciples. Disciples make disciples.

The word disciple means learner or follower and occurs throughout the gospels and in the first chapters of Acts. Then at Antioch the disciples are given the derisive title "Christian" (Acts 11:26). Shortly the disciples came to love the name

> The disciples suffered and died for His cause because they were transformed from, you guessed it, the inside out.

because it captures the fact that Christ's followers follow because Christ lives in them. The disciples suffered and died for His cause because they were transformed from, you guessed it, the inside out. This transformation produces a characteristic lifestyle or pattern, we sometimes call this discipleship.

Paul wrote to the Philippians enjoining them to imitate his life, "Brothers and sisters, join in following my example, and observe those who walk according to the pattern you have in us." (Phil 3:17)[1]. He wrote the same to the Corinthians: "Be imitators of me" twice in the same book (1Cor 4:16, 11:1), and sent Timothy to remind them of his "ways in Christ, as I teach everywhere in every place" (4:17). This "pattern" is the only thing Paul teaches everywhere in every place he goes. Most believers and Christian leaders are acutely aware of their short-comings and loath to use themselves as walking examples of how to live. But to those humble leaders, Paul's exhortation was not to perfection but direction. He wrote, "Not that I have attained ...but I press on" (Phil 3:12-14); "Be followers of me as I am of Christ" (1Cor11:1).

'The most important thing in analyzing how we should live as believers is that the most important thing remains the most important thing. Failure in the Christian life may often be traced to a believer allowing the urgent or the pressing to usurp the position of the essential. The most important things in the Christian life may be buried in the dust of good, or even useless activity. Important things compete for our attention and com-mitment, and we must prioritize our Christian focus. In making decisions, the most important thing must first be identified then kept as the priority.

As Christians, we live from the inside out. The med-itations of our hearts

> The most important things in the Christian life may be buried in the dust of good, or even useless activity.

compel our being. Solomon wrote: "Keep your heart with all

diligence; for out of it spring the issues of life" (Prov 4:23 NKJV). External disciplines can never reform an evil heart. Bathing a pig will not make it a sheep. Teaching a criminal will only make him a smarter criminal—if his heart is not changed. By a miraculous act of creation God brings forth physical life, and through regeneration He brings forth spiritual life. But Christians are commanded to work out their salvation with fear and trembling knowing that it is God who is at work within them, "both to will and do of His good pleasure" (Phil 2:13 KJV).

What did Jesus, Paul, Timothy, and the leaders referred to above have in common? They had hearts filled with love for God and people, hearts humble before God seeking His will above all, hearts of faith which obey the promptings of his Holy Spirit. Though we speak of love, humility, faith, and holiness or obedience as distinct, we will see that they are in fact aspects of one heart, a heart that pleases God.

Just as there are four internal qualities that characterize the Christian, four external human activities marked the life of the early church: And they were continually devoting themselves to the apostles' teaching and to fellowship, to the breaking of bread and to prayer (Acts 2:42). These external priorities (apostle's teaching, fellowship, breaking of bread, and prayer), like the internals of the heart, may often be crowded out by both good and bad activities. As we examine the Scriptures and the life of the early church, we realize these externals not only demonstrate the reality of the internals, but they also nourish

> Though we speak of love, humility, faith, and holiness or obedience as distinct, we will see that they are in fact aspects of one heart, a heart that pleases God.

Living Inside Out

them. Apart from the miracle of new birth in Christ, they are merely religious activities, but when combined with the internals in the life of the believer, they define greatness in the Kingdom of God. Section one of this work examines the four internals and section two examines the four externals.

Section 1, The Four Internals — Love, Humility, Obedience, and Faith

Love

Jesus was once asked, "Teacher, which is the greatest commandment in the law" (Matt 22:36 NIV)? His response was immediate and straightforward. He said, "You shall love the Lord with all your heart, and with all your soul, and with all your mind. This is the great and foremost commandment" (Matt 22:38). He added, "The second is like it, you shall love your neighbor as yourself" (Matt 22:39), and concluded, "On these two commandments, depend the whole Law and the Prophets" (Matt 22:40). "Love is the great and foremost commandment" and everything else hangs on a believer's ability to love God and love people.

> "Love is the great and foremost commandment" and everything else hangs on a believer's ability to love God and love people.

Humility

On another occasion, Jesus taught, "Whoever then humbles himself as this child, he is the greatest in the Kingdom of Heaven" (Matt 18:4). Again, according to scripture, the greatest

Introduction, Internals And Externals

commandment is love, but the greatest individual is the Christian with the most humility. How are they linked? "The sacrifices of God are a broken spirit; a broken and a contrite heart, O God, you will not despise" (Ps 51:17). Just as all the law is fulfilled in the command to love, so the sacrifices under

> Just as all the law is fulfilled in the command to love, so the sacrifices under the law of God amounted to a broken and contrite heart.

the law of God amounted to a broken and contrite heart. Notice that sacrifices (plural) are a broken spirit (singular). A broken spirit is not a single isolated sacrifice. Today, all of a believer's sacrifices in life amount to a broken and contrite heart. "To him whose mind is humble, scripture recognizes it as though he were to bring all offerings at once."[2]

Micah's definition of the good that is required by God, ties together the commitments to justice, mercy, and humility. "He has told you O man what is good and what does the Lord require of you, but to do justice, to love kindness, and to walk humbly with your God?" (Mic 6:8).

Justice and insight are a natural outworking of the spiritual believer because God "leads the humble in justice and teaches the humble His way" (Ps 25:9). Justice or righteousness in the New Testament is revealed to be an obedience of faith. Loving kindness and humility complete Micah's definition of the good. Chapter three examines the priority of humility and its interaction with faith and love.

Living Inside Out

Obedience

"Whoever therefore shall break one of these least Commandments and shall teach man, so he shall be called the least in the kingdom of heaven. And whoever shall do and teach them the same shall be called great in the Kingdom of Heaven" (Matt 5:19 KJV). Jesus does not call the one who is obedient the greatest in the kingdom, but the one who is disobedient is called the least. When the disciples ask him about the greatest, He responds by saying, "But the greatest among you shall be your servant. And whoever exalts himself shall be humbled; and whoever humbles himself shall be exalted" (Matt 23:11-12).

> Jesus does not call the one who is obedient the greatest in the kingdom, but the one who is disobedient is called the least.

Interestingly, the humble and contrite of spirit are those who tremble at the word of God. The implication is that they tremble and obey. "But to this one I will look, to him who is humble and contrite of spirit, and who trembles at My word." (Isa 66:1-2) According to scripture, the spiritual believer does not take God's Word or God's Commandments lightly. In the same way, those who fail to tremble at God's Word are proud, self-sufficient, and disobedient. According to scripture, they are the least in the kingdom of God.

> Obedience, then, is not a matter of one or two actions. It is a matter of being led by the Spirit in a life of faith.

Obedience is not external conformity but internal conformity. It is "not of the letter but the spirit."[3]

Introduction, Internals And Externals

Obedience is living from the inside out! Jeremiah prophecies that under a New Covenant, the Law of God will be "written on the heart" (Jer 31:33). If we are led by the Spirit, we are not under the law but having life from the Spirit we are to walk, or act, according to the leading of the Spirit (Gal 5:18, 25). Obedience, then, is not a matter of one or two actions. It is a matter of being led by the Spirit in a life of faith.

The process by which this occurs involves both the Spirit and the believer. The fact that we are commanded to "imitate" addresses our responsibility. Peter commands believers to apply all diligence in adding the qualities of Christ-likeness: "Now for this very reason also, applying all diligence, in your faith supply moral excellence, and in your moral excellence, knowledge, and in your knowledge, self-control,

> We must cultivate a heart of love, humility, and obedience. This is a process of transformation which begins from the inside and emanates inside outward.

and in your self-control, perseverance, and in your perseverance, godliness, and in [your] godliness, brotherly kindness, and in your brotherly kindness, love. For if these qualities are yours and are increasing, they render you neither useless not unfruitful in the true knowledge of our Lord Jesus Christ. For he who lacks these qualities is blind or short-sighted, having forgotten his purification from his former sins. Therefore, brethren, be all the more diligent to make certain about His calling and choosing you; for as long as you practice these things, you will never stumble" (2 Pet 1:5-10).

We must cultivate a heart of love, humility, and obedience. This is a process of transformation which begins from the inside and emanates inside outward. The Spirit of Christ is prompting

Living Inside Out

and empowering us in this process, but to obey it is our individual responsibility. This obedience from the heart is often termed "sanctification" or "holiness". The book of Leviticus is taken up with the theme of holiness in terms of obedience to Gods Law. "Sanctify yourselves therefore and be ye holy: for I am the Lord your God. And ye shall keep my statutes and do them: I am the Lord which sanctifies you" (Lev 20:7-8 KJV).

Here the joint responsibility is clear as well as the mechanism. God works and man works. God sanctifies Israel by giving her His law. She sanctifies herself by obeying that law. Under the Old Covenant, obedience was not separated from love but was to be motivated by love. Therefore, thou shalt love the Lord thy God, and keep his charge, and his statutes, and his judgments, and his commandments, always. (Deu 11:1 KJV)

Under the New Covenant we are sanctified not only by the Law but by the indwelling Spirit who empowers us to love and obey. The New Covenant is the fulfillment of God's desire for a right heart. "O that there were such a heart in them, that they would fear me, and keep all my commandments always, that it might be well with them, and with their children forever" (Deu 5:29 KJV). Even under the Old Covenant the responsibility for a right heart is laid upon the people in terms of a spiritual circumcision. "Circumcise your-selves to the Lord and remove the foreskins of your heart" (Jer 4:4). Love will grow

> Anything that prevents a heart from being sensitive to God's leading should be removed from the life of the believer.

as we humble ourselves before God acknowledging our desperate need for Him; as we believe that Christ has died for our sins, that He has been raised for our justification, that we have died and been resurrected with Him; and as we obey from the heart the

Introduction, Internals And Externals

promptings of the Holy Spirit. Anything that prevents a heart from being sensitive to God's leading should be removed from the life of the believer.

Faith

Saving faith[4] is valued by God precisely because it is inseparably linked to love, humility, and obedience. Different aspects of faith have been emphasized throughout history. One of the interesting problems in studying faith in the Old Testament is that it is not mentioned as such though it is clearly in evidence. We learn in Hebrews that it was by faith

> We would expect pride to be contrasted with humility, righteousness with unrighteousness, and faith with unbelief, but in this case—the heart of the proud is contrasted with the heart of the just who live by faith.

that Abel offered a more excellent offering, Enoch was translated, Noah built an ark, Abraham obeyed, Sarah conceived, and so on (Heb 11). But the word "faith" does not appear in the original stories! Faith is at the heart of each of these relationships since without it, it is impossible to please God. Twice in the book of Romans, faith is referred to as an act of obedience: Through whom we have received grace and apostleship to bring about the obedience of faith among all the Gentiles, for His name's sake (Rom.1:5). But now is manifested, and by the Scriptures of the prophets, according to the commandment of the eternal God, has been made known to all the nations, leading to obedience of faith. (Rom 16:26)

Habakkuk, who prophesied at the time of the Babylonian invasion of Israel, is sometimes called the philosopher prophet because he struggles with the great philosophical question: "Why art Thou

Living Inside Out

silent when the wicked swallow up those more righteous than they?" (Hab1:13). From Habakkuk's perspective, though Israel is not perfect, she is more righteous than her Babylonian conquerors. He brings his complaint to the Lord and awaits a reply. God answers with a call for faith as He works His sovereign plan of judgment and deliverance. He will use the Babylonians but will certainly judge them as well.

The call for faith is couched in a revealing dichotomy: "As for the proud, his heart is not right within him, but the righteous will live by faith" (Hab2:4). We would expect pride to be contrasted with humility, righteousness with unrighteousness, and faith with unbelief, but in this case—the heart of the proud is contrasted with the heart of the just who live by faith. Today the link between righteousness and faith is cemented in the minds of Christians because the second half of the passage is quoted three times in the New Testament and taken up as the watchword of the Protestant reformation. "The just shall live by faith!"

Entrance into the Kingdom is by faith alone. The humble childlike faith that Jesus contrasts with the proud controlling spirit of the world reaffirms the scriptural dichotomy between faith and pride. In the world the kings of the earth lord over their subjects, but it is not so in the Kingdom of God. While the proud heart is not right with God, the humble heart believes, trusts, and relies on God. It is the humble who live by faith. They are the righteous, childlike members of the Kingdom of God.

> While the proud heart is not right with God, the humble heart believes, trusts, and relies on God. It is the humble who live by faith.

Zephaniah echoes this sentiment saying: Seek the LORD, all you humble of the earth. Who have carried out His ordinances;

Introduction, Internals And Externals

seek righteousness; seek humility" (Zep 2:3). I will remove from your midst your proudly exultant ones...but I will leave in your midst a people humble and lowly. They shall seek refuge (trust) in the name of the Lord. (3:11-12)

Faith is graphically portrayed by the image of sheep "grazing and lying down with none to make them afraid" (Zep 3:13 KJV). Jesus said, "Whoever then humbles himself as this child, he is the greatest in the Kingdom of Heaven" (Matt 18:4). Why is humility of such value in God's eyes? "Behold, as for the proud one, His soul is not right within him; but the righteous will live by his faith" (Hab 2:4). Pride is the opposite of being right with God and living by faith.

As Luther points out; "humility is the essence of faith."[5]

Just as Love is an essential attribute of God, humility is a defining attribute of humanity in right relationship to God on the same level as faith. The publican who humbly made his plea for God's mercy went to his home justified (Luke 18:14), a con-

> When a child obeys but does not love or trust—it is cause for concern. A profession of love without obedience would be equally troubling.

dition possible only through faith. Faith is dependent upon love, humility, and obedience. "Faith works through love" (Gal 5:6).

The interdependence of these qualities may be demonstrated in our expectations of our children. What does a parent want from a child? Most of all, parents hope for love, obedience, trust, and a degree of humility. When a child obeys but does not love or trust—it is cause for concern. A profession of love without obedience would be equally troubling. The possibility of any one of the four in the absence of the others is difficult to picture. These four qualities are aspects of one character, the character of a Christian.

Living Inside Out

Together they define greatness in God's eyes. "The greatest is love" (1Cor 13:13, Matt 22:36). "He who humbles himself will be greatest in the Kingdom of God" (Matt 18:4). The one who teaches and does these things will be called great (as opposed to least) in the Kingdom of God (Matt 5:19).

How can these all be the greatest unless they are intimately connected? They represent aspects of one character. "Without faith it is impossible to please Him" (Heb 11:6). We cannot even begin to talk about greatness without faith. Since they are all interdependent, as one grows so do the others; and to the extent that one is missing, so are the others. Far from being able to judge another's heart we are unable to judge even our own hearts. The general direction for our behavior is outlined in Malachi, "to do justly, to love mercy, and to walk humbly with God" (Mic 6:8 KJV). This is the same message at the heart of the Mosaic Law (Deu 11:1, 3, 18-22), embodied in Christ (John 13:12-17), and imitated and enjoined by Paul (Phil. 4:9). "If we live in," or have our realm of being in the Spirit; "let us walk in the spirit."[6]

Though the inner being is spiritually minded there must be an intentional engagement with time and space. The walk must be walked externally, 'with our feet on the ground' so to speak. Life is an observable righteousness. Section two takes up four basic external activities that reveal the condition of the heart and the real presence of love, humility, faith, and obedience. They are the activities to which the early church devoted itself as listed in Acts 2:42.

Section 2, The Four Externals — Apostles Teaching, Fellowship, Breaking of Bread, and Prayer

Acts 2:42-47 may be seen as a snapshot of the early church: "And they were continually devoting themselves to the apostles'

Introduction, Internals And Externals

teaching and to fellowship, to the breaking of bread and to prayer. And everyone kept feeling a sense of awe; and many wonders and signs were taking place through the apostles. And all those who had believed were together and had all things in common;

> This is the defining statement of life in the earliest church. They devoted themselves to four activities: the apostles teaching, fellowship, breaking of bread, and prayer.

and they began selling their property and possessions, and were sharing them with all, as anyone might have need. And day by day continuing with one mind in the temple, and breaking bread from house to house, they were taking their meals together with gladness and sincerity of heart, praising God, and having favor with all the people. And the Lord was adding to their number day by day those who were being saved."

This is the defining statement of life in the earliest church. They devoted themselves to four activities: the apostles teaching, fellowship, breaking of bread, and prayer.

- The Apostles teaching is contained not only in the New Testament Epistles and the Gospels but includes their commitment to the Old Testament as well.

- Fellowship in its original context involved a partnership or sharing in an endeavor which involved all that an individual brought to the table.[7]

It would include the use of our time, talents, and treasures in a sacrificial communion.

Living Inside Out

- The Breaking of Bread is not simply a meal, but a reference to the ordinance of worship imbedded in the Jewish Passover and reinstituted at the Last Supper in such a way as to join Jew and Gentile into one body in Christ and create a foundation for worship in the Church, the body of Christ, the Assembly of the Firstborn, The Israel of God.

- Finally, a devotion to prayer, both personal and corporate, will characterize the true Christian.

The second half of this work considers how each of these external activities are energized by the internals of the heart, and in turn, these externals nourish the internals.

The Apostles Teaching (Scripture)

Devotion to the Apostles Doctrine or the Word of God springs first from a love for God: "If you love me you will keep my commandments" (John 14:15); second from humility: "To this one I will look, to the one who is humble and contrite of spirit and who trembles at my word" (Isa 66:2); from obedience of heart: "Oh that there were such a heart in them, that they would fear me and keep all my commandments always" (Deu 5:29), and faith: referring specifically to the Apostles doctrine Paul writes, "We also believe and so we also speak" (2Cor 4:13). The priority of the Scriptures in the life of the church has commonly marked its vitality whereas its neglect has marked its demise.

> The priority of the Scriptures in the life of the church has commonly marked its vitality whereas its neglect has marked its demise.

Introduction, Internals And Externals

If the Great Commandment embodies the Old Covenant; the Great Commission may be seen to embody the New. It mandates that all of Christ's disciples make disciples of all nations teaching them to observe all that he has commanded. The Doctrine of the Apostles reiterates the teachings of Jesus. The proclamation of the Kingdom of God begins with the Gospels, the four portraits of the King, the founding of the church in the book of Acts, and the Epistles which address ongoing questions of the churches as they seek to fulfill the commission and record their teaching.

Fellowship

Fellowship, in the same way, will be seen to flow out of a heart of love, humility, obedience and faith: "If there is any encouragement in Christ, any comfort from love, any participation (koinonia-fellowship) in the spirit, any affec-

> The life worthy of the gospel of Christ is a life of unity, both in standing firm and striving side by side for the faith of the gospel.

tion and sympathy, complete my joy by being of the same mind and having the same love, being in full accord and of one mind. Do nothing from selfishness or conceit but in humility count others better than yourselves." (Phil 2:1-3 RSV) This passage summarizes the idea that external behavior is motivated by an inner work of the Holy Spirit which entails love and humility. Obedience appears later in verse 8. Christ's obedience is an act of faith in God's promise of exaltation in verses 9-11. The life worthy of the gospel of Christ is a life of unity, both in standing firm and striving side by side for the faith of the gospel. This striving "side by side" is a description of true fellowship, not a casual social interaction, but a costly endeavor which anticipates conflict.[8]

Living Inside Out

A life of fellowship is a life of engagement. It is sharing in conflict and in suffering. The conflict here results from the proclamation of the gospel. There is an anticipated rejection of this message, not a casual rejection but a violent rejection. Jesus was sent into a world which would reject and crucify Him. So, it was "granted to us, not only to believe, but also to suffer for His sake", we are engaged in conflict. Fellowship in this context is not a fringe benefit. As we share abundantly in Christ's sufferings, so we share abundantly in comfort (2Cor 1:7). Both these words "share", are from the root word koinonia.

In commenting on Acts 2:42, Bonhoeffer writes, "It is instructive to note that fellowship – koinonia- is mentioned between word and sacrament. This is no accident for fellowship always springs from the word and finds its goal and completion in the Lord's Supper. The whole common life of the Christian fellowship osculates between word and sacrament. It begins and ends in worship. It looks forward in expectation to the final banquet in the kingdom of God. When the community has such a source and goal it is a perfect communion of fellowship even material goods fall into their appointed place. In freedom, joy, and the power of the Holy Spirit a pattern of common life is produced where neither was there any among them that lacked."[9]

Breaking of Bread (Communion)

The taking of the bread and the cup was given a special significance when Jesus said, "this bread," which at the time of the first century not only reminded him of the manna from Heaven but also the Passover lamb itself.[10]

It was symbolic of His own body which was given for them. The cup of redemption–the third cup taken after the meal which

Introduction, Internals And Externals

spoke of the blood of the Passover lamb found its antitype in the blood of the Messiah. This was no mere addendum but a reinterpretation of crucial elements of the ancient Passover. It is no wonder then that early Christians continued to celebrate the Passover, and to see in it the fulfillment of a second Passover that delivered them not from bondage in Egypt but from bondage to the sin which enslaves not only the Jewish people but every human being.

Reference is made to crucial elements of the Passover throughout the New Testament. The Passover marks the beginning of the "new life, the new year" (Exo 12:2). Receiving of Messiah as Lord marks the beginning of a new life for every believer

> You are in fact unleavened.

(2 Cor. 5:17). Prior to the taking of the Passover meal the Jewish people were instructed to search their homes and to purge out the leaven (a type of sin) (Exo 12:15). Paul refers to this tradition he exhorts the Corinthians to a holy life. He writes, "You are in fact unleavened. Christ our Passover is sacrificed for us therefore let us keep the Feast not with the leaven of malice and wickedness but with the unleavened bread of sincerity and truth (1Cor 5:7-8)"

His reference is to the purging of the leaven at the Feast of Unleavened Bread which continues for seven days following the Feast of Passover. The leaven is purged prior to the evening of Passover and the people eat only unleavened bread for the following week. Paul takes this as a picture of the holiness of the Corinthian church extended to the church in general and challenges the church to a life of moral purity based upon this very ceremony which would have been common knowledge to not only the Jewish but also the Gentile church of the first century.

The lamb slain for the first born in Exodus 12:5-6 is a type of

Living Inside Out

Christ slain for each of us (2Cor 5:21).[11]

The blood of the lamb applied to the lentil and door post is a picture of the blood applied to our own heart. The feasting on the lamb in the house over which God hovers prefigures our abiding in Christ in John 15. Paul writes, "As often as we eat this bread and drink this cup, we 'proclaim' the Lord's death"[12] in the same way that the taking of the Passover meal proclaims God's redemptive hand to the children of Israel.[13]

All of these truths were the meditation of the early Christian community every time they took the bread and the wine of Passover in their weekly communion

> The blood of the lamb applied to the lentil and door post is a picture of the blood applied to our own heart.

service. Unfortunately, the first century saw a hardening of the Jewish leadership opposed to the minority Messianic movement which was entirely Jewish in the early years.[14]

With the conversion of Cornelius a door was opened for the Gentiles as promised to Abraham: "In you all the families of the earth shall be blessed (Gen 12:3)." This expectation is repeated throughout the Seder[15].

Prayer

The apostles devoted themselves to four activities: "the apostle's doctrine, fellowship, breaking of bread, and prayer."[16]

For them prayer was not a casual, haphazard, religious activity attached to their busy careers. Rather, prayer was the heartbeat of their lives. It was an activity to which they were devoted because it was essential to the life of the church and the individual. It was seen on the same par with the apostle's doctrine, fellowship, and

Introduction, Internals And Externals

with breaking of bread. Over the centuries prayer has played an essential role to the ongoing ministry of the church just as prayerlessness has characterized the church in times of carnality and corruption.

By His Spirit God leads us to pray according to His will. And by that same Spirit He answers working all things according to His will. In the final chapter prayer is examined as an outworking of love, humility, faith, and obedience. These externals can never produce the internals except as the Holy Spirit miraculously brings them to life.

> Internal rebirth is invariably revealed in an external transformation.

People may spend hours in the Word of God, in the company of Christians, in the celebration of the Lord's Supper, and prayer without experiencing the life of a child of God. True Spiritual life is lived from the inside out—here's how.

It begins as one becomes humbly obedient to the faith, and forsaking all, abandons itself to the love of God. Internal rebirth is invariably revealed in an external transformation. In the context of these activities, as they flow from a heart of love, humility, faith, and obedience to God, Christians discover the will of God, their ultimate salvation, sanctification, and maturity so that they become models of Christ and usable servant leaders in the Kingdom of God.

SECTION I
THE INTERNALS

CHAPTER 2

DEFINING LOVE, THE MOST IMPORTANT THING

L ove defines us. What we love, how we love, who we love ultimately defines who we are and what we become. This explains why Solomon said, "Watch over your heart with all diligence for from it flow the springs of life". (Pro. 4:23 NASV)

"Which is the greatest commandment in the law?" (Matt 22:36 NIV) This was the question posed to Jesus. But behind it was the ageless question, "What is most important?" Where should I focus my attention? What is my purpose? There are so many voices, both good and bad, vying for attention. Jesus' response was immediate and straightforward. He said, "You shall love the Lord your God with all your heart, and with all your soul, and with all your mind. This is the great and foremost commandment. The second is like it, you shall love your neighbor as yourself. On these two commandments, depend the whole law and

> What we love, how we love, who we love ultimately defines who we are and what we become.

the prophets" (Matt 22:37-38). The Apostle Paul adds, "The purpose of our teaching is Love" ITim 1:5.

God

Neighbor ← YOU → Neighbor

Figure 1. We might illustrate the great commandment this way: Love God, first and foremost, and neighbor as oneself.

We are commanded "to love God with all the heart and soul and strength" (Deu 6:5). This must be an all-consuming love as signified by the combination of the heart, soul, and strength. The Hebrew word "is the richest biblical term for the totality of inner or immaterial human nature. In biblical literature, it is the most frequently used term for our immaterial personality functions as well as the most inclusive term for them since, in the Bible, virtually every immaterial function of man is attributed to the heart."[17]

> The Great Problem with the Great Commandment is our Great Sin: In our fallen condition we are guilty and self-centered.

Secondly, it will require my soul—sometimes translated life or breath. We might say, "with every breath" or "all my life." Lastly, it will require my everything, utmost effort, my strength. One ancient translator rendered it "your money." The Hebrew is literally, and with all your very. At the heart of this love for God is intimate communication. God communicates with me in His word and applied by His in-dwelling Spirit, and I communicate with Him in prayer, worship, and service.

Defining Love, The Most Important Thing

The Great Problem with the Great Commandment is our Great Sin: In our fallen condition we are guilty and self-centered. We want and need God's love and our neighbor's support and approval. However, sin alienates us from both God and our neighbor. Rather than loving them, we use them. We would have both God and neighbor serve us. We love the world, and everything in it, and want it to serve us. The great commandment, like all the rest of the Law exposes our sinfulness. The second graphic illustrates the problem.

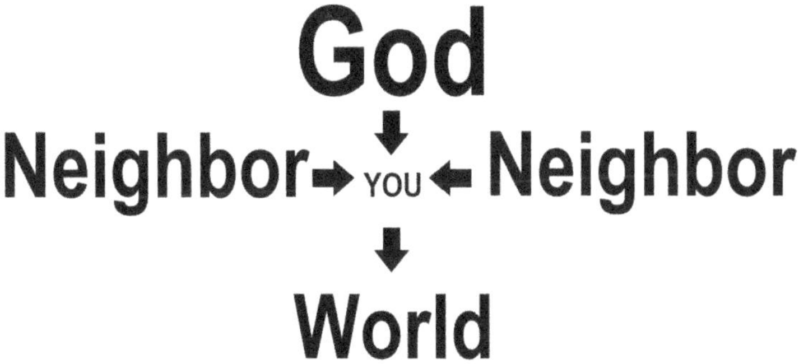

God
Neighbor→ YOU ←Neighbor
World

Figure 2. Self-centeredness is the essence of our sinful condition.

The third graphic imposes the cross on our sinfulness.[18] The solution is the Gospel or the Great Commission. Only death to our self-centered life and resurrection with Christ can enable us to love as God would have us love. Jesus transforms the great commandment as He does many other commandments—He expands them. He commands

> Just as rightly focused love fulfills the law: wrongly focused love is at the heart of all our problems.

Living Inside Out

us to love not just as we love ourselves but as He loved us and gave himself for us.

Love is the most important thing in life: loving God with all your heart and loving others as you love yourself. However, the focus of our love is essential. Just as rightly focused love fulfills the law; wrongly focused love is at the heart of all our problems. The Apostle Paul wrote, "The love of money is the root of all evil" (1Tim 6:10). Paul did not say "money is the root of all evil", but "the love of money". In his second letter to Timothy, Paul writes that in the last days, difficult times will come. These times will be characterized by multiple evils including people becoming lovers of self...lovers of money... and lovers of pleasure rather than God (II Tim 3:1-5).

Figure 3. The third graphic imposes the cross on our sinfulness.

At the heart of Jesus' message was this unsettling image which would divide the crowd: And he summoned the multitude with his disciples and said to them, "If anyone wishes

Defining Love, The Most Important Thing

to come after me, let him (1) deny himself, (2) take up his cross and (3) follow me. For whoever wishes to save his life shall lose it. But whoever loses his life for my sake and the Gospel's shall save it. For what does it profit a man to gain the whole world and forfeit his soul? For what shall a man give in exchange for his soul?" (Mark 8:34-37)

Mark Shaw writes: At heart, self-denial is the question of ownership. Who is really in charge of my life, God, or me? Denial of self leads to specific denial of our self-concern and self-will. We need to be concerned with God's name and will and agenda and not our own.[19]

In the Mark 8 passage above, Jesus defines self-denial in terms of crucifixion. He had their attention! Their eyes were most likely wide open as they searched their minds for some other possible meaning. His Jewish disciples understood perfectly what Roman crucifixion involved. They had probably seen it on a regular basis. And it stood in stark contrast to their hope for a Messiah that was going to save them from life's problems. Their expectation of the kingdom of God did not involve death but life, a glorious life, not failure but success, not loss but overwhelming gain.

> Jesus' message made as little sense to those listening two thousand years ago as it does to most people considering following Christ today.

They looked forward to an escape from their poverty and deliverance from their subjugation to Rome (Luke 1:68-75). Jesus' message made as little sense to those listening two thousand years ago as it does to most people considering following Christ today.

Despite the popularity of pop culture's graphic descriptions of crucifixion, as with Mel Gibson's "The Passion of the

Christ"[20], our expectation of the Kingdom of God today is, for the most part, an expectation of peace, prosperity, and deliverance from our perceived problems. There is little discussion of an *exchange*, especially of our life. The cross is to us a popular symbol, a pretty piece of jewelry—probably the best-selling piece of jewelry on the market—but trading our life as a Holy sacrifice is hardly a subject of everyday contemplation for most Christians. Matthew, Mark, and Luke all record the command, **"take up your cross."** Luke adds that we must take up the cross **"daily"** and follow Jesus. So, it is not a command which can be fulfilled in a literal crucifixion or even in martyrdom. Rather, Jesus must have intended a **sacrificial application** to our daily lives.

> I am crucified with Christ, nevertheless, I live. Yet not I, but Christ lives in me,

Paul explains daily crucifixion in terms of living by faith. His is a faith which not only believes that Jesus died for him; but that he died with Jesus and rose to a life motivated by the love Christ exemplified on the cross. He writes, "I am crucified with Christ, nevertheless, I live. Yet not I, but Christ lives in me. The life which I now live in the flesh, I live by faith in the son of God, who loved me and gave himself for me" (Gal 2:20).

People who say they love God demonstrate their love in different ways. Jesus himself said that to keep His commandments is to love him. John, who refers to himself as the disciple Jesus loved, wrote "We know love by this that he laid down his life for us: and we ought to lay down our lives for the brethren" (1John 3:16). Just as John 3:16 has become a defining text for God's love for us, 1 John 3:16 is the defining text for our love for others. A life of love is essentially a life laid down, consumed, exactly as a sacrifice is laid down and consumed.

Defining Love, The Most Important Thing

The horizontal beam of the cross point to the two kinds of neighbors: the lost and the saved—those who know Christ, and those who do not. Both groups of people require love which will be costly to the giver of love.

> A life of love is essentially a life laid down, consumed, exactly as a sacrifice is laid down and consumed.

The lost require the Gospel which will cost the giver's life: "for whoever wishes to save his life shall lose it but whoever loses his life for my sake and the gospel's will save it" (Mark 8:35). The saved require fellowship, instruction, service, and support; costly again: "we ought to lay down our lives for the brethren" (1John 3:16). This love for the brethren will require our life.

Love for the world **can** consume our lives but it **must not**. The lower vertical beam of the cross with the jagged arrow illustrates this point. John admonishes us, "Do not love the world or anything in the world. If anyone loves the world, the love of the father is not in him. For all that is in the world, the lust of the flesh, the lust of the eyes, and the boastful pride of life is not from the father but from the world. The world, and also its lusts, are passing away, but the one who does the will of God abides forever" (1John 2:15-17).

The ultimate purpose for our lives is love. This love is first toward God, secondly to my neighbor saved and unsaved, and lastly away from the world and its indulgences. The New Testament is the record of this love modeled in the life of Christ; the life of

> The ultimate purpose for our lives is love.

Paul; the lives of the of the early church leadership; and all the

Living Inside Out

examples of those who follow in their steps. This love is modeled throughout early church History.

The Example of Jesus

Jesus' love for the Father motivated all that He did. He came not to do His own will, but the will of the Father. His relationship with people may be summarized in the two texts which refer to His purpose. In Luke 4:43, we read, "But He said to them, 'I must preach the Kingdom of God to the other cities also for **I was sent for this purpose**;'" and in John 12:27, "My soul has become troubled and what shall I say? 'Father, save me from this hour?' But **for this purpose, I came** to this hour." All that Jesus did in His time on the earth may be summarized in these two purposes. In short, He came (1) to proclaim the kingdom and (2) to die to establish His kingdom. His miracles of healing, feeding the multitudes, calming the storm, and so on, are part of the proclamation of the Kingdom.[21]

> Jesus' purpose was to become their purpose.

His sinless life, His death, and His resurrection establish the Kingdom. The Holy life and ministry of Christ and the death and resurrection are both undertaken on behalf of His lost sheep.

His purpose is equally clear for His followers: "And he appointed twelve that they might be with him, and he might send them out to preach" (Mark 3:14). Jesus' purpose was to become their purpose. In the same way He has been sent into the world, so they will also be sent into the world. As he has

Defining Love, The Most Important Thing

loved, so they are also to love. As his life has been consumed, so their lives also will be consumed ... by love (John 15, 16).

The Example of Paul

One of the clearest explanations of what love is and how it works in life appears in 2Cor 5:14-19: "For the love of Christ controls us, having concluded this, that one died for all, therefore all died; and he died for all, that they who live should no longer live for themselves, but for him who died and rose again on their behalf. Therefore, from now on we recognize no man according to the flesh; even though we have known Christ according to the flesh. Yet now

> For the love of Christ to control us, we must die to our love for ourselves.

we know him thus no longer. Therefore, if any man is in Christ, he is a new creature; the old things passed away; behold, new things have come. Now all these things are from God who reconciled us to himself through Christ and gave us the ministry of reconciliation, namely that God was in Christ reconciling the world to Himself; not counting their trespasses against them, and He has committed to us the word of reconciliation."

How should the love of Christ control our lives? It controls us to the extent that we conclude not simply "that Christ died for us," but "that we died with Him." If that is true, we should no longer live for ourselves but for Him. For the love of Christ to control us, we must die to our love for ourselves. We must die to the world: "the lusts of the flesh, the lust of the eyes, and the boastful pride of life" (1John 2:16). For the Christian who desires to live Christ's love from the inside out, these misplaced

Living Inside Out

"loves" "war against the soul" (1Pet 2:11), and against the "real" love of God. They take us captive and choke the work of God in our lives (1Pet 2:11, 2Tim. 2:22-3:17, Matt 13:18-23).

What does "living for Him" entail? Paul explains. It is our reorientation to all of life in such a way that we recognize no one and nothing in the way we previously did. Instead, we see everything now from the perspective of the "ministry of reconciliation" (2Cor 5:11; 2Cor 5:28). "Old things, the things of the world, have passed away" (2Cor 5:17). The love of Christ controlled Paul so completely that his life was consumed

> The love of Christ has never moved to their hearts, to the core of their being. It is simply consigned to the religious cubbyholes of their souls.

with the proclamation of the gospel and with the building up of those who received his word of reconciliation. Paul concludes that while God was in Christ reconciling the world to Himself, He was at the same time committing to us the "word of reconciliation."

Many professing Christians would like to think that the love of Christ controls them, when in fact they are very much alive to the lusts of the flesh, the lusts of the eyes, and the boastful pride of life. The radical, life-changing conclusion that Paul had reached is only a theoretical construct for some professing Christians. The love of Christ has never moved to their hearts, to the core of their being. It is simply consigned to the religious cubbyholes of their souls.

A life of self-denial changes the way we relate to others. Calvin noted pride, jealousy, and envy and the rivalry they produce are endemic in human relationships: But there is no one who does not cherish within some opinion of his own pre-eminence. Thus, each individual, by flattering himself, bears a kind of kingdom in his breast. For claiming as his own what pleases him, he censures the character and morals of others (3.7.4). This being the case, gentleness, humility, and lowliness before others are the primary marks of self-denial in relationships.[22]

This logic is not by chance when addressed by Paul to the Corinthian church. The Corinthian church of Paul's time was marked by carnality, division, superficial spirituality, and prosperity-not unlike our present day. Numerous outlines of both First and Second Corinthians have been proposed,[23] but the underlying theme that gives cohesion to both books is Paul's lifestyle—the example of the apostle in contrast to the life of the Corinthians.[24]

In the first book, Paul addresses a series of concerns, some of which are posed by the Corinthian church, and some a matter of Paul's fatherly compassion for the people. What characterizes the book is Paul's pattern of using himself as an example. He repeatedly offers a theoretical answer followed by an appeal to his own lifestyle and example which the Corinthians have forgotten.

What doctrine did Paul teach **everywhere** in **every church?** The answer is explicitly stated in 1Cor 4:15 -17: "For if you were to have countless tutors in Christ, yet *you would* not *have* many fathers; for in Christ Jesus, I became your father through the gospel. I exhort you, therefore, be imitators of me. For this reason, I have sent to you Timothy, who is my beloved and faithful child in the Lord, and he will remind you of **my ways** which are in Christ, just as **I teach everywhere in every** church."

Living Inside Out

Paul was concerned not only that they understood the life of Christ historically, but that they reproduced the life of Christ experientially. Timothy was sent to Corinth not merely to resolve the theological conflict or to deliver a written epistle, but rather to remind the church of the lifestyle of the apostle. He did this not only in word but in conduct. Paul later reminds his young brother to be an example to believers in "speech, conduct, love, faith and purity" (1 Tim 4:12).

These were the ways of Paul. The love of Christ and love for people directed his life. He repeats the expectation in 1 Cor. 11:1: "Be imitators of me, just as I also am of Christ." Notice that the context here relates to the social question of "eating meat offered to idols." Initially he deals with theological issues then his conclusion returns to the argument of lifestyle based upon **purpose**.

> These were the ways of Paul. The love of Christ and love for people directed his life.

So, whether you eat or drink or whatever you do, do all to the glory of God. Give no offense to Jews or to Greeks or to the Church of God just as I try to please everyone and everything not seeking my own interests but the interest of the many that they may be saved (1 Cor 31-33). Be imitators of me as I am of Christ (1 Cor 10:13). "Do as I do," he repeats, "for the sake of the gospel."

The context of chapter four is even more convicting. He argues that all the apostles are set forth as models "exhibits to the world" (4:9). Paul facetiously rebukes the Corinthian church because they stand in contrast to the apostle's lifestyle:

"We are weak, but you are strong; you are distinguished, but we are without honor. To this present hour we are both hungry

Defining Love, The Most Important Thing

and thirsty, and are poorly clothed, and are roughly treated, and are homeless; and we toil, working with our own hands; when we are reviled, we bless; when we are persecuted, we endure; when we are slandered, we try to conciliate; we have become as the scum of the world, the dregs of all things, *even* until now. I do not write these things to shame you, but to admonish you as my beloved children. For if you were to have countless tutors in Christ, yet *you would* not *have* many fathers; for in Christ Jesus, I became your father through the gospel. I exhort you, therefore, be imitators be imitators of me. For this reason, I have sent to you Timothy, who is my beloved and faithful child in the Lord, and he will remind you of my ways which are in Christ, just as I teach everywhere in every church." (1Cor 4:10-17)

Paul is not saying these things to set himself apart from the Corinthians as an unreachable model. Rather, he instructs like a *father* who expect his children to follow in his footsteps. Timothy is a beloved and *faithful son*. He is faithful in following Paul's model. He will teach the Corinthians by word and by example.

Paul tells the Colossian church, "And we proclaim Him, admonishing every man and teaching every man with all wisdom that we may present every man complete in Christ. And for **this purpose,** also I labor, striving according to His power, which mightily works within me" (Col 1:28-29). Paul's **purpose** was to proclaim the Gospel to every person, then build to completeness every one that trusted in Christ. (Do not let the chapter break distract you from the unity of Paul's thought.) He continues in chapter two, "For I want you to know how great a struggle I have for you and for those at Laodicea and for those who have not seen me face to face that their hearts may be encouraged being knit together in love to reach all the riches of full assurance of understanding, and the knowledge of God's mystery that is Christ, in whom are hidden all the treasures of wisdom and knowledge" (2:1-3). Paul's **purpose** and his struggle are that Christ may be formed in the lives of his followers—that their hearts may be knit together in love. **Examples in the Early Church—Imitators.**

> Paul's purpose and his struggle are that Christ may be formed in the lives of his followers—that their hearts may be knit together in love.

The great commandment to love God with all your heart, soul, and mind, and to love others as we love ourselves is actualized in the ministries of both Jesus and Paul. They represent a template for each of us. Jesus called people to follow His example. Paul claimed that he was doing exactly that!

Is this view of perfect love from Jesus and applied love from the Apostle Paul impractical—if not impossible—for anyone else? One might argue, "I am not the Messiah, and certainly not an apostle, not even a pastor. I have a job and a family. I have other interests. How can this "life of love from the inside out work in my life?"

A third generation[25] of Christians in leadership in the early Church embraced this model. Unlike the Corinthian church, which is characterized by carnality, the Philippian church is marked by maturity. There are no rebukes or corrections in the letter to the Philippians, but simply exhortations to continue in what they have received.

"Brethren, join in following my example and observe those who walk according to **the pattern** you have in us. For many walk, of whom I often told you, and now tell you even weeping,

Defining Love, The Most Important Thing

that they are enemies of the cross of Christ, whose end is destruction, whose God is their appetite, and whose glory is in their shame, who set their minds on earthly things. For our citizenship is in heaven, from which we eagerly wait for a savior, the Lord Jesus Christ, who will transform the body of our humble state into conformity with the body of his glory, by the exertion of the power that he has

> In being friends of the world, they are enemies of the lifestyle demonstrated by Jesus and Paul.

even to subject all things to himself" (Phil 3:17-21). Paul's lifestyle had become a pattern for the elders at Philippi; and the Philippians are exhorted to imitate "those who walk according to the pattern you have in us." This is clearly a reference to the leaders in the Philippian church.[26]

The alternative is to be counted with those who are enemies of the cross of Christ. Rather than "loving God with all their heart, soul, mind, and strength and their neighbor as themselves," God's enemies love only themselves. "Their God is their appetite," and they set their minds on earthly things. They love this world (Phil 3:19). Just as John wrote, "If anyone loves the world, the love of the Father is not in him" (1John 2:15), so it is in their lives. They are enemies of the cross and therefore enemies of the love of God. In being friends of the world, they are enemies of the lifestyle demonstrated by Jesus and Paul. By contrast, the Philippians follow Paul's example and the example of those who walk according to this Christ-like pattern.

In the same book, Paul calls attention to two of his coworkers, Timothy and Epaphroditus. The people already know them not only by their talk but by their walk, by their sacrificial service. His description of these men is revealing.

They are not just letter carriers, they are models. They too are walking according to the pattern: "But I hope in the Lord Jesus to send Timothy to you shortly, so that I also may be encouraged when I learn of your condition. For I have no one else of kindred spirit who will genuinely be concerned for your welfare. For they all seek after their own interests, not those of Christ Jesus. But you know of his proven worth, that he served with me in the furtherance of the gospel like a child serving his father. Therefore, I hope to send him immediately, as soon as I see how things go with me" (Phil 2:20-23). Paul is sending one who has a genuine love.

> Christians are exhorted to be "imitators of God and to walk in love as Christ loved us and gave Himself an offering and a sacrifice for us.

He describes Epaphroditus in similar terms: "Receive him then in the Lord with all joy, and hold men like him in high regard; because he came close to death for the work of Christ, risking his life to complete what was deficient in your service to me" (Phil 2:29-30). These men are **imitators**. This is repeated in the book of Ephesians, where Christians are exhorted to be **"imitators of God** and to walk in love as Christ loved us and gave Himself an offering and a sacrifice for us."

In writing to the Thessalonian church Paul says, "You know what kind of men we proved to be among you for your sake. And you became **imitators** of us and of the Lord, for you received the word in much affliction with the joy of the Holy Spirit, so that you became an **example** to all the believers in Macedonia and Achaia" (1Thes 1:5-6). Paul repeats this same message **"everywhere in every church"** (1Cor 4:17).

Defining Love, The Most Important Thing

With such frequent repetition, how can this concept be missed? "The love of Christ controls us **having concluded** this, that one died for all therefore all died, and He died for all that those who live should no longer live for themselves but for Him who died for them and rose again" (2Cor 5:14).

> But whoever loses his life for my sake and the Gospel's shall save it.

Christ's love controls us to the extent that we conclude and remain firm in our conclusion in Mark 8:34-37: "Jesus summoned the multitude with his disciples and said to them, 'if anyone wishes to come after me, let him deny himself, take up his cross and follow me. For whoever wishes to save his life shall lose it. But whoever loses his life for my sake and the Gospel's shall save it. For what does it profit a man to gain the whole world and forfeit his soul? For what shall a man give in exchange for his soul?"

Living inside out is an act of faith: just as we believe He died for us we believe we died with Him. Faith here is a confident resolve, a conclusion in the sense of a final decision with ongoing consequences. It is an act of humility in that it requires the death and denial of self.

> Living inside out is an act of faith: just as we believe He died for us we believe we died with Him.

Unbelief and pride then keep us from living God's love.

Love is consuming. Either love of the world will consume our life, or the love of God will consume our life. Everyone loves something; this is the way we are built. This is why the "first and foremost commandment" is that we "love God with all our heart, all our soul, and all our strength." (Deut. 6:5, Mk.

12:30). The fall represents a turning from the love of God to the love of self. The essence of redemption is that we turn to God from idols, especially the idol of self. Augustine wrote, "We are renewed day by day by making progress in our love from temporal things to eternal things, from visible things to invisible things, from fleshly things to spiritual things."[27]

This love of Christ and the imitation of Christ are so central to our lives in Christ that we are named Christians. The change in terminology from disciple to Christian reflects a perception that the disciples were not merely learners or students, not even followers of a particular teacher or teaching, but men who believed that Jesus was the Christ who had been crucified, resurrected, and, by the power of the Holy Spirit, made to

> This love of Christ and the imitation of Christ are so central to our lives in Christ that we are named Christians.

live within them. Hence the name Christian: "And the disciples were first called Christians in Antioch" (Acts 11:26).

The fact that we are commanded to "imitate" addresses our responsibility. We do this by applying the utmost measure of strength in our loving. Peter commands believers to **apply all diligence** in adding the qualities of Christ-likeness: "Now for this very reason also, **applying all diligence**, in your faith supply moral excellence, and in your moral excellence, knowledge, and in your knowledge, self-control, and in your self-control, perseverance, and in your perseverance, godliness, and in your godliness, brotherly kindness, and in your brotherly kindness, love. For if these qualities are yours and are increasing, they render you neither useless nor unfruitful in the true knowledge of our Lord Jesus Christ. For he who lacks these qualities

Defining Love, The Most Important Thing

is blind or short-sighted, having forgotten his purification from his former sins. Therefore, brethren**, be all the more diligent** to make certain about His calling and choosing you; for as long as you practice these things, you will never stumble." (2 Pet 1:5-10)

We must cultivate a heart of love, humility, faith, and obedience. This is a process of transformation from the inside out. The Spirit of Christ is prompting and empowering us in this process, but to do it is our individual responsibility.[28]

Love grows as **we humble ourselves** before God acknowledging our desperate need for love; as **we believe** not only that Christ has died for our sins and been raised for our justification, but that we have died and been resurrected with Him; and finally, as **we listen and obey from the heart** the personal promptings of the Spirit. Externally this will be observable in our commitment to the apostles' doctrine (in the Scriptures), fellowship (with the Church), the breaking of bread (in Worship), and prayer (to our Father in heaven). The fulfillment of the Great Commission and a spiritual fulfillment of the Sabbath/Rest (not simply a day but a life) will follow naturally. It will not do simply to take up the activities, or even to be consumed with the activities without the heart; nor will it suffice to profess the internals without the externals.

> We must cultivate a heart of love, humility, faith, and obedience. This is a process of transformation from the inside out.

Examples in Church History—Imitators

As we review church history it is easy to see elements of this pattern of imitation. It is equally simple to see the deficiencies in following the pattern. In the early centuries, the church was often marked by a love which sustained it through open persecution. For example, in an anonymous Letter to Diognetus dating from the second century, there is a reference to imitating God:

"To be happy does not, indeed, consist in lording it over one's neighbors, or in longing to have some advantage over the weaker ones, or in being rich and ordering one's inferiors about. It is not in this way that any man can *imitate God*, for such things are alien to his majesty. But if a man takes his neighbor's burden on himself and is willing to help his inferior in some respect in which he himself is better off, and, by providing the needy with what he himself possesses because he has received it from God, becomes a god to those who receive it—then *this man is an imitator of God.* Then, while your lot is cast on earth, you will realize that God rules in heaven; then you will begin to talk of the mysteries of God; then you will love and admire those who are being punished for their refusal to deny God . . . And when you love him, you will be an imitator of his goodness. And do not be surprised to hear that a man can become an imitator of God. He can because God wills it."[29]

Clearly the imitation of God is a pattern of life to be lived in the midst of the culture. It is counter-cultural, yet it serves to redeem the culture.[30]

It is holy but not in the sense of being separate or withdrawn; but pure, uncorrupt, and innocent. It is the persistence in the face of the threat of death which is irresistible. The martyrs of the early

> Jesus has many who love His kingdom in heaven, but few who bear His cross.

centuries have much to teach us about love and discipleship.

Defining Love, The Most Important Thing

Ignatius in facing martyrdom wrote to his fellow Christians, "Pray that I will have the strength both outwardly and inwardly so that I may not just talk about it but want to do it, that I might not merely be called a Christian, but actually prove to be one."[31]

"We call martyrdom perfection, not because the man comes to the end of his life as others, but because he has exhibited the perfect work of love."[32]

They are filled with love having concluded that one died for all, and therefore all died. Thomas à Kempis (1379-1471) wrote: "We must abandon all we love for the one we love, for Jesus wants us to love him only above all other things....Jesus has many who love His kingdom in heaven, but few who bear His cross. He has many who desire comfort, but few who desire suffering. He finds many to share His feast, but few His fasting. All desire to rejoice with Him, but few are willing to suffer for His sake. Many follow Jesus to the breaking of bread, but few to the drinking of the cup of His passion. Many admire His miracles, but few follow Him to the humiliation of His cross. Many love Jesus as long as no hardship touches them."[33]

Thomas discovered the priority of love as an imitation of Christ. This was love which would manifest itself in a deep personal piety, separation from the pollutions of the world as well as a humble heart of servanthood to his fellow Christians and a sacrificial proclamation of the gospel to his world.

Movements of revival paved the way for the Reformation. In the late fourteenth century, the *Devotio Moderna*[34] (the modern way of serving God) rose in northern Europe emphasizing personal piety and service to God and man. Thomas represents the pinnacle of this movement. He was exposed to the movement at the age of twelve, entered an Augustinian monastery at nineteen and remained there, except for three years

Living Inside Out

writing, preaching, and counseling till his death in his nineties. He produced one of the most widely read devotional books of all times: *The Imitation of Christ*, a classic work first printed at Augsburg in 1471, the year of Thomas' death.

Within a few decades it was read and loved throughout Europe. *The Imitation* is a product of the contemplative and monastic emphasis on the interior life and its disciplines. Unlike the "Brethren of the Common Life",[35] who sought to live devout lives in the middle of bustling cities, the spiritual teaching of the *Imitation* emphasizes withdrawal from the distractions and dangers of the world. However, the writing had such a wide audience that Thomas has influenced more over the centuries than most of his contemporaries who lived among the people. Though he lived a monastic life he was available to many who came to him for counsel and instruction.

The first chapter of *The Imitation of Christ* entitled, *"Imitating Christ and Despising All Vanities on Earth,"* speaks for itself: "Yet whoever wishes to understand fully the words of Christ must try to pattern his whole life on that of Christ."[36]

The cross of Christ has meant different things to Christians throughout the ages. Paul said, "But may it never be that I would boast, except in the cross of our Lord Jesus Christ, through which the world has been crucified to me, and I to the world" (Gal 6:14). In the early centuries the cross became a symbol of martyrdom. By the time of Constantine, the cross would be a symbol of the Empire. Throughout the

> At times when the church has lost its fervor, its holiness, its piety, it has been the theme of the cross which has stirred the faithful and brought revival.

Defining Love, The Most Important Thing

Middle Ages, the cross was a defining element of daily life as the place of an ongoing atonement in the mass.

For Luther, the cross became a symbol of the work of God in justifying us by faith alone. It has been a symbol of God's presence with us in suffering, God's love for us in the midst of tragedy, victory over death, and the resurrection itself. For Bonhoeffer, the cross is the essence of the call of God. "When God calls a man, He calls him to come and die."[37]

At times when the church has lost its fervor, its holiness, its piety, it has been the theme of the cross which has stirred the faithful and brought revival.

But in every case the love of God has been central to understanding the meaning of the cross. It is this love which must capture, fill, and control our lives if we are to imitate Christ Jesus. Saint Augustine, wrote in 413AD, "Two cities have been formed by two loves—the earthly by the love of self even to the contempt of God; and the heavenly, by the love of God even to the contempt of self. The former, in a word, glories in itself, the latter in the Lord."[38]

> It is love for the world which consumes and destroys without benefit but love for God which leads us to life.

The love empowered through obedience to the will of God is just the opposite of the love for the world. It is love for the world which consumes and destroys without benefit but love for God which leads us to life.

"And He summoned the multitude with His disciples, and said to them, 'If anyone wishes to come after Me, let him deny himself, and take up his cross, and follow Me. For whoever wishes to save his life shall lose it; but whoever loses his life for My sake and the gospel shall save it. For what does it profit a man to gain the whole world, and forfeit his soul? For what shall a man give in exchange for his soul?" (Mark 8:34-37) John writes that whoever loves is born of God and whoever does not love does not know God (I John 4:7).

> We tend to romanticize the past and confuse true greatness in God's eyes with success.

We tend to romanticize the past and confuse true greatness in God's eyes with success. God's leaders are concerned, above all else, with loving Him and those in His image. Their humble concern is that their own sin is the chief impediment, and they flee to the cross as their only hope, finding Christ their sole reward. It is this humble concern, this humility of mind we will discuss in the next chapter as we seek to live from the inside out.

CHAPTER 3

DISCOVERING HUMILITY, PREREQUISITE FOR GUIDANCE

In the words of St Augustine, "If you ask me, what is the first precept of the Christian religion, I will answer, first, second, and third, Humility."[39]

Jesus said, "Whoever then humbles himself as this child, he is the **greatest** in the Kingdom of Heaven" (Matt 18:4). Why is humility of such value in God's eyes? It is because humility describes dependence on God as opposed to independence from God.

The humble admit their inability to do anything of value apart from God. Humility is "aptness for grace" according to Luther. It is a result of seeing sin as God sees it, acknowledging its ever-present deceit and power, and realizing that only He can deliver us from it. When the mind of Christ controls us (Phil. 2:5) we walk in a loving humility: we love and value others above ourselves. Paul describes this to the Corinthians, "We no longer live for ourselves but for him who died for us" (2 Cor. 5:15). John explains, "We know love by this that he laid down

> The humble admit their inability to do anything of value apart from God.

45

his life for us, and we ought to lay down our lives for the brethren" (1John 3:16).

Moses' Ways and the Word of God

"Moses was very humble, more than any man who was on the face of the earth." (Num. 12:3). The fact that Moses, who was without question one of the greatest prophets and leaders of Israel, is described as the most-humble man on earth should put an end to the thinking that humility requires a rejection of prominence or leadership.

> If humility requires primarily a dependence upon God and his word, it is a prerequisite for leadership.

In fact, the opposite is true. If humility requires primarily a dependence upon God and his word, it is a **prerequisite** for leadership.

Moses was born into slavery in Egypt and by the decree of the king should have been killed at his birth; but by the hand of God, he was protected and raised as a son in the house of the pharaoh. He was dependent upon God for his life and his position, and he knew it. He expected that his brethren would appreciate his calling, but they did not.

After his people's rejection, he spent 40 years raising sheep for Jethro in Midian and discovered on a deeper level the meaning of dependence. At the call of God from the burning bush, he returned to Egypt in

> When Moses was charged with pride by his siblings, he was silent. It is in this context we learn that he was the most-humble man on earth.

total dependence upon God to deliver a group of slaves from

Discovering Humility, Prerequisite For Guidance

the most powerful nation on earth with only the promise of God's presence. When Moses was charged with pride by his siblings, he was silent. It is in this context we learn that he was the most-humble man on earth.

Remember, Moses wrote the Pentateuch, so he is describing himself as the meekest man on the earth. This is not a boast but a statement of his dependence upon God. Moses had no response to Miriam and Aaron: the response came from God. Moses humble dependence led to an intimacy with God which also distin-guished him from the people. "He made known His ways to Moses, His acts to the sons of Israel" (Ps 103:7). The children of Israel saw the works of God, but Moses knew His ways. God revealed himself to the nation, but He revealed himself to Moses on a completely different level.

> Moses knew God intimately and he constantly sought a deeper more personal relationship.

God spoke to Moses face-to-face. "Hear my words: If there is a prophet among you I the Lord make myself known to him in a vision; I speak with him in a dream. Not so with my servant Moses. He is faithful in all my house. With him I speak mouth to mouth, clearly and not in riddles, and he beholds the form of God" (Num.12:6-8). Moses knew God intimately and he constantly sought a deeper more personal relationship. He found it because of his humble heart.

The humble are led because humility is a willingness to follow. "He leads the humble in justice, and He teaches the humble His way" (Psalm 25:9). The meekest man in all the earth was the one who knew the ways of God. "All the kings of the earth will give thanks to You, O Lord, when they have heard the words of your mouth. And they will sing of the ways

Living Inside Out

of the Lord, for great is the glory of the LORD. For though the LORD is exalted, yet He regards the lowly; but the haughty He knows from afar" (Ps 138:4-6).

The reference to the "ways of God" is remarkable in this context since it is tied to His glory. His glory is great in that He regards the lowly though He Himself is exalted. He has no need of man, especially lowly men; yet He regards the lowly. This grace is in contrast to the rich and powerful of the world who trample the weak and powerless. An attitude of pride is exactly what condemns them. God's nature is such that though he is exalted, he regards the lowly. And this is his glory, in fact the greatness of his glory is precisely this regard for the lowly!

We are prone to think of Moses in terms of Hollywood's portrayal of him either in The *Ten Commandments* (1956) if we have grey hair or the more recent Disney production, if not. We imagine of his bold confrontations with Pharaoh as he storms in and out of the royal palace or his confrontation with the people as he returns from Mount Sinai and in anger smashes the stone tablets – in neither instance does he seem particularly humble. But the scene may have played out in a completely different tone.

The Hebrew word in Numbers 12 is a term used to describe the afflicted, the poor of the land who must trust God as deliverer. It is the spiritual goal of physical affliction.[40]

It is common to look upon poverty as humility because of this basic link between the poor and the humble. Commentators have struggled over Jesus' meaning of "Blessed are the poor in spirit," in Matthew, as opposed to "the poor" in Luke[41].

Poverty alone does not guarantee poverty of spirit or humility.

Discovering Humility, Prerequisite For Guidance

At the same time, Jesus warns against the dangers of wealth. It is easier for a camel to go through the eye of a needle than a rich man to enter the kingdom of heaven, because the kingdom of Heaven belongs to the '*ani*'-poor/humble." Perhaps one of the greatest struggles we face as Evangelicals in the 21st century is our relative wealth when compared to the rest of the world.[42]

> Perhaps one of the greatest struggles we face as Evangelicals in the 21st century is our relative wealth when compared to the rest of the world.

Moses had been raised in the court of Pharaoh then banished to the desert. He knew wealth and poverty. Humility on the part of the wealthy requires a responsive generosity, compassion on a social level, and fellowship in suffering. And Moses, we are told, chose to suffer with the people of God. The link between physical poverty and spiritual poverty or humility is seen throughout the pages of scripture as well as the history of the church over the centuries.[43]

Beyond physical poverty is the poverty of spirit which yearns for communion with God and so hungers for a word from God. The humble heart not only listens but responds. Isaiah describes this as trembling at the Word of God. "To this one I will look: to the one who is contrite of spirit and who trembles at my word" (Isa 66:2). Humility in God's eyes is judged by our response to His voice.

> "To this one I will look: to the one who is contrite of spirit and who trembles at my word" (Isa 66:2).

This may be a clue as to how Moses could be seen as the most-humble man on the face of the earth. In spite of their

Living Inside Out

professed devotion, God saw the heart of the people and responded, "Oh that there was such a heart in them, that they would fear Me and keep all my commandments always, that it might be well with them and their children forever" (Deu 5:29). Moses exhorted, "Circumcise therefore the foreskin of your heart, and be no longer stubborn" (Deu 10:16). All the prophets called Israel to repentance, not a superficial spirituality but a wholehearted turning from sin described by humility.

The Prophets and Reformers

Paradoxically, God sees the heart of the humble not as a position of disdain but as a "high and holy place." "Thus says the high and exalted One who lives forever, whose name is Holy, I dwell on a high and holy place, and also with the contrite and lowly of spirit in order to revive the spirit of the lowly and to revive the heart of the contrite" (Isa 57:15). He indwells the humble, gives grace to the humble, revives the humble, and sustains them in conflict.

The reformers cry of *Sola Scriptura*[44] is a statement of their humility–their captivity to the Word of God. When placed before the Diet of Worms, Luther refused to recant his views, "unless I am convinced by the testimony of Scripture, here I stand, I can do no other.[45]"

In spite of innumerable physical ailments, Calvin led one of the most arduous lives of devotion to the word of God ever recorded.[46]

Ulrich Zwingli (1484-1531) began the Swiss reformation in 1519 with a new approach to preaching. He would no longer follow the lectionary but preach straight through the text of the Bible. This was a radical departure from the norm of his

Discovering Humility, Prerequisite For Guidance

day. It was the humble reverence for the Word of God over the traditions of men which set the reformers apart. They could have been independent of God and dependent on their traditions, but their humble dependence on God made them independent from men.

Micah's definition of the good ties together the commitments to justice, mercy, and humility. "He has told you O man what is good and what does the Lord require of you, but to do justice, to love kindness, and to walk humbly with your God?" (Mic 6:8) Justice is intuitive to the prophets because God leads the humble in justice

> It was the humble reverence for the Word of God over the traditions of men which set the reformers apart.

and "teaches the humble His way" (Psa 25:9). The justice they call for usually involves humility in its execution: the rich and powerful are called to treat the weak and poor with respect and fairness. (Isa.1, Jer. 2-5, Amo. 2-9, Mic. 7:2-6)

The law is fulfilled not only in love but in a loving humility. The sacrifices of God–the entire sacrificial system–amounts to a broken and contrite heart. "The sacrifices of God are a broken spirit; a broken and a contrite heart, O God, you will not despise" (Ps 51:17). Notice that sacrifices (plural) are a broken spirit (singular). A broken spirit is not simply a sacrifice, but all of the sacrifices together amount to a broken and contrite heart. I believe this is the reason the day of atonement on which a sacrifice was made for the entire nation was a day of fasting and humbling. It is the only prescribed fast on the holy days and emphasizes the appropriate inner response to sin even today when Israel has no temple and no sacrifice.

Sacrifice apart from humility is never acceptable to God. "The sacrifice of the wicked is an abomination to the Lord but the prayer of the upright is His delight" (Pro. 15:8). The wicked here bring a sacrifice without a broken and contrite heart, without intending to turn from sin. The external act though outwardly good, is an abomination because of the heart. The humble man comes in total dependence on the grace of God and his prayer is a delight because he comes to a loving forgiving Father who delights to show his mercy to the one who has hope in nothing but God.[47]

> On a very practical level a sense of separation from God, should always generate in his children a reexamination of the heart to see if sin has crept in and been unnoticed.

Just as God honors humility, He despises pride. "Though the Lord is exalted, yet He regards the lowly; but the haughty He knows from afar" (Psalm 138:6). Moses experienced an intimacy with God, the proud experience a separation: God seems far away. On a very practical level a sense of separation from God, should always generate in his children a reexamination of the heart to see if sin has crept in and been unnoticed. This is the reason for regular searching of the heart and confession before partaking of the Lord's Supper. This distancing takes the form of resistance in Proverbs 3:34 "Though He scoffs at the scoffers, yet He gives grace to the afflicted" (the "humble, RSV"). Luther wrote, "Humility is 'aptness for grace,' the essence of faith."[48]

Discovering Humility, Prerequisite For Guidance

Habakkuk: Humility and Faith

Habakkuk, who prophesied at the time of the Babylonian invasion of Israel, struggles with the philosophical question, "Why do the wicked prosper and the righteous suffer?" From Habakkuk's perspective, though Israel is not perfect, she is more righteous than the Babylonian conquerors all around her. He brings his complaint to the Lord and awaits a reply. God replies by calling for faith as He works His sovereign plan of judgment and deliverance. He will use the Babylonians but will certainly judge them as well. Notice the way the Lord describes the two parties "As for the proud his soul is not right within him but the righteous shall live by faith" (Hab 2:4). We would expect that pride would be contrasted with humility, that righteousness would be contrasted with unrighteousness, and that faith would be contrasted with unbelief. But in this case the heart of the proud is contrasted with the heart of the just who live by faith. The heart of pride is a heart of unbelief which we should associate with wickedness whereas the humble heart is a heart broken before God, a heart of faith, right with God.

> The heart of pride is a heart of unbelief which we should associate with wickedness

Today the link between righteousness and faith is cemented in the minds of Christians because the second half of the verse is quoted three times in the New Testament and taken up as the watchword of the reformation. "The just shall live by faith!" Entrance into the Kingdom is by faith alone. We must remember that in the Scriptures, faith is contrasted with a heart of pride. It is the humble childlike faith that Jesus contrasts with the proud controlling spirit of the world. In the world, the kings of the earth lord it over their subjects but it is not so in the Kingdom of God. While the proud heart is not right with God, the humble heart believes, trusts, and relies upon God. It is the humble who live by faith. They are the righteous the childlike members of the Kingdom of God. As Luther points out, "humility is the essence of faith."

The just not only have faith: they live by it. Not only are they justified by it: they walk in it. In Psalm 25, we see faith waiting; in Psalm 26 we see it walking. This is referred to as integrity: "I have walked in my integrity" (Psa. 26:1).[49]

> The just not only have faith: they live by it. Not only are they justified by it: they walk in it.

This intangible quality of integrity is often termed "obedience of the heart." It is the third component of the heart that pleases God which we will consider in depth in the next chapter.

Christ's response of obedience to the Father's will is a response of delight. As the Psalmist writes, "I delight to do Thy will, O my God; Thy Law is within my heart" (Psa 40:8). This heart humbly and joyfully submits to the will of God. It is not a grudging, legalistic obedience, but a delight. Jesus repeatedly confronts the "religious" leaders of his day with superficial obedience apart from a heart of love and humility towards God. "Woe to you, scribes and Pharisees, hypocrites! For you tithe mint and dill and cumin and have neglected the weightier provisions of the law: justice and mercy and faithfulness; but these are the things you should have done without neglecting the others" (Matt 23:23).

Chapter twenty-three of Matthew addresses the shortcomings of the Pharisees not in their external obedience to the law but their internal heart of disobedience which He terms lawlessness. "Even so you too outwardly appear righteous to men, but inwardly you are full of hypocrisy and lawlessness" (Matt 23:28). Lawlessness here is a characteristic of the heart. Just as the mouth speaks from what fills the heart, our activities of obedience or disobedience reveal hearts of love, humility, and obedience—or of lawlessness. Jesus's obedience to the point of death is a model of humility of mind. "If therefore there is

> Jesus's obedience to the point of death is a model of humility of mind.

any encouragement in Christ, if there is any consolation of love, if there is any fellowship of the Spirit, if any affection and compassion, make my joy complete by being of the same mind, maintaining the same love, united in spirit, intent on one purpose. Do nothing from selfishness or empty conceit, but with humility of mind let each of you regard one another as more important than himself; do not *merely* look out for your own personal interests, but also for the interests of others. Have this attitude in yourselves which was also in Christ Jesus, who, although He existed in the form of God, did not regard equality with God a thing to be grasped, but emptied Himself, taking the form of a bondservant, *and* being made in the likeness of men. And being found in appearance as a man, **He humbled Himself by becoming obedient to the point of death, even death on a cross"** (Phil 2:1-8).

Jesus: His Yoke and His Mind

When we learn of Christ, we learn humility. "Take My yoke upon you and learn from Me, for I am gentle and humble in

Living Inside Out

heart, and you will find rest for your soul" (Matt 11:29). We cannot be disciples simply by listening to his words; we must take His yoke. When we learn from him, we learn gentleness and humility. The humility of God is a mystery, but we see a glimpse of it in the interaction of the

> Humility defines the mindset of Jesus. So those who would walk as Jesus walked—must think as Jesus thought.

three persons of the Godhead: The Son submits to the cross in obedience to the Father. The Father has committed all judgement to the Son. The Spirit does not speak of himself but glorifies the Son. There is a beautiful interdependence within the Trinity in love and humility.

Paul's exhortation to humility is based upon the "mind" of Christ. Humility defines the mindset of Jesus. So those who would walk as Jesus walked—must think as Jesus thought. "Do nothing from selfishness or empty conceit, but with humility of mind regard one another as more important than yourselves. Do not {merely} look out for your own personal interests, but also for the interests of others. Have this attitude in yourselves which was also in Christ Jesus, who, although He existed in the form of God, did not regard equality with God a thing to be grasped, but emptied Himself, taking the form of a bondservant, and being made in the likeness of men. Being found in appearance as a man, He humbled Himself by becoming obedient to the point of death, even death on a cross. For this reason also, God highly exalted Him, and bestowed on Him the name which is above every name" (Phil 2:3-9).

Notice here that humility is defined in terms of obedience to the Father's will. In the same way, Paul called on the Corinthian church to imitate his lifestyle of love; he calls the

Discovering Humility, Prerequisite For Guidance

Ephesians and Philippians to imitation in terms of humility. "Therefore I, the prisoner of the Lord, entreat you to walk in a manner worthy of the calling with which you have been called, with all humility and gentleness, with patience, showing tolerance for one another in love" (Eph 4:1-2).

> Humility before God is submission to His word. He in turn reveals himself to the humble.

Humility is the first characteristic of the walk "worthy of our calling." It is the humble heart which moves us to a life of love, to a life of obedience, and to a living faith. Humility before God is submission to His word. He in turn reveals himself to the humble. Humility before others is a life crucified: dead to our pride and selfishness which alienates us not only from God but from others.

Humility before the world acknowledges the threat the system poses to holiness. It abstains from fleshly lusts, flees youthful lusts, walks circumspectly knowing the devil prowls about as a lion seeking whom he may devour (1Pet 2:11, 2 Tim 2:22, Eph 5:15, 1Pet 5:8). James compares the temptation process in terms of a lure used in catching

> Humility before the world acknowledges the threat the system poses to holiness.

an animal in a snare or a fish on a hook. When we are lured and enticed by our own desires we are caught in the sin process which leads to certain death (Jam. 1:13-15). Humility acknowledges the terrible consequences and flees...it doesn't lick the bait.

Living Inside Out

The Process

Humility is a function of love, obedience, and faith. We have seen in Isaiah 66 how humility is defined in terms of trembling and obedience to God's word. Paul, in discussing spiritual gifts with the Romans, exhorts them to humility as they examine their allotment of faith.

> Here Paul says in effect, if you would like a humbling thought, look at just how much faith God has given you compared to others.

"For through the grace given to me I say to everyone among you not to think more highly of himself than he ought to think; but to think so as to have sound judgment, as God has allotted to each a measure of faith" (Rom 12:3). Here Paul says in effect, if you would like a humbling thought, look at just how much faith God has given you compared to others. Somehow each of us realize that our measure of faith is much less that we would like it to be. We realize that our exercise of faith comes short when we compare ourselves to Moses, Noah, Abraham, or for that matter many of our contemporaries. If we judge rightly, Paul says, our littleness of faith will be humbling.

Both Peter and James quote Prov 3:34; "God is opposed to the proud but gives grace to the humble."[50]

Peter does it in a context of service to others. He exhorts; "You younger men likewise be subject to your elders and all of you (younger and older) cloth yourselves with humility towards one another."

> In the same way, our humility as Christians is our clothing and to appear without it is to appear naked.

Peter sets humility in the context of clothing. Probably the first thing we notice about

Discovering Humility, Prerequisite For Guidance

a person is clothing (or lack thereof). In the same way, our humility as Christians is our clothing and to appear without it is to appear naked. Our pride is as offensive as our nakedness and our humility should be as obvious as our clothing.

James narrates a process by which we humble ourselves. He says first, "God gives grace to the humble." Next, he describes the process, then concludes, "Humble yourselves in the presence of the Lord and He will exalt you". Notice this structure: "God is opposed to the proud but gives grace to the humble. Submit therefore to God. Resist the devil and he will flee from you. Draw near to God and He will draw near to you. Cleanse your hands, you sinners; and purify your hearts, you double-minded. Be miserable and mourn and weep; let your laughter be turned into mourning and your joy to gloom. Humble yourselves in the presence of the Lord, and He will exalt you" (James 4:6-10).

> When a person turns from sin he turns from rebellion to humble submission.

The process begins with submission to God. The essence of sin is rebellion against God. When a person turns from sin he turns from rebellion to humble submission. The love of God revealed at the cross captures the heart which concludes by faith that it should no longer live for itself in rebellion against God but for the one who died for him (2Cor 5:17). The grace of God makes this possible—hence Luther's insight that "humility is aptness for grace, the essence of faith." Salvation in this text encompasses not only the initial act but the ongoing process of resisting the devil and drawing near to God. The truly regenerate take up the cross dying daily to self and in the process learn of Christ who is humble of heart. These believers find rest for their souls—rest from their living death of slavery to sin. They resist the devil who now flees. They draw near to God in faith and subsequent holiness cleansing their hands and hearts in obedience. And finally in deep repentance, they mourn and weep as they realize the vastness both of their sin and the grace of God. This is the process in a nutshell.

Humility and Spirituality

Richard Lovelace sees spirituality as "the indispensable foundation of Christianity."[51]

Humility is the heart of spirituality. In addition to love for God, the mystics of the counter-reformation valued a true humility that was foreign to much of the Catholic Church and to many Protestants as well. Lovelace notes that though Luther traced many of the distortions arising in the church's life to the loss of the doctrine of Justification by Faith, "what he may not have fully realized was that the understanding of justification was one of a complex of factors determining spiritual vitality, and that if others of these were missing or unarticulated in the church's experience—such as the deep conviction of God's holiness and human need which drove Luther himself to sanc-tification—then, even while the church held to justification by faith alone, it would suffer distortion in other dimensions."[52]

This is exactly what happened to mainstream Lutheranism within 100 years of his death. The Lutheran church consol-idated around it's doctrinal distinctives and descended into a dead orthodoxy. Both German Pietism and Puritanism are responses to this distortion.

According to Lovelace, "This approach would never have satisfied the Puritans and Pietists who were convinced their primary responsibility was to be *ecclesiareformata semper reformada,* a reformed church always reforming.[53]

As they prayed for the destruction of the papal antichrist, they were increasingly aware of the antichristian remnants still clinging to them and deforming the Church's witness."[54]

By the end of the 16th-century Protestants in both the Lutheran and Reformed spheres were referring to the "half reformation," which had reformed their doctrines and not their lives and were seeking for a revitalization of the church.[55]

The church of the 21st century faces a similar pseudo–spirituality which can be addressed only by a recovery of the "complex of factors" or the internal priorities which undergird the external activities we are discussing. "We must remember our history because it calls us to humility."[56]

Zwingli, Luther, and Calvin are names we most commonly associate with the reformation and the development of our protestant tradition. We sometimes refer to them as Magisterial Reformers because they acknowledged the role of the church in the magistrate and subsequently developed state churches. A second group of men are termed radical reformers because they not only separated from Rome but from the association of church and state. They were condemned by both Catholics and Protestants as anarchists, but their radicalism went far beyond "separation of church and state" to a radical level of discipleship calling for separation from the world and a life of practical holiness. We will meet them in the next chapter as we take up the topic of Holiness/Obedience as a third aspect of the heart God values.

CHAPTER 4

DISCERNING HOLINESS, OBEDIENCE

Menno Simons describes his conversion with these words: "My heart trembled within me. I prayed to God with sighs and tears that he would give to me, a sorrowing sinner, the gift of His grace, create in me a clean heart, and graciously through the merit of the Crimson blood of Christ forgive my unclean walk and frivolous easy life."[57]

This broken heart which "trembled within", spurred Menno to a life of humble service to the persecuted brethren who would one day take his name calling themselves Mennonites. Because of intense persecution he had no permanent home but traveled extensively, "I with my poor wife and children have for eighteen years endured excessive anxiety, oppression, affliction, misery, and persecution. Yes, when the preacher's repose on beds and soft pillows, we generally have to hide ourselves in out-of-the-way corners. We have to be on our guard when a dog barks for fear the arresting officer has arrived. In short, while they are gloriously rewarded for their services with large incomes and good times, our recompense and portion be but fire, sword, and death."[58]

Though many of those who gave him lodging were captured and killed, Menno eluded capture. He also managed to write numerous tracts and three major works including Foundation of Christian Doctrine which not only lays the foundation of non-violence but defines the nature of discipleship, "Ah dear sir, it will not help a fig to be called Christians, boast of the Lord's blood, death, merits, grace, and gospel, so long as we are not converted from this wicked, immoral, and shameful life. It is in vain that we are called Christians that Christ died, that we were born in the day of grace, and baptized with water, if we do not walk according to His law, counsel, admonition, will, and command, and are not obedient to His Word."[59]

> It is in vain that we are called Christians that Christ died, that we were born in the day of grace, and baptized with water, if we do not walk according to His law, counsel, admonition, will, and command, and are not obedient to His Word.

Obedience Under the New Covenant

Obedience is not external conformity but internal conformity. It is not of the letter but the spirit.[60]

It is living from the inside out! This is why, under the New Covenant, the "Law of God is written on the heart" (Jer 31:33). If we are led by the Spirit, we are not under the law, but having life from the Spirit we are to walk, or act, according to the leading of the Spirit (Gal 5:18, 25).

> Obedience is not external conformity but internal conformity. It is not of the letter but the spirit.

Discerning Holiness, Obedience

Obedience, then, is not a matter of one or two actions. It is a matter of being led by the Spirit in a life of faith. This obedience is intimately connected to love, humility, and faith, so much so that without it the others are incomplete.

> It is living from the inside out!

During the time of the Apostles, Jews who rejected the Gospel and clung to the externals of Judaism, sought to impose circumcision on new Gentile believers.[61]

Later centuries saw a conscious effort by the church to distance itself from its Jewish roots.[62]

But in so doing, other legalisms or "rules" were introduced by religious Orders.

The situation in the Church became similar to what was described in Israel: "but Israel, pursuing a law of righteousness, did not arrive at that law. Why? Because they did not pursue it by faith, but as though it were based on works. They stumbled over the stumbling stone, just as it is written, Behold, I lay in Zion a stone of stumbling and a rock of offense, and he who believes in Him will not be disappointed" (Rom 9:31-33).

> External legalisms obscure the truth that obedience from the heart amounts to holiness in life.

During the Middle Ages, common vows associated with these "Rules" included poverty, chastity, and obedience. External legalisms obscure the truth that obedience from the heart amounts to holiness in life.

God's holiness encompasses His being and His doing: He is holy and does righteousness. A man who is holy does righteousness by obedience from the heart (which is an obedience of love, humility, and faith). The outworking of this conflict for

Living Inside Out

sinful yet redeemed man has taken many forms in the history of the church. The monasticism[63] of Augustine, Benedict,[64] and Loyola; and Methodism and Pentecostalism are all examples.

What are we to make of the monastic endeavor in light of Christ's obedience and the example of the early church? Augustine's experience of grace led to a simple rule calling for discipline but leaving room for personal freedom. Augustine concludes that those who accept the rule must go forth "not as slaves living under the law but as men living in freedom under grace."[65]

Later rules became more restrictive calling for celibacy, dictating times for rising and sleeping, excluding certain foods, and limiting travel to isolate the monk from the world. In addition to the traditional vows of poverty and chastity, Ignatius Loyola[66], founder of the Jesuits, required a special oath of absolute obedience to the Pope. Still other Rules focused on a particular discipline like poverty while sending the monk back into society with the goal of spreading the gospel. This was characteristic of early Celtic monasticism.[67]

> Obedience to the Gospel must be an obedience of faith which springs from a humble heart in love with Jesus.

By 1200 AD, after the peak of Benedictine monasticism, the new mendicant or begging orders of Francis and Dominic were taking hold. These orders represented a return to the simplicity of the gospel with the attending emphasis on poverty. The original rule of Francis consisted only of a few instructions from the gospels[68].

Obedience to the Gospel must be an obedience of faith which springs from a humble heart in love with Jesus. It subjects

Discerning Holiness, Obedience

itself to the will of God and the desperate need of its fellow man to bring salvation to the world. Disciplines in the form of law imposed on the unregenerate may serve as a schoolmaster to bring them to Christ, but for the Christian, the return to law apart from the Spirit is a departure from Christ. This is not to say that the Christian is not in need of discipline and self-control. By seeking God with brief retreats to the wilderness and services of love for God and man, the Monastic experiment represented one of the purist expressions of obedience in the history of the church. But these must proceed from the spirit and not from the flesh.

Much like a pendulum swinging back and forth, the history of the Church is a history of action, reaction, and overreaction. For many in the monasteries of the Middle Ages, life was an overflow of a true spirituality springing from a heart of faith and a deep love for God. For others the rules without inner life became bondage. With the reemphasis on faith at the time of the Reformation, the pendulum swung back to center and the disciplines of the previous age were built into the lives of the faithful.

Generally, the leaders of the Reformation believed that the monastics did not in fact conform to a simple gospel rule of life, that their repetitive prayers, fasts, and ceremonies were meaningless and that they had no real value to society. The vast wealth which they had accumulated seemed better spent on general public needs. Those monastics who had kept their vows were seen as cut off from true Christian freedom in lives that were futile and unfulfilled. Wherever the Reformation was triumphant, the monasteries were disestablished.[69]

For most contemporary evangelicals, the pendulum has swung so far in the direction of freedom that there is a desperate need to recover obedience in its biblical form. It is time for a reexamination of the nature of spirituality's internal workings and their effect on behavior. The faith that saves and sanctifies is not merely superficial intellectual consent. Transforming faith invites God to bring hardship, struggle, and discomfort, to the life of the believer and results in obedience/holiness.

Obedience: Greatness in the Kingdom

The Kingdom is promised to the obedient. As the scripture says, "Not everyone who says to me, 'Lord, Lord,' will enter the kingdom of heaven, but only the one who does the will of my Father who is in heaven (Matthew 7:21). God requires obedience, a heart of obedience that is an obedience of faith. It is an obedience that springs from a humble heart which hears the voice of God and acts. What could be more reasonable? But the Bible is essentially the story of humanity's disobedience to the voice of God. Obedience seems to be the rare exception! From the fall of Adam and Eve to the flood, only three people hear and obey the voice of God. The remainder of Genesis centers on the lives of Abraham, Isaac, Jacob, and Joseph, four men who narrowly escape the wrath of God by their occasional obedience. Wholehearted obedience is a rare but distinguishing exception. The great promise to Abraham was given specifically because he obeyed the voice of God (Gen 22:15-18).

By the time of Exodus, when a detailed law is given, the people of God, who are far from being the model of obedience,

> It is time for a reexamination of the nature of spirituality's internal workings and their effect on behavior.

Discerning Holiness, Obedience

are characterized as rebellious! As God's voice becomes clearer, humanity's hearing seems to fail proportionately. The heroes are still the exceptions to the rule, but when obedience occurs, we have a miraculous story of faith, humility, or love. The text is engaging because it matches

> But the Bible is essentially the story of humanity's disobedience to the voice of God. Obedience seems to be the rare exception!

our personal experience. G. M. Burge argues that "the whole of biblical theology" depends on obedient hearing[70].

Listening to the voice of God and obeying is critical to the Christian living inside out.

The interdependence of love, humility, obedience, and faith may be demonstrated in our expectations of our children. What does a parent want from a child? Obedience? Imagine a child who obeys but does not love or trust the parent. That would be very disturbing to any parent. A profession of love for the parent without obedience should be equally troubling. So too, a profession of love for God without obe-

> Listening to the voice of God and obeying is critical to the Christian living inside out.

dience should set off alarms in the Spirit. The possibility of any one of the four—love, humility, obedience, and faith, in the absence of the others is difficult to picture. These four qualities of love, humility, obedience, and faith are aspects of one character, the character of a Christian living from the inside out.

Wouldn't you love to be great in God's eyes? Together, these four traits, define greatness in God's eyes. "The **greatest** is love". He who humbles himself will be **greatest** in the kingdom of God (Matt 18:4). He who teaches and does these things will be called **great** (as opposed to least) in the Kingdom of God (Matt 5:19). Without faith it is impossible to please God (Heb 11:6), thus we cannot even begin to talk about greatness without faith. How can these all be the greatest unless they are inherently connected? They represent aspects of one character. Since they are interdependent (faith works by love), as one grows so do the others; and to the extent that one is missing, so are the others.

> These four qualities of love, humility, obedience, and faith are aspects of one character, the character of a Christian living from the inside out.

Obedience: The Foundation of Life

At the conclusion of the Sermon on the Mount, Jesus tells a story of two men who build their houses on two different foundations, one of sand and the other of rock. "Not everyone who says to Me, "Lord, Lord," will enter the kingdom of heaven, but he who does the will of My Father who is in heaven will enter. Many will say to Me on that day, "Lord, Lord, did we not prophesy in your name, and in Your name cast out demons, and in Your name perform many miracles?" And then I will declare to them, "I never knew you; depart from me, you who practice lawlessness." **Therefore, everyone who hears these words of Mine and acts on them, may be compared to a wise man who built his house on the rock.** And the rain fell, and the floods came, and the winds blew and slammed against that house; and yet it did not fall, for it had been founded on the rock. Everyone who hears these words of mine and does not act on them will be like a foolish man who built his house

Discerning Holiness, Obedience

on the sand. The rain fell, and the floods came, and the winds blew and slammed against that house; and it fell—and great was its fall" (Matt 7:21-27 KJV).

In the Book of 1Corinthians, Jesus is called both a rock and a foundation. But that is NOT the point of this illustration. In this illustration, **the foundation of rock is obedience ("everyone who hears these words of Mine and acts on them").** It is acting on the truth Jesus has just presented. The foundation is...foundational! It is the rock upon which everything else rests! Obedience is the marker of love, faith, and humility. The one who has the commandments and keeps them is the one who truly loves. The one who believes and obeys is the one who truly believes. And the one who humbles himself becomes obedient ...to the point of death.

> the foundation of rock is obedience ("everyone who hears these words of Mine and acts on them").

Earlier in the sermon Jesus introduces obedience with these words: "Whoever therefore shall break one of these least Commandments and shall teach man so, he shall be called the least in the kingdom of heaven. And whoever shall do and teach them the same shall be called great in the Kingdom of Heaven" (Matt 5:19).

He does not call the one who is obedient the greatest in the kingdom, but the one who is **disobedient** is called the **least**. When the disciples ask him about the greatest, He responds by saying, "The **greatest** is the one who humbles himself and becomes the servant of all" (Matt.23:11). Interestingly, the humble and contrite of spirit are those who tremble at the word of God. The implication is that they tremble and **obey**. "Thus says the Lord, "Heaven is My throne and the earth is My footstool. Where then is a house you could build for Me? And where is a place that I may rest? For My hand made all these things, thus all these things came into being," declares the Lord. "But to this one I will look, to him who is humble and contrite of spirit, and who trembles at My word" (Isa. 66:1-2).

They do not take God's Word or God's Commandments lightly. In the same way, those who fail to tremble at God's Word and those who are proud and self-sufficient are disobedient; they are the least in the kingdom of God.

Any discussion of law (rules) in evangelical circles raises the immediate concern that grace will be endangered. Debate about the exact place of God's law in the Christian life is not a new subject.[71]

In His discussion of Commandments[72] throughout Matthew 5, Jesus emphasizes not the legalistic details of law, but the heart of obedience and the desire to go beyond the letter of the law to the spirit of the law; beyond external conformity to an internal conformity. Jesus defined it clearly. Adultery is not merely the external act but the looking and lusting. The prohibition against murder becomes a prohibition against hatred. Obedience is an **attitude of the heart** and not simply an act of external conformity to commands.[73]

Discerning Holiness, Obedience

This is the attitude that characterized the Lord. "I delight to do Your will, O my God; Your Law is within my heart" (Ps 40:8). Under the New Covenant the law is written on our hearts. (Jer. 30:33, Isa 59:21) Interestingly, Abraham is said to have "obeyed my voice" and kept my charge, my commandments, my statutes, and my laws" (Gen 26:5) before the giving of the Mosaic law. This is in keeping with Paul's comment to the Corinthians that he was "not himself under the law (the Mosaic Law)" while at the same time "not outside the law of God, but under the law of Christ" (I Cor 9:20-21).

We think of justification by faith as the central theme of the Epistle to the Romans. However, Paul begins, concludes, and affirms in the middle of the text that he is speaking about an obedience of faith: "By whom we have received grace and apostleship for obedience to the faith among all nations for his name" (Rom 1:5). "But now is made manifest by the Scriptures and the prophets. According to the commandment of the ever-lasting God, made known to all nations for the obedience of faith" (Rom16:26). "But God be thanked that though you were the servants of sin, you have obeyed from the heart that form of doctrine, which was delivered to you" (Rom 6:17 KJV).[74]

The context here is important. Paul notes that slavery to sin results in death, but slavery to obedience leads to righteousness. Clearly this obedience is that of faith.

The Example of Christ

What is the perfection of Christ? Is it his holiness, love, humility, or his obedience? It includes all of these and more. He is perfect in all his ways. He is the perfect Son of God. Yet we read, "Although He (Jesus) was a Son, He learned obedience from the things which He suffered. And having been made perfect, He became to all those who obey Him the source of eternal salvation" (Heb 5:8-9). Christ's obedience[75] is a common theme.

He learned obedience; He was perfected; and He became the source of eternal salvation to those who obey Him! If the perfection of our Lord was somehow tied to his obedience, obedience should be important to us.

> If the perfection of our Lord was somehow tied to his obedience, obedience should be important to us.

In fact, this text ties our eternal salvation not to our faith in Christ but to our obedience to him, just as Romans 6:16 does "Do you not know that when you present yourselves to someone as slaves for obedience, you are slaves of the one whom you obey, either of sin resulting in death, or of obedience resulting in righteousness?

The reference to his obedience in the context of suffering is repeated in Philippians: "Being found in appearance as a man, He humbled Himself by becoming obedient to the point of death, even death on a cross" (Phil 2:8). Christ's obedience occurs in the context of a loving sacrifice for the salvation of the world. Though he began his ministry in the desert and often retreated to the desert to pray,

> Christ's obedience occurs in the context of a loving sacrifice for the salvation of the world.

His passion for the Father's will drove Him to the multitudes and to the cross. Christ is our faithful and merciful high priest who accomplishes our salvation in obedience to the Fathers will. Sacrifice and meal offering you have not desired; my ears You have opened; Burnt offering and sin offering You have not required. Then I said, "Behold, I come; in the scroll of the book—it is written of me. I delight to do Your will, O my God; Your Law is within my heart. I have proclaimed glad tidings of righteousness in the great congregation; Behold, I will not restrain my lips, O Lord, You know. I have not hidden Your righteousness within my heart; I have spoken of Your faithfulness and Your salvation; I have not concealed Your lovingkindness and Your truth from the great congregation" (Ps 40:6-10, quoted in Heb 10:5-7).

> Intimacy with God is not possible apart from submission to God.

Matthew: Intellect and Will

Intimacy with God is not possible apart from submission to God. The Gospel of Matthew constantly addresses behavior. Matthew is an ethicist.[76]

His gospel is structured around five sermons introduced by narratives which serve as the introduction to these discourses. Principle subjects include the reign of God (or of Heaven), God's will, justice, commandments, and the challenge to be perfect, to surpass, excel, observe, keep, to bear fruit, and to teach.

Is this a kind of rabbinic salvation by works? No. But it is a gospel which calls for submission to God's will. Though the sermons are central, the focus of the teaching is not the intellect but the will. For Israel the will of God is contained in the Torah; for Jesus it is in love, but it is a love marked by humble obedience to the law of Christ. These five discourses parallel the five books of the Pentateuch. He is the only evangelist to use the term church because he sees the church as the true Israel.[77]

Living Inside Out

Jesus stands in the shoes of Moses–the infancy narrative with the massacre of the children and God's son called out of Egypt prefigure the Prophet like Moses; after 40 days he ascends the mount and proclaims a new Law, in his transfiguration, Matthew adds, "his face shone like the sun" just as Moses face. Yet it is clear, one greater than Moses is here. And He proclaims a Law of Love on the same level, or truthfully— on a higher level, than Moses.

At the heart of the book of Matthew (11:25-30) is the prayer of Jesus, thanking his Father, that He has hidden these things from the wise and understanding and revealed them to children, the same children, who in Matthew 18 are characterized as being humble and greatest in the kingdom of God. He then issues an invitation: "Come to me, all who labor and are heavy laden and I will give you rest. Take my yoke upon you and learn from me for I am gentle (or meek) and lowly in heart and you will find rest for your souls for my yoke is easy, and my burden is light" (Matt11:29). Here it is in the obedience of coming and taking the yoke that rest is discovered. We are not called simply to observe but to plow, to take the yoke, to hear and to obey.

> Disciples are not merely scribes; they are obedient doers.

Matthew concludes his work with the Great Commission: "Go and make disciples… teaching them to observe all that I commanded you" (Matt 28:19-20). Disciples are not merely scribes; they are obedient doers. "Today scholars agree that the entire gospel points to these final verses: all the threads woven into the fabric of Matthew, from chapter one onward, draw together here."[78]

There is a danger for us in the comfort of our homes and culture to become occupied with the study of God's word apart from obedience. When our hearts are disobedient, we question the command. This was the approach of the serpent with Adam and Eve in the garden. He questioned the command, the structure and intent of the command. "Has God said, 'You shall not eat'" (Gen 3:1)? We may discuss its form and content, to distract from our sin, our failure to hear and obey. This is the essence of the teaching of the Pharisees and Sadducees which Jesus condemned as hypocrisy. (Matt 23:23-28).

David and Saul

In a "Walk Through the Bible"[79] lesson: Saul, David, and Solomon were pictured as having "no heart," a "whole heart," and a "half heart" respectively. Why is it that we say that Saul had no heart for God? It is because his 'obedience' was not obedience at all but *rebellion and insubordination* in God's sight. Then Samuel said to Saul, "Wait, and let me tell you what the Lord said to me last night." And he said to him, "Speak!" Samuel said, "Is it not true, though you were little in your own eyes, you were made the head of the tribes of Israel? And the Lord anointed you king over Israel and the Lord sent you on a mission, and said, 'Go and utterly destroy the sinners, the Amalekites, and fight against them until they are exterminated. **Why then did you not obey the voice of the Lord**, but rushed upon the spoil and did what was evil in the sight of the Lord?" Then Saul said to Samuel, "**I did obey** the voice of the Lord, and went on the mission on which the Lord sent me, and have brought back Agag the king of Amalek, and have utterly destroyed the Amalekites. **But** the people took some of

Living Inside Out

the spoil, sheep and oxen, the choicest of the things devoted to destruction, to sacrifice to the Lord your God at Gilgal." Samuel said, "Has the Lord as much delight in burnt offerings and sacrifices as in obeying the voice of the Lord? Behold, **to obey is better than sacrifice**, and to heed than the fat of rams. For rebellion is as the sin of divination, and insubordination is as iniquity and idolatry. **Because you have rejected the word of the Lord, He has also rejected you** from being king" (1 Sam 15:6-23).

Do you wonder why God may seem distant in your life? Consider your life choices. Disobedience is rejection of the word of God. It results in rejection by God; just as "God resists the proud and draws near to the humble." It is a manifestation of a heart of rebellion. It is especially dangerous because we are prone to think that what we are doing is in fact what God has commanded: "I did obey." Obedience is dependent upon our hearing the voice of God. The similarity between this passage and Romans 10:16-21 is striking. The obedience in question is obedience of and from the heart. When God chose David over Saul, Samuel said to Saul. "You have acted foolishly; you have not kept the commandment of the Lord your God, which He commanded you, for now the Lord would have established your kingdom over Israel forever. But now your kingdom shall not endure. The Lord has sought out for Himself **a man after His own heart**, and the Lord has appointed him as ruler over His people, **because you have not kept what the Lord commanded you**" (1 Sam 13:13).

Paul refers to this episode in his sermon at Antioch: "Then they asked for a king, and God gave them Saul the son of Kish, a man of the tribe of Benjamin, for forty years. After He had removed him (Saul), He raised up David to be their

Discerning Holiness, Obedience

king, concerning whom He also testified and said, I have found David, the son of Jesse, **a man after my heart, who will do all My Will**" (Acts13:22).

This issue of total submission, total obedience to the will of God gripped the heart of David. He could say in one breath,

> I have found David, the son of Jesse, a man after my heart, who will do all My Will" (Acts13:22).

"I desire to do your will, O my God; your law is within my heart," (Ps 40:8) and with the next, "My iniquities have overtaken me, they are more than the hairs of my head" (Ps 40:12).

Wesley: Perfectionism, and Pentecostalism

Obedience from the heart, total obedience to the will of God, or "Perfection," is the subject which is most often associated with John Wesley. His classic work *A Plain Account of Christian Perfection* is the record of his reflections on his teaching. He never uses the term "sinless perfection" but rather "Christian Perfection."[80]

Wesley introduced the concept of *entire sanctification.*

There was a remedy for the sickness of systemic sinfulness – a personal definitive work of God's sanctifying grace by which the war within oneself might cease and the heart be fully released from rebellion into wholehearted love for God and others. This relationship of perfect love could be accomplished, not by excellence of any moral achievements, but by the same faith in the merits of Christ's sacrifice for sin that initially had brought justification and the new life in Christ. It was a 'total death to sin and an entire renewal in the image of God"[81]

Living Inside Out

Wesley also concluded that this state of holiness was a step beyond the initial experience of conversion and could in the same way be experienced instantaneously just as conversion. "To this day both my brother and I maintained,

1. That Christian perfection is that love of God and our neighbor, which implies deliverance from *all* sin.

2. That this is received merely by *faith*.

3. That it is given *instantaneously*, in one moment.

4. That we are to expect it, not at death, but *every moment*; that *now* is the accepted time, *now* is the day of this salvation."[82]

It is this second work which becomes the focus of subsequent movements of holiness. Augustus M. Toplady penned these words in a well-known hymn:

Rock of Ages, cleft for me, let me hide myself in thee.

Let the water and the blood, from thy wounded side which flowed,

Be of sin the double cure; save from wrath and make me pure.[83] What did he mean by "the double cure?" The following line answers: "save from wrath and make me pure." "Double Cure" theology originates with John Wesley. It is this second instantaneous experience of deliverance or *entire sanctification.* **The heart of the holiness movement from Wesley's time until today is the *double cure*.**[84]

Holiness revivals and camp meetings characterized the nineteenth century. Francis Asbury in the early Methodist

Discerning Holiness, Obedience

movement carried Wesley's teaching throughout the United States. A third element was added and popularized by Charles F. Parham, who began a small Bible school in Topeka, Kansas in 1900 with forty students. "Fire baptism" with the Holy Spirit as evidenced by speaking in tongues burst on the scene December 31, 1900, when Agnes Ozmen asked for prayer that she might receive the baptism of the spirit. She became the first documented person to speak in tongues in the 20th century.[85]

This did not occur in a vacuum.[86]

Synan traces the reappearance of some of the charismatic gifts to Edward Irving in the 1830s and to Charles Spurgeon in 1857 who stated in a sermon titled, *The Power of the Holy Spirit*: "Another great work of the holy spirit which is not accomplished in the *bringing on of the later day glory* in a few more years, I know not when and I know not how, the Holy Spirit will be poured out in far different style from the present. There are diversities in operations and during the last few years it has been the case that the diversified questions have consisted of very little pouring out of the spirit…. My eyes flash with the thought that very likely I shall live to see the outpouring of the Spirit. When' the sons and daughters shall prophecy and the young men shall see visions and the old men shall dream dreams."[87]

The Cane Ridge revival which began as a communion service erupted into what some called "a frolic of faith" where thousands experienced 'manifestations of the Spirit' which included falling, jerking, dancing, barking, running, and singing.[88]

"The first revivalist to change this formula (from the Wesley second blessing) was Benjamin Hardin Irwin, founder of the "Fire-Baptized Holiness Church."[89]

Charles Parham who began his Bible school in Topeka in 1900, opened another school in Houston, Texas in 1905 where WJ Seymour, a black student from Louisiana would receive his training. Having accepted the "divine call" to go to Los Angeles, he was instrumental in the revival which broke out at Azusa Street and continued for three and a half years.

Though speaking in tongues was the main attraction, reports of all of the other gifts soon followed.[90]

Modern Pentecostalism traces its roots to this meeting. The Pentecostal movement is the largest of the renewal movements in modern time, with over half a billion members around the world. At its roots is the concern for holiness or the *entire sanctification* as defined by John Wesley.

Wesley had divided from his Puritan reformation roots. "Reformed theologians commonly insist that sanctification continues throughout a believer's life in distinction from justification, which is a definitive act of God, occurring once for all."[91]

The Keswick movement of "Higher Life" conferences in England began in the summer conventions of 1875 as a British counterpart of the American holiness movement.[92]

Popular speakers were Robert Pearsall Smith and his wife Hannah Whitall Smith. The Keswick position represented a major stand of holiness teaching within the United States which is separate from the bulk of Pentecostalism. The Keswick emphasis displaced the concept of the second blessing as an eradication of the sinful nature in favor of a baptism in the Holy Spirit as and enduement of power for service. The experience anticipated by the ardent seekers at Keswick was cast not so much in terms of cleansing as in the anointing by the Spirit. Further, the spirit-filled life was not a state of perfection but a maintained condition.[93]

Discerning Holiness, Obedience

These various positions represent the church's ongoing understanding of obedience, sanctification, and holiness. One of the difficulties involves translating our will to obey into active obedience. On an even deeper level is the difficulty of maintaining an obedient heart. All agree that this must be an inner work of the Spirit of God as David prayed, "Create in me a clean heart, O God and renew a right spirit within me" (Ps 51:10 ESV). He continues, "Uphold me with a willing spirit" (Ps 52:12 ESV).

> A man after God's heart is a man who wills to do all His will.

A man after God's heart is a man who wills to do all His will. It amounts to being willingly obedient. In the case of David, it meant that he expanded the boundaries of Israel defeating the enemies surrounding him and preparing the way for his son to build the temple. David wanted to build it himself and because it was in his heart, God said He would build Him a house. God rewards the intent of the heart. This was David's heart; his delight was to do God's will; to do whatever was on the heart of God. This is exactly what he did. "For David, after he had served the purpose of God in his own generation, fell asleep" (Acts 13:36).

> Obedience from a heart of humility and love is an obedience of faith. It is the result of a circumcised heart, union with Christ, and the Baptism of the Spirit.

This is not to say that he never sinned. He failed as we all do, but overall, he had a different heart than Saul. The issues of the exact application of the law to the Christian or even of external disciplines of the monastic life are secondary to the

Living Inside Out

heart issue of obedience. One of the characteristics of the new covenant is that God's law is internalized—it is written on the heart. Every Christian cannot now recite the text or the letter of the law, but the law is a delight to the heart. The heart is humbled and changed, it is opened to believe, to obey, to love. And it is in the heart of the humble that God dwells. The Kingdom of God is revealed as we live from the heart, from the inside out.

Obedience from a heart of humility and love is an obedience of faith. It is the result of a circumcised heart, union with Christ, and the Baptism of the Spirit. Though all of these are instantaneous, their effect is an ongoing result of faith exercised moment by moment. Therefore, we turn to an examination of that which is essential to greatness, the fourth and final internal: Faith.

CHAPTER 5

DELIVERING FAITH, THE MYSTERY

Though Martin Luther lived an exemplary life as a monk, inside he felt he could never live up to God's requirement of righteousness. God's righteous judgment proclaimed in the gospel seemed cause for despair until he realized that the righteousness offered in the gospel is not active (something we must do), that is, not a result of our external struggle; but passive, that is, righteousness received by faith in Christ's finished work something He and only He did). "I began to understand that the righteousness of God is that by which the righteous live by a gift of God, namely by faith."[94]

> This revelation of a faith which rests in God's gift rather than striving in religious activity transformed all of life for Luther. He referred to it as a 'new birth'.

This revelation of a faith which rests in God's gift rather than striving in religious activity transformed all of life for Luther. He referred to it as a 'new birth'.

> Faith lies at the heart of our being but remains a spiritual secret for many.

Living Inside Out

This rest of faith is the fourth aspect of the heart God seeks in the believer living inside out.

Faith is the *sine qua non* for pleasing God. It is that mysterious ingredient which makes the unseen visible and the visible sign, like baptism and communion, a spiritual reality. It reveals the hidden things of God. Faith originates with God, but is exercised by humankind, and transforms our physical world. Faith lies at the heart of our being but remains a spiritual secret for many. In this final chapter of section one, we will explore the relationship of faith to love, humility, and obedience; and discuss the operation of faith in creative work, Sabbath rest, and spiritual growth.

Faith Works by Love

Faith springs from love, humility, and obedience.

- LOVE- "Faith works through love" (Gal 5:6).

- HUMILITY- "I will leave in your midst a meek and humble people, and they shall trust in the name of the Lord" (Zeph 3:12).

- OBEDIENCE- "Through whom we have received grace and apostleship to bring about the obedience of faith among all the Gentiles, for His name's sake" (Rom 1:5).

Faith is valued by God precisely because it is intimately linked to love, humility, and obedience.

Jesus' teaching that the entire law could be summarized in the commandments, to love God with all our heart and our

Delivering Faith, The Mystery

neighbor as ourselves, would have come as no surprise to His hearers since this is precisely what Moses taught.[95]

The people who believed gladly heard the Lord because their hearts bore witness to this truth whereas the unbelieving in the place of leadership rejected Him. When we love someone, we trust them. A steady faith is a sure sign of intimacy with God.[96]

Love believes in all circumstances

> One of the interesting problems in studying faith in the Old Testament is that it is not mentioned as such when it is clearly in evidence.

(1Cor 13:7). Faith is contrasted with works in Galatians and Romans; but James demonstrates the impossibility of true faith apart from works. This is further developed in the book of Hebrews. Different aspects of faith are emphasized throughout the scriptures. At times faith is explicitly demonstrated in loving obedience (Deut 30:11-16).

One of the interesting problems in studying faith in the Old Testament is that it is not mentioned as such when it is clearly in evidence. We learn in Hebrews that it was by faith that Abel offered a more excellent offering, Enoch was

> Without faith, it is impossible to please God. So, every case wherein a man or woman is pleasing to God is an example of "faith".

translated, Noah built an ark, and Moses was hidden from Pharaoh. **But the word "faith" does not appear in the original stories.** Nevertheless, according to scripture, "faith" is at the heart of each of these relationships. Without faith, it is impossible to please God. So, every case wherein a man or woman is pleasing to God is an example of "faith". Often though, faith is professed but not actually possessed. Jesus confronted the Jews of his day with their unbelief: "If you believed Moses, you would believe me; for he wrote of me. But if you do not believe his writings, how will you believe my words" (John 5:46-47)?

It is possible to be occupied with God's law without faith. One of the purposes of God's law is to bring us to a humble awareness of our depravity and the extent of our sin: "by the law is the knowledge of sin" (Rom 3:20). The law was a tutor to lead us to faith in Christ, but faith preceded the law and characterized all who pleased God in every age. Paul writes that the Gentiles have, "attained a righteousness that is by faith; but Israel, who pursued a law that would lead to righteousness, did not succeed in reaching that law. Why? Because they did not pursue it by faith, but pursued righteousness based upon works" (Rom 9:30-32).

The relationships between faith and works, grace and law, love and obedience go to the heart of our relationship with God.[97]

The requirement to work out our salvation in obedient service sometimes displaces the faith/rest aspect evidenced in moment-by-moment yielding to the Spirit of God, but the two must not be separated.

In the same way, the content of faith, must not eclipse the object or person of our faith[98].

Biblical faith is both objective (content-full) and subjective—confidence or trust in God. Beyond the historical content of the Christian faith lies the person of Christian faith. Paul said, "believe on the Lord Jesus Christ and you will be saved" (Acts 16:31). Jesus said, "Have faith in God" (Mark 11:22). The Hebrew concept of faith is weighted toward the second aspect, the confident trust in the person whereas the Greek, though including the latter, focuses on the first, the content or proposition.[99]

Both aspects are crucial, but the Hebrew, confident trust in God, is especially important to our understanding of the interdependence of love, humility, and obedience in faith.

Faith is reliance upon God; a casting of oneself upon God. It is in this sense that faith works by love. When one is gripped by the love of God in giving His son, the believer responds in faith. When a person realizes that he is living a life of pride exalting himself above God and humbles his heart, confessing his sin he responds in faith. When a person understands the reality of his rebellion against God, and then obeys the gospel by submitting to Christ as Lord, he acts in faith. Faith then is a manifestation of love, humility, and obedience.

This resignation to God himself, this "casting of ourselves", upon God is sometimes seen as a "Higher Life" principle or a part of a "second work of grace," but it is simply a proper appreciation of the nature of biblical faith. A Puritan prayer summarizes it well, "Thou hast taught me that faith is nothing else than receiving thy kindness; that it is an adherence to Christ, a resting on him, love clinging to him as a branch to the tree to seek life and vigor from him."[100]

Watchman Nee writes, "Christianity begins not with a big 'do', but with a big 'done'."[101]

"The all-important rule is not to 'try' but to 'trust', not to depend upon our own strength but upon His."[102]

"Our task is one of holding, not of attacking. We do not fight for victory, we fight from victory."[103]

His insights are reflective of Hudson Taylor a generation before him.[104]

The source of strength in the Christian life is Christ Himself, living His life by the power of His Spirit in the yielded heart of the believer. Ian Thomas described it as "The Saving Life of Christ" referring to Romans 5:10.[105]

> The source of strength in the Christian life is Christ Himself, living His life by the power of His Spirit in the yielded heart of the believer.

Variations of this "faith in God" theme occur under many different headings in Scripture: resting, waiting, trusting, and hoping. Elements of Sabbath, Sukkoth, Canaan, walking in the Spirit, living in the Kingdom of God, even Heaven itself reflect this amazing theme. It is often presented in graphic images and paradox.

We are commanded to wait on God. Waiting on God is contrasted with disobedience and synonymous with seeking Him, returning to Him, trusting Him, hoping in Him, observing justice and kindness, and results in inheriting the land:

- Ps 37:9-For evildoers will be cut off, but those who **wait** for the Lord, they will inherit the land. Ps 25:3-Indeed, none of those who **wait** for Thee will be ashamed; those who deal treacherously without cause will be ashamed.

- He gives power to the faint and to him who has no might he increases strength. Even the young men will faint and be weary. The young men will fall and be exhausted. But they who **wait** for the Lord will renew their strength. They will mount up with wings like eagles. They will run and not be weary. They will walk and faint (Isaiah 40:29-31).

Delivering Faith, The Mystery

- Lam 3:25-The Lord is good to those who **wait** for Him; to the person who seeks Him.

- Hosea 12:6-Therefore, return to your God, observe kindness and justice, and **wait** for your God continually.

- Psalm 130:5-**Wait** for the LORD, my soul does **wait**, and in His word, do I hope.

One text is especially interesting because of the way it is quoted in the New Testament: Isa 64:4, "For from of old they have not heard nor perceived by ear, neither has the eye seen a God besides Thee, who acts on behalf of **the one who waits for Him**." Paul, citing this same text writes,1Cor. 2:9- "Things which eye has not seen, and ear has not heard, and which have not entered into the heart of man, all that God has prepared **for those who Love Him**." This is a fascinating commentary on the concept of waiting in the Old Testament passage, equating it with loving God in 1Corinthians.

The Great Illustration: The Sabbath

The best illustration and one which has become one of the greatest sources of controversy is the Sabbath itself. The Sabbath as an illustration of our life of faith in Christ is most concisely captured in Hebrews 4:4-11.

"For He has thus said somewhere concerning the seventh *day*, and God rested on the seventh day from all His works; again, in this *passage*, "They shall not enter My rest. Since therefore it remains for some to enter it, and those who formerly had good news preached to them failed to enter because of disobedience, He again fixes a certain day, today, saying through David after so long a time just as has been said before, Today, if you hear His voice, do not harden your hearts. For if Joshua had given them rest, He would not have spoken of another day after that. There remains therefore a Sabbath rest for the people of God. For the one who has entered His rest has himself also rested from his works, as God did from His. Let us therefore be diligent to enter that rest, lest anyone fall through *following* the same example of disobedience."

The author recalls three references to Sabbath/rest and concludes that under the new Covenant, the observance of Sabbath is fulfilled by exercising faith. First, referring to the creation account, he writes that "God rested on the seventh day from all of His works." Next, He then quotes Ps 95 which refers to the land of Canaan as a place of rest from the slavery of Egypt. This was denied to the first generation of those who came out of Egypt because of disobedience and unbelief (Num 14). The next generation, under the leadership of Joshua, did enter the land. Finally, he calls attention to the first part of Ps 95, spoken in the time of David, long after the land of Canaan had been possessed, and another promise is made. "Today if you hear His voice, do not harden your hearts." He then argues in verses 8-11, "For if Joshua had given them rest, he would not have spoken of another day after that. There remains therefore a Sabbath rest for the people of God. For the one who has entered His rest has himself also rested from his works, as God did from His. Let us therefore be diligent to enter that rest, lest anyone fall through following the same example of disobedience."

This rest was not the rest from warring enemies (Deu 25:19). Having conquered all of the enemies around him, David knew firsthand what that kind of rest would mean, but he looked toward another rest.[106]

This Sabbath rest is intimately linked with the rest of God on the seventh day but is intentionally distinct from it. The command to keep the Sabbath was given in Exodus 16, 17, and 20 to those very people the writer of Hebrews states did not enter the rest. The next generation which entered and possessed the land, those not included in the oath, "they shall not enter my rest" (Hebrews 3:11), did not enter the rest, though they certainly had the (literal seventh day) Sabbath. Third, this rest is entered by faith! "We who have believed enter that rest" (Hebrews 4:3). Again, it is to be entered today; not just on the seventh day but every day. In fact, it is to be entered continually. "We who have believed (do) enter," or enter continually that rest. Dale Ratlaff points out as well, "The author (of Hebrews) is showing how much better the new covenant is than the old. I believe the truth he is trying to convey is that 'Sabbath' (sabbatismos, Gr.) of the new covenant is better than the Sabbath (*sabbaton,* Gr.) of the old covenant."[107]

The entire book of Hebrews is an exhortation to faith, to drawing near, to holding fast, to enduring under persecution. Here too, the exhortation is to "be diligent," "to strive" (RSV), or "to labor" (KJV). But the goal to this striving is to enter rest.

This seems on the surface a paradox. If the rest is in fact rest, what work is involved? He answers, 'the rest of faith', agreeing with Jesus; this is the work of God that you believe on him whom He has sent (John 6:29). It is repentance, the rest of ceasing from our sin and self, taking the yoke of Christ, and finding rest for the soul. This rest requires the work; the labor of ceasing from self, turning from the incessant demands of sin,

Living Inside Out

Satan, and the world. This rest of faith encompasses all that the Sabbath was intended to teach.

Psalm 92 which is titled A Psalm for the Sabbath, reveals this broad application: "A Psalm, a song for the time that is to come for the day that shall be all Sabbath and rest in the life everlasting."[108]

Isaiah reflects this broad understanding of Sabbath as well: the keeping of Sabbath is associated with the keeping of justice and the doing of righteousness in all of life. Thus, says the Lord, "Preserve justice, and do righteousness, For My salvation is about to come And My righteousness to be revealed. How blessed is the man who does this, And the son of man who takes hold of it, who keeps from profaning the Sabbath: And keeps his hand from doing any evil" (Isa 56:1-2).

> Sabbath is associated with the keeping of justice and the doing of righteousness in all of life.

The Sabbath commandment given in Exodus 20 and repeated in Deuteronomy 5 enjoins rest. It is based on a remembrance of the Sabbath in which God rested from His work of creation (Exod 20:1-11). Secondly, it is an observance of the Sabbath in which all are freed from work in keeping with God's deliverance of His people from bondage in Egypt (Deut 5:12-15). For the Jewish nation, the Sabbath became a sign of the covenant at Sinai. "So, the sons of Israel shall observe the Sabbath, to celebrate the Sabbath throughout their generations as a perpetual covenant. It is a sign between Me and the sons of Israel forever; for in six days the Lord made heaven and earth, but on the seventh day He ceased from labor and was refreshed" (Exod 31:16-17).

The keeping of the Sabbath came to represent the entirety of the covenant, or the heart of the law. The Maccabeans would keep it to the point of refusing to attack enemies on the Sabbath.[109]

The Books of Jubilees, the Damascus Document, and later Rabbinic works give detailed lists of prohibited tasks—grouped and subdivided, so that even carrying small objects for minute distances may be forbidden. Oral tradition surrounding the Sabbath and the Torah itself is referred to as a "fence" set around the law whose many restrictions serve to keep one from even approaching violation of the command to sanctify the Sabbath.[110]

It was these interpretations of scripture that Jesus confronted.

The weekly Sabbath pointed back to the rest of the creation before sin's resulting curse and the deliverance from bondage to the enemies which results from that fall. Jesus fulfilled the righteousness of the Sabbath and proclaimed Himself "Lord of the Sabbath." He repeatedly healed on the Sabbath to expose the erroneous legalism which had come to surround not only Sabbath but many other elements of Judaism. Beyond that He transcends authority in interpreting Sabbath and in fulfilling it in terms of freeing individuals from bondage to their physical disease and spiritual blindness.[111]

Many have taken up the discussion of how and if Jesus actually violated the Sabbath law as a statement of His authority over the Sabbath. Most agree that He fulfills the Sabbath when rightly interpreted.[112]

The crux of the matter is that Jesus was continually involved in activities the Jews considered a violation of the Sabbath (John 5:18). His response was two pronged. First, judgment should not be superficial, not according to appearance but, according

Living Inside Out

to righteousness with consideration of the heart/motivation (John 7:24); and with this in view, the Messiah, Jesus himself is the final judge and final authority (John 5:22, 27).

In the early church, Sabbath was quickly abandoned for the Lord's Day or Sunday.[113]

Any discussion of continuity and discontinuity between God's covenants requires care in defining the analogies. Controversies over keeping Saturday Sabbath a Holy Day or transferring the laws of the Seventh Day Sabbath to a first day or Sunday Sabbath often miss the point of the fulfillment of Sabbath in Christ. The literal physical rest of Sabbath pictures the rest of salvation both from works of flesh and from the temporal toil of earth. Celebration of "The Lord's day," proclaims the rest we now enjoy because of Christ's death and resurrection as well as the anticipation of heaven's rest. Both are acts of faith but should not be confused or consolidated. The Messianic movement has sought to recover elements of Sabbath celebration with a goal of understanding their fulfillment in Christ. But the celebration of the day points to the reality of faith.

In short, the physical rest of the Old Testament Sabbath has become the salvation rest of the true Sabbath. Believers in Christ can now live in God's Sabbath that has already dawned.

Delivering Faith, The Mystery

Jesus' working to accomplish this superseded the OT Sabbath (John 5:17) and so does the doing of God's work that He now requires of people- believing in the one God has sent (John 6:28-29). In fact, the Sabbath keeping now demanded is the cessation from reliance on one's own works. (Hebrews 4:9-10)[114]

The Land of Canaan

The rest of faith is also illustrated by the land of Canaan. "For ye are not as yet come to the rest and to the inheritance, which the Lord your God gives you. But when ye go over Jordan, and dwell in the land which the Lord your God gives you to inherit, and when he gives you rest from all your enemies round about, so that ye dwell in safety" (Deut 12:9-10). Once they arrived in the Promised Land, they began to fight the fight of faith. It is interesting that Canaan is called "a rest." Unfortunately, many Christian hymns reflect the common notion that Canaan should be interpreted as a picture of Heaven. Canaan though is not only a type of heaven, but of the victorious life of faith. The book of Hebrews is concerned with the 'better' promise, priest, sacrifice, land, and so forth. The message of Hebrews 3 and 4 is: watch out, be careful to trust and obey, because God is calling us to a better Sabbath, a rest of faith and obedience.

> It is interesting that Canaan is called "a rest." Unfortunately, many Christian hymns reflect the common notion that Canaan should be interpreted as a picture of Heaven. Canaan though is not only a type of heaven, but of the victorious life of faith.

Living Inside Out

"Today if you hear his voice, do not harden your hearts as in the rebellion in the day of testing in the wilderness where your fathers put me to the test, saw my works for forty years. I was provoked with that generation. I said they always go astray in their heart. They have not known my ways and I swore in my wrath they are not going to enter my rest. Take care brethren, lest there be in any of you an evil unbelieving heart" (Heb 3:7-12).

The land of Canaan prefigures the rest entered by faith and obedience we discover in Christ as we learn God's ways. "Exhort one another daily while it is called today lest any you be hardened through the deceitfulness of sin" (Heb 3:13 KJV). The hardening effect of sin can be avoided by daily exhortation, assuming a humble response of faith. "For we share in Christ if indeed we hold our original confidence firm to the end as it is said, "Today if you hear his voice do not harden your hearts as when they provoked me" (Heb 3:14-15). And to whom did He swear that they should not enter His rest, but to those who were <u>disobedient</u>? So we see that they were not able to enter because of <u>unbelief</u> (Heb 3:18-19 NASB).[115]

Here, disobedience is synonymous with unbelief just as faith is synonymous with obedience. "Therefore, while the promise of entering his rest still stands, let us fear lest we should fall short. For the good news came to us just as it did to them, but the message did not benefit them because it was not united by faith. For we who have believed enter the rest" (Heb 4:2-3).

By faith and patience, we inherit the promise…the rest, Canaan. We enter a condition of resting. The rest in Canaan is not sitting and doing nothing but taking up our swords and shields and conquering the Promised Land. Our rest in faith lies

Delivering Faith, The Mystery

in taking up the sword of God's word, and the shield of Faith, and building the Kingdom. It is done only in God's power.

Plowing is done in the power of the strongest oxen. "Take my yoke upon you and learn of me" (Matt 11:29). An ox does not sit down to plow. A soldier does not fight by falling asleep in battle. These are pictures of faith which allows us to rest and to work at the same time. We ought to fear going through a day or a life in unbelief, not entering His rest. It is possible for us to live life in the flesh just as it was for Israel. After they did it long enough, God took them out of the picture. For each of us, there is a challenge every day to believe God, to lay down the burden of sin, our own interests, and agendas, and submit to Him. As we do His will in His power and strength, in returning and rest, we are saved. They that wait upon the Lord renew their strength; they run and are not weary. They walk and do not faint (Isa 40:31).

Worn out Christians are often "worn out" because they are not living out the Christian life in the power of Christ. The Christian life is just that: Christ living within. In the same way we were saved we must rise each day praying, "Lord, save me again from my own agenda, my own business, and myself." We must stop and listen to the voice of God. We must spend our day in the conscious presence of God, in Shabbat, in the Land of Promise, listening to the Word of God, celebrating Him. But it is in this condition that the real work is done, the important battle is engaged.

"Behold, the dwelling place of God is with man" Revelation 21:3. This is our confident expectation and our experience of faith. Shabbat, *Sukkot*,[116] Canaan, or the fullness of the Spirit, must not be reduced to a day, a season, a place, or even a transient ecstatic experience. It is the ongoing daily experience of

Living Inside Out

God living and dwelling in me in all His power, love, and holiness. It is living…from the inside out. And once we learn the rest of faith we can move to the walk of faith.

The Great Exercise of Faith

Some understand faith as a natural ability, which resides in all. This is true to the extent that faith involves action based upon evidence. People constantly sit on chairs they have not personally assembled based upon the evidence that the chair is beside a table and in no apparent disrepair. Scripture speaks of another level of faith exercised by sinners in response to the gospel. This faith is not common to all men but is a gift of God: "For to you it has been granted for Christ's sake, not only to believe in him, but also to suffer for his sake" (Phil 1:29). "For through the grace given to me, I say to every man among you not to think of himself more highly than he ought to think; but to think so as to have sound judgment as God has allotted to each a measure of faith" (Rom 12:3).

Faith is granted or allotted. Having received it we give thanks. We ask God for greater faith. We pray that our friends might believe. But we never boast that we simply had the common sense to believe. Faith is given by God. Jesus is the author of our faith. "Fixing our eyes on Jesus, the author and perfecter of faith, who for the joy set before him endured the cross, despising the shame, and has sat down at the right hand of the throne of God" (Hebrews 12:2).

Not only is He the author, but also the perfecter of our faith. Faith changes—it grows and is perfected. One of the most important commentaries on the life of Abraham is found in the fourth chapter of Romans; "Yet with respect to the promise of

Delivering Faith, The Mystery

God, he did not waver in unbelief, but grew strong in faith, giving glory to God" (Rom 4:20). Abraham had been promised a son in his old age. He was one hundred years old and his wife ninety. But this did not cause him to doubt. He was convinced that God was able to do what he promised. Growing strong in faith, he glorified God. Notice two things: First, his faith grew, or he grew strong in faith; and second, this growth in faith glorified God. God is glorified as we exercise our faith, and as it grows. Paul writes to the Thessalonians. "We have always to give thanks to God for you brethren, as is only fitting because your faith is greatly enlarged, and the love of each one of you toward one another grows even greater" (2Thess1:3).

> God is glorified as we exercise our faith, and as it grows.

Our faith grows in the same way that our bodies grow. Faith is a gift in the same sense that our bodies are gifts. We did nothing to obtain the body that we have. Some bodies are genetically superior to other bodies; some bodies are afflicted from birth. But much of what we end up with is dependent on our attitude, desire, diet, and exercise. Though many bodybuilders are endowed with an outstanding genetic makeup, the final product is the result of hours, months, and years of training and discipline. Apart from those grueling hours of training they would never develop the mass and symmetry that leads to a world title. Bodybuilding requires that the muscles be

> In much the same way as a body builder, a young Christian's faith is challenged: broken down and built-up by exercise.

Living Inside Out

challenged. Muscle fibers are broken down with each training session then repaired and enlarged in the recovery phase.[117]

In much the same way as a body builder, a young Christian's faith is challenged: broken down and built-up by exercise. Just as a coach guides athletes, Jesus acts as the perfecter of our faith. He directs the challenges before us, but we must exercise faith; and as we do, it grows. We grow strong in faith, giving glory to God—living inside out.

In 1 and 2 Thessalonians, we read that faith is enlarged and love grows: they seem to go hand-in-glove. Faith works through love. This is more difficult to appreciate than the growth of the physical body. Our faith and love are not obvious in every situation. And sometimes when we think our love and faith are weakest, they are at their best.

Unlike the physical body, which is visible to the naked eye, faith is invisible. Jesus compares it to a mustard seed, the smallest of the common seeds in ancient Israel. Jesus once said, "If you had faith like a mustard seed, you could say to this Mulberry tree, 'Be uprooted and be planted in the sea', and it would obey you" (Luke 17:6). Moreover, "If you have faith the size of a mustard seed, you will say to this mountain, 'Move from here to there,' and it will move; and nothing will be impossible to you" (Matt 17:20).

Was Jesus speaking allegorically, or has no one ever had mustard seed faith? Perhaps faith is more like nuclear power than conventional power. One does not require many nuclear bombs to move a mountain or a mulberry tree, so it is with faith. We need very little and in fact, we are given little. But with exercise, it grows. And the growth and exercise of our faith glorifies God.

Delivering Faith, The Mystery

God gives faith to be exercised. As He gives bodies capable of sitting, walking, standing, and running, so he gives faith, capable of glorifying Him. What a shame it would be to have faith and not exercise it. It would be as tragic as having the potential to be an Olympic champion, and never going to the gym.

The Righteous and The Unrighteous

The righteous live by faith. "As for the proud his soul is not right within him; but the righteous will live by his faith" (Habakkuk 2:4). This text is quoted three times in the New Testament.[118]

In Romans the righteous result of faith is emphasized. In Galatians, the faith is emphasized as the process by which we become righteous. And in Hebrews, the life of faith is emphasized. The righteous live by faith, day by day. God expects it of them.

Consider the story of Peter walking on the water in the midst of a storm. "Immediately Jesus stretched out His hand and took hold of him, and said to him, 'You of little faith, why did you doubt?'" (Matt 14:31). Look at the context here. Rebuking Peter for his little faith, Jesus questioned why he doubted. Jesus acts surprised as if he were expecting a different outcome. The boat was some distance from land and was being beaten by the waves. It was dark, between three and six in the morning when Jesus came to them walking on the sea. When the disciples saw Him, they were terrified and said, "It is a ghost." They cried out in fear, but immediately Jesus spoke to them saying "Take heart, it is I, do not be afraid." Most of them were terrified but Jesus calmed them. In the midst of this, Peter spoke up, "Lord, if it is you, command me to come to you on the water." This

Living Inside Out

is "Great Faith," the kind of attitude that sets Peter apart. Jesus said to him, "Come." Peter got out of the boat to walk on the water to Jesus.

The other apostles must have been amazed at what Peter did initially. "But when he saw the wind, he was afraid and beginning to sink he cried out 'Lord save me.'" This seems a natural enough response. But when Jesus reached out and took hold of him, He said, "Oh, you of a little faith, why did you doubt?" One would expect that Jesus would have been encouraged with Peter, even with his failure. The attempt was more than any of the other disciples dared. But Jesus did not say, "That was great for your first time; good effort!" Jesus expected faith from Peter, and he said, "You of a little faith, why did you doubt?" God expects great things of His children to whom He has given a measure of faith. He expects faith to be exercised daily moment by moment.

The honor roll of Hebrews 11 is repeated in the pages of church history in the daily faith of people like George Mueller of Bristol, England who without ever mentioning his needs to men called on God and saw Him provide on a daily basis for hundreds of England's orphans over a period of twenty years; or the British politician William Wilberforce and his supporters who in the face of overwhelming opposition and repeated defeat saw the abolition of the slave trade in the British Empire by diligent public debate; or David Brainerd, who in his mission to the American Indians sometimes tied himself to his horse journeying from village to village in blizzard conditions; or Adoniram Judson, who over 40 years, in spite of illness and imprisonment, continued his work of translating the entire Bible into the Burmese language and founding a church of over 7,000 members and 100 trained national pastors. Time would

Delivering Faith, The Mystery

fail to tell of these and countless others like Mother Teresa, C.T. Studd, Richard Allen, Susanna Wesley, Watchman Nee, men and women across all ages and races, who glorified God in loving, humble, obedient faith.[119]

"And leaving the multitude, they took Him along with them, just as He was, in the boat; and other boats were with Him. And there arose a fierce gale of wind, and the waves were breaking over the boat so much that the boat was already filling up. And He Himself was in the stern, asleep on the cushion and they awoke Him and said to Him, "Teacher, do You not care that we are perishing?" And being aroused, He rebuked the wind and said to the sea, "Hush, be still." And the wind died down and it became perfectly calm. And He said to them, "Why are you so timid? How is it that you have no faith?" And they became very much afraid and said to one another, "Who then is this, that even the wind and the sea obey Him" (Mark 4:36-41)?

> Jesus expected faith from his disciples, and Jesus expects the same from us.

Here again we see Jesus address the disciples about their lack of faith while they were at sea. The disciples were seasoned fishermen, not newcomers to the Sea of Galilee. They had been in storms in their small fishing boats before. Notice their assessment of the situation. "Do you not care that we are perishing?" They had reason to believe they were in imminent danger. As fishermen addressing a carpenter, they expected Him to trust their seasoned judgment. As the son of God, addressing his disciples, He expected them to act in faith. "Why are you so timid? How is it that you have no faith?" He did not say weak faith or little faith. He said, "no faith!" And again, He acted surprised.

Living Inside Out

Jesus expected faith from his disciples, and Jesus expects the same from us. Jesus has given us faith to begin a relationship with Him, and He expects the exercise of it as a daily part of life.

Finally, at the end of His time on the earth, He exhorts two of His disciples as they face a seemingly hopeless future. "But also, some women among them amazed us. When they were at the tomb early in the morning, and did not find His body, they came, saying that they had also seen a vision of angels, who said that He was alive. And some of those who were with us went to the tomb and found it just exactly as the women also had said; but Him they did not see. And He said to them, O foolish men and slow of heart to believe in all that the prophets have spoken! Was it not necessary for the Christ to suffer these things and to enter into His glory? And beginning with Moses and with all the prophets, He explained to them the things concerning Himself in all the Scriptures. And they approached the village where they were going, and He acted as though He would go farther. And they urged Him, saying, "stay with us, for it is getting toward evening, and the day is now nearly over." And He went in to stay with them. And it came about that when He had reclined at the table with them, He took the bread and blessed it, and breaking it, He began giving it to them. And their eyes were opened, and they recognized Him; and He vanished from their sight. And they said to one another, "Were not our hearts burning within us while He was speaking to us on the road, while He was explaining the Scriptures to us" (Luke 24:22-34)?

Here Jesus speaks to two of his disciples as they walk on the road to Emmaus. The disciples are puzzled by reports of the resurrection. They have been grieving the loss of their master after witnessing his crucifixion. Does Jesus comfort them in

Delivering Faith, The Mystery

their unbelief? No, he rebukes them! "Oh, foolish men, slow of a heart to believe!" Jesus expected faith even in the storms of life and in the face of death because he had given faith. Since he was the perfecter of faith He expected the exercise of faith. Take note that the problem was in their hearts. He describes them as "slow of heart."

Israel was exhorted, "circumcise the foreskins of your heart and be no longer stubborn" (Deut 10:16). Uncircumcision is counted as pride and circumcision of heart is equated with humility (Lev 26:41); and with love (Deut 30:6). Jeremiah exhorted the nation, circumcise yourselves to the Lord and remove the foreskin of your hearts. God promised to circumcise the hearts of his people, so we would love and obey Him. It was no new revelation when Paul wrote, "For no one is a Jew who is merely one outwardly, nor is circumcision outward and physical, a Jew is one inwardly, and circumcision is a matter of the heart, by the Spirit, not by the letter" (Romans 2:28-29). The command to circumcise our hearts and the promise that God will circumcise the heart is parallel to the commands to believe and the promises that God will give faith.

On the two occasions in which Jesus commended "great faith" He observed it in humble hearts. When the centurion said, "I am not worthy that you should come under my roof," Jesus replied, "I have not found so great faith, no, not in Israel!" (Matt 8:8, 10) Likewise with the woman who argued out of humility, "Lord, the little dogs eat of the crumbs" He said, "Oh woman, great is your faith" (Matt 15: 27-28).

The heart is the center of humanity including our minds, our emotions, and will. It is the immaterial part of humanity. Some have sought to draw fine distinctions between soul and spirit, but this is difficult since many of the same attributes are assigned to both.[120]

When we are commanded to love God with all the heart, soul, mind, and strength (Mark 12:30 citing Deut 6:4) the heart refers to all we are within, the soul to our length of days, the mind and strength is a translation of the word that normally means "very." It means our "everything," our energy, our ultimate, so it is often translated here "mind and strength."[121]

Faith springs from the inner being, the heart. "With the heart man believes, resulting in righteousness" (Romans 10:10). We are commanded to believe in our hearts that God raised Jesus from the dead. A heart left to itself is corrupted by sin, enslaved, and darkened.

Jesus was clear on this matter. When his enemies confronted him in unbelief, he responded, "You do not believe because you are not part of my flock. My sheep hear my voice, and I know them, and they follow me; and I give them eternal life" (John 10:26, 27). Unbelief is contrasted with hearing the voice of God and following him.

Paul is equally clear on this issue when he writes to the Thessalonians. Paul instructs the Thessalonians to pray, "That we may be delivered from perverse and evil men for not all men have faith" (2 Thess 3:2). Faith is natural to the sheep. The just shall live by faith. And when they fail to exercise their faith, they are rebuked for being slow of heart. In fact, the rebuke takes an even stronger form in the book of Hebrews where we read,

"Take care brethren lest there should be in anyone of you an evil unbelieving heart, in falling away from the living God" (Heb 3:12). A heart of unbelief is an evil heart. In the same chapter, unbelief is synonymous with disobedience. To whom did he swear that they would not enter his rest but to those who were disobedient? So, we see that they were unable to enter because of unbelief (Heb 3:18, 19). Unbelief is disobedience and faith, living inside out, is a matter of obedience.

Prosperity and Crucifixion

How do we go about guarding our hearts, taking care of our hearts, and growing in faith? Examples of faith confront us in every generation. Sometimes faith triumphs: it takes the form of conquest. At other times we read of faith in the context of martyrdom: "They conquered kingdoms, enforced justice, obtained promises, stopped the mouths of lions, quenched the power of fire, escaped the edge of the sword, were made strong out of weakness, became mighty in war, put foreign armies to flight. Women received back their dead by resurrection" (Heb 11:33-35).

This goes beyond prosperity gospel to a dominion theology. But in the same chapter we read: "All these died in faith, without receiving the promises, but having seen them and having welcomed them from a distance and having confessed that they were strangers and exiles on the earth—they were stoned, they were sawn asunder, they were tempted. They were put to death with the sword: they went about in sheep skins, and goat skins, being destitute, afflicted, ill-treated, man, of whom the world was not worthy, wandering in deserts and mountains and caves and holes in the ground. And all these, having gained approval through their faith, did not receive what was promised" (Heb. 11:13, 37-39).

This is not a "prosperity gospel", and no one is "claiming their healing".[122]

Living Inside Out

Here, they are not prospering by faith, but are impoverished, and not healed, but afflicted and killed.

How can these two contrasting outcomes, conquering (in verse 33) and suffering (in verse 37) be reconciled? It seems to be a matter of timing. The ultimate goal of our faith is not martyrdom but triumph. But the triumph may involve martyrdom for some. Faith enables us to endure the martyrdom that

> The ultimate goal of our faith is not martyrdom but triumph. But the triumph may involve martyrdom for some.

the kingdom of God may triumph. Just as Jesus did not suffer simply for the sake of suffering, but to redeem His own and establish the kingdom, so we do not suffer simply for the sake of suffering but to establish the kingdom. Jesus endured the cross, despising the shame, because he looked forward to the prize. We too endure hardness looking forward to the prize: "While we look not at the things which are seen, but at the things which are not seen; for the things which are seen are temporal, but the things which are not seen are eternal" (2Cor 4:18). Pain and suffering in the believer produce character when endured by faith. We might lose the use of our legs but learn to walk by faith. We might lose our eyes but gain spiritual insight: We might lose our money but gain spiritual riches.

The faith of Hebrews 11 is a faith which at times leads to victory, triumph, and prosperity; and at other times enables the believer to endure persecution, poverty, and in some cases martyrdom. Ultimately, the faith of the believer will rescue him and reward him with riches and honor and life. The problem is that deliverance may not be in this world. The timing of the fulfillment is crucial. The teaching of "prosperity" in light of

Delivering Faith, The Mystery

the entirety of scripture cannot be defended without an eternal perspective—our reward is in heaven. The "Prosperity Gospel"-the "Name it and Claim it" theology of many contemporary churches can be a hindrance to biblical faith.

This same disregard for God's sovereign timing leads to the error of the "Health and Wealth" gospel.[123]

Here, not only is wealth a result of faith, but healing as well. There can be no question that God does heal in many cases; however, in most cases he allows the normal course of sickness and disease for believers and unbelievers alike. Healing and resurrection as benefits of faith must await God's sovereign timing.

The Apostle Paul relates his own exercise of faith. "The life that I now live in the flesh, I live by faith in the Son of God" (Gal 2:20). This exercise of faith is the affirmation of the first half of the verse: "I am crucified with Christ, nevertheless I live, yet not I but Christ lives in me." I am alive in a physical sense, yet from a faith perspective, I have died with Christ. His resurrected life is my life. It is this exercise of faith which empowers the Christian to live a life of holiness considering Himself dead to the things of the world and alive to the things of God. Far more profitable than believing God will give you a raise or make you rich, it is this exercise of faith which causes love to be operational in the Christian's life: "The love of Christ controls us having concluded this that one died for all, therefore all died" (2 Cor 5:14). It is this exercise of faith that produces a life from the inside out.

The "conclusion" is a conclusion of faith. Just as faith works by love, so love works by faith. Christians are tempted to live by sight, as though Christ were not resurrected since He is unseen. However, they are not dead to sin but alive to it.

Spiritual circumcision is likewise an activity of faith in which God cuts off the "body of the flesh" yet we are commanded to, "put to death what is earthly in you."[124]

It is this exercise of faith, hour by hour and day by day, which causes the formation of Christ in every Christian. And as Bonhoeffer put it, "only those who obey can believe, and only those who believe can obey"[125]

Conclusion

All these things are prompted by the Spirit of God in regeneration, but they are the responsibility of the believer in response to the promptings of the Spirit. Unfortunately, only God can see the heart. Far from being able to judge another's heart, we are unable to judge even our own hearts. The general direction for our behavior is outlined in Malachi, "to do justice, to love mercy, and to walk humbly with God." This is the same message at the heart of the Mosaic Law (Deut 11:1, 13, 18-22), embodied in Christ (John 13:12-17), and imitated and enjoined by Paul (Phil 4:8-9).

There are however some basic external activities that reveal the condition of the heart and the presence of these qualities of love, humility, faith, and obedience. They are in a nutshell the activities of the early church as listed in Acts 2:42. The Apostles doctrine, broadly understood, includes not only the New Testament Epistles and the Gospels but their commitment to the Old Testament as well. Fellowship in its original context represented a partnership, sharing in an endeavor involving all that an individual brought to the table. It would include the use of our time, talents, and treasures in a sacrificial communion. The Breaking of Bread is a reference to the ordinance of worship imbedded in the Jewish Passover and reinstituted at the last supper in such a way as to join Jew and Gentile into one body in Christ and create a foundation for worship in the Church, the body of Christ, the Assembly of the Firstborn, The Israel of God. Finally, a devotion to prayer, both personal and corporate, will characterize the true Christian. In section two we will examine these visible manifestations of the inner life.

SECTION II
THE EXTERNALS

CHAPTER 6

THE APOSTLE'S DOCTRINE, THE WORD OF GOD

"Now as they were traveling along, He entered a certain village; and a woman named Martha welcomed Him into her home. And she had a sister called Mary, who moreover was listening to the Lord's word, seated at His feet. But Martha was distracted with all her preparations; and she came up to Him, and said, Lord, do You not care that my sister has left me to do all the serving alone? Then tell her to help me. But the Lord answered and said to her, Martha, Martha, you are worried and bothered about so many things; but **only a few things are necessary,**

> The good part is not just the better part, but the best part, the priority, "Only a few things are necessary, really only one": Listening to the word of God.

really only one, for Mary has chosen the good part, which shall not be taken away from her (Luke 10:36-42 ESV)".[126]

Here is Jesus' commentary on priorities; the priority of listening to God's word. **"Only a few things are necessary, really only one!"** Mary, "sat at the Lord's feet and listened to His teaching" (Luke 10:39). Martha, distracted with her service, eventually asked that Mary be excused to help her. Jesus responded,

115

"No! Mary has chosen the good part, which shall not be taken away from her". The good part is not just the better part, but the best part, the priority, "**Only a few things are necessary, really only one**": Listening to the word of God.

In Section 1, we examined the inner life, the heart, in terms of the four, "greatest" qualities: love, humility, faith, and obedience. We saw how all of these are interrelated and define aspects of one character. In the second section, we will examine the outworking of this character—priorities to which the early church was "devoted." These four "externals" are manifestations of a healthy individual and a healthy church. They cannot produce the internals of love, humility, faith, and obedience, except as the Holy Spirit miraculously brings them to life, but they may be seen to **nourish** them.

The Word of God itself, as proclaimed in the Gospel, is instrumental in producing love. We love because He first loved us, and we discover that love when we encounter the Gospel. We discover holiness when we encounter the Law of God and the incarnate Son of God. We are humbled when we see the glory and majesty of God as revealed in scripture. Finally, we believe the message of the Gospel. In essence, the Word of God is essential to our initial love, humility, holiness, and faith. The subject of this chapter is our ongoing devotion to the Word of God. The word not mixed with faith will not profit us (Heb 4:2).

People may spend hours in the Word of God, in fellowship with Christians, in the celebration of the Lord's Supper, and even in prayer without experiencing the life of God. Spiritual life begins in the heart, but it is lived from the inside out. "They devoted themselves to the apostles teaching, fellowship, the breaking of bread, and prayer. Awe came upon every soul and many wonders and signs were being done by the apostles. And all who believed were

The Apostle's Doctrine, The Word Of God

together and had all things in common. They were selling their possessions and belongings and distributing the proceeds to all as they had need. And day by day attending the temple together breaking bread in their homes, they received their food with gladness and generous hearts, praising God and having favor with all the people. And the Lord added to their number day by day those who were being saved" (Acts 2:42-47).

> In today's culture, we become distracted with many activities but are often devoted to none.

This is the defining statement of life in the first century church. They **devoted** themselves to four activities: the **apostles teaching, fellowship, breaking of bread,** and **prayer**. In today's culture, we become distracted with many activities but are often devoted to none. Devotion to the externals is essential to spiritual health in the same way exercise is essential to physical health. The first of these fundamentals is the apostles' teaching which will be discussed under the heading of The Word of God in this chapter.

A heart of love, humility, obedience, and faith will result in devotion to God's word. Why? We listen to those we love. A loving spouse cannot ignore the words of a husband or wife. A loving child will not despise his parent's command. So, no one who genuinely loves God will ignore God's word, but will long to hear his voice—not casually perusing the scriptures—but diligently studying them. The humble tremble at His voice (Isa 66:2). They confess sin, literally saying the same thing God says, agreeing with His word about it. They willingly submit knowing their absolute dependence on God for sustenance, direction, perspective, and meaning to their life. The humble "do not lean on their own understanding but in all their ways acknowledge Him" (Prov 3:6).

Living Inside Out

The proud ignore God, despising His law. A heart of obedience requires a word to obey. Knowledge of God's law facilitates obedience: the more fully it is understood, the better it can be obeyed. Finally, it is only those who believe who will be devoted to God's word. The word "not mixed with faith" did not historically profit Israel (Heb 4:1), nor will it profit men today. But those who believe will see His salvation, His glory, and His power. Christians who believe will cling to His word—especially when all else is lost!

The Apostles' Doctrine—Scripture: The Word of God

Both, Roman Catholic and Orthodox communities argue that the true church preserves the tradition of the apostles in their communities and in their authoritative interpretations of Scripture. The Protestant Reformers argued that the scriptures alone[127] define the apostles teaching. Though protestant denominations disagree in their interpretation of Scripture, they confess its authority over their traditions. By the 14th century, papal decrees and canon law proceeding from ecumenical councils came to have more authority than the Bible. Having strayed from the scriptures, the Church became increasingly corrupt.[128]

> The Protestant Reformers argued that the scriptures alone define the apostles teaching.

Wycliffe responded by translating the scriptures into the common tongue of the people. "Englishmen learn Christ's law best in English. Moses heard God's law in his own tongue. So did Christ's apostles."[129]

The Vulgate itself was Jerome's translation into the common or vulgar Latin. Wycliffe died peacefully before the translation was completed, and it was left to Jan Hus [130]to continue his teachings.

Martin Luther, as a young monk, discovered a volume of sermons by Jan Hus who had been condemned as a heretic. He was astonished that "they had burnt so great a man, who explained the scriptures with so much gravity and skill."[131]

Luther would rediscover and proclaim the same truths. Some think of the Reformation as beginning with the posting of his ninety-five theses, but the seeds were planted much earlier. Luther was able to confront the church and escape with his life. In his escape, he was also to give the German people a complete translation of the scriptures from the Hebrew and Greek. The legacy of the reformation is most clearly seen in the explosion of translations. By 1990, at least one book of the Bible had been translated into almost 2000 languages. The entire Bible today is in 310 languages—and growing.[132]

The apostles' doctrine is not merely the writing and traditions of the apostles but includes the gospels which in turn are rooted in "the law, the prophets, and writings"[133] comprising the entirety of Scripture. It is authoritative because it is the Word of God.[134]

The apostles' doctrine finds its exclusive source in the Canonical Scriptures.

The Functions of The Scripture

Why is the scripture so important to us? Moses explains this way: "Take to heart all the words by which I am warning you today, that you may command them to your children, that they may be careful to do all the words of this law. For it is no empty word for you, but **your very life**, and by this word you shall live long in the land that you are going over the Jordan to possess" (Deuteronomy 32:46-47).

Living Inside Out

The word of God is your very life! It is not a compartment of your life. It is not even one of many priorities, for the Christian living from the inside out, it **is** your life. In our highly sub-specialized American culture, it is not uncommon to hear someone say, "medicine is his life," or "her family is her life," or even "football is his life." We know immediately what is meant. This text should be understood in the same way. One might say, "He reads it constantly, speaks of it constantly, evaluates everything by it, and relates everything to it."

> The word of God is your very life! It is not a compartment of your life.

Four functions recur amplifying the priority of God's word. These four functions then, represent recurrent themes: The Word is food, nourishment for the spirit; it gives victory, success, peace, comfort, hope and direction, ultimately producing purity, holiness and Godliness in the individual and the church. Table 6-1 lists four functions of the Word of God which recur as themes.

Table 6-1 The Functions of the Word

1. Food (1Peter 2:2; Job 23:12; Jeremiah 15:16; Matthew 4:4).

2. Success, Victory, and Direction (Joshua 1:8; Isaiah 55:11; Jeremiah 23:29; 2Timothy 3:16).

3. Peace, Comfort, and Hope (Psalm 119, 165; Romans 15:4; Psalm 78:5-11).

4. Godliness and Purity (2Peter 1:4) (Psalm 119:1-11, 128; John 17:17).

The Apostle's Doctrine, The Word Of God

The first function of the Word is that of nourishment: it is food for the child of God. From the days of Job, who lived in the time of Abraham, the saints have realized that a word from God is more necessary than literal food. Job said in chapter 23:12, "I

> If a Christian is too busy for their daily portion from God, then they are too busy.

have treasured the words of his mouth more than my portion of food," literally my daily portion.[135] (Certainly this was his portion of food, perhaps his portion of breath or life). It is his "daily requirement".

David, in referring to The Word of God says, "More to be desired are they than gold, even much fine gold, sweeter also than honey and the drippings of the honeycomb" (Ps19:10). Not only is it food but it is like honey, the sweetest of foods.

When facing personal rejection, the fall of the nation of Israel, and certain captivity, Jeremiah said, "Your words were found, and I ate them, and your words became to me the joy and delight of my heart" (Jer 15:16). Here again, the word is eaten as food but beyond nourishment, it is strength, joy, and delight to the heart.

After fasting forty days in the wilderness Jesus was hungry. Satan came to him and tempted him saying, "Turn these stones into bread." But Jesus responded, "Man shall not live by bread alone but by every word that comes from the mouth of God" (Matt. 4:4). In the world of marketing, this text is commonly quoted to sell most anything…. "Man shall not live by bread alone," he needs a new car. "Man shall not live by bread alone," he needs a new house, a new dress, sex, makeup, a vacation, or whatever the world is selling. The second half of this verse is rarely quoted. "Man shall not live by bread alone, **but by every**

Living Inside Out

word that comes from the mouth of God." How seldom we hear that last phrase!

This principle is particularly helpful in discovering your priority. Have you ever felt, "I just do not have time to spend reading the bible? I wish I had more time for it, but my life is so busy." If God's word is more important than daily food, we might refrain from eating each day until we partake of the word? If a Christian is too busy for their daily portion from God, then they are too busy. This discipline inevitably yields new "found" time for God's word by about 4 pm.

The reality is that we do not value God's word as much as we do food. Americans spend hours eating and minutes in the Word of God. The apostle Peter counseled young Christians: "Like newborn babes, desire the sincere milk of the Word, that by it you may grow up into salvation" (1Pet 2:2). How often do infants drink milk? Continuously! We should desire the milk of the Word of God in the same way a newborn desires physical milk.

> "Meditate in the Word of God, day and night, that you may observe to do according to all that is written therein, for then you will make your way prosperous and then you will have good success."

The second function of the Word of God is to give direction, wisdom, and success in life. Moses, giving Joshua a sort of pep talk as he is about to assume the leadership of the people of God, says, "This book of the law shall not depart out of your mouth but you shall meditate in it day and night that you my observe to do according to all that is written therein, for then you will make your way prosperous and then you will have good success" (Joshua 1:8-9). There is no better counsel for

The Apostle's Doctrine, The Word Of God

success. "**Meditate** in the Word of God, **day and night,** that you may observe to **do** according to **all** that is written therein, for then you will make your way prosperous and then you will have good success." Consider it continuously. Consider it with a view to obedience. Consider it in its entirety that you might do according to all that is written therein, for **then** you will make your way prosperous and **then** you will have good success.

The Book of Proverbs is devoted to the theme of wisdom, direction, and success. Invariably these themes are related to the Word of God–to hearing it, to receiving it, practicing it, and understanding it. This is seen especially in the first three chapters. "My son if you receive my words, if you treasure up my commandments with you, making your ear attentive to wisdom, inclining your heart to understanding. If you call out for insight and raise your voice for understanding and seek it like silver and search for it as hidden treasure, then you will understand the fear of the Lord and find the knowledge of God" (Prov 2:1-5). "Then you will understand righteousness and justice and equity in every good path "(Prov 2:9)

Some people wish God would give them miraculous guidance, a blinding light, a vision. Jeremiah, in seeking direction and in counseling the people of God, contrasts the wisdom and direction one might receive from visions and dreams with the direction and wisdom of the Word of God. "Let the prophet who has a dream tell the dream, but let him who has my Word, speak my Word faithfully. What has straw in common with wheat declares the Lord. Is not my Word like fire declares the Lord and like a hammer that breaks the rock in pieces?" (Jer 23:28-29).

In the same way that Moses counseled Joshua, Solomon counseled his son, and Isaiah counseled the nation, so Paul counsels his young disciple, Timothy. "All scripture is breathed out by God and is profitable for teaching, for reproof, for correction, and training in righteousness that the man of God may be competent and equipped for every good work" (2 Tim 3:16-17). What is the source of instruction, correction, and direction? It is God's word, the Scriptures.

The third function of the Word of God is the production of peace, comfort, and hope during difficulty, conflict, and despair. "Great peace will they receive that love thy law and nothing will cause them to stumble" (Ps 119:165). For those who are offended, discouraged, or who stumble in the race, the Word of God functions to restore hope and peace. As we love God's word, feed on it, committing ourselves to it, and saturating ourselves with it, we begin to see things from God's perspective. The immediate circumstances are placed in broader context. It is a context in which the living God always triumphs for the good of His people. This theme of hope and comfort is probably best captured in Psalm 78:7-11, which is a statement of the purpose for which the Word of God is written: "He established a testimony in Jacob and appointed a law in Israel which He commanded our fathers to teach their children that the next generation might know them, the children yet unborn, and rise and tell them to their children so that they should set their hope in God and not forget the works of God but keep his commandments that they should not be like their fathers as stubborn and rebellious generation, a generation whose heart was not steadfast and whose spirit was not faithful to God."

> **The third function of the Word of God** is the production of peace, comfort, and hope during difficulty, conflict, and despair.

Why are we given story after story rather than simply commands? This text explains that the law and the testimony are given that we might have a perspective on history. The Wall Street Journal provides an economic perspective. US News and World Report presents an American perspective, BBC a British perspective, Entertainment Tonight: Hollywood's perspective. The Word of God provides God's perspective on history and current events. Unlike other perspectives which often provoke depression, despair, or envy, God's perspective is designed to produce hope.

> Unlike other perspectives which often provoke depression, despair, or envy, God's perspective is designed to produce hope.

How does that happen? The scriptural history of the people of God as they interact with the nations around them reveals how God has continually acted on their behalf. He led them through times of difficulty and success, teaching them to turn from sin and to trust Him. Scripture reassures us that when we fail, God does not give up on us but works behind the scenes to bring His people back to Himself. He never loses control of the circumstances but simply waits for His children to humble their hearts and return to their first love, to trust their loving father, set their hearts aright and put their hope in God. This is perhaps one of the clearest explanations of the purpose of the Word of God. "He established a testimony in Jacob ... that they should set their hope in God" (Ps 78: 5-7 ESV). Paul reflects the same awareness when he writes, "Whatever was written in former days was written for

> The Word of God is given to purify us, sanctify us, keep us from sin, and make us holy.

our instruction that through the endurance and encouragement of scripture we might have hope" (Rom 15:4).

The fourth and final function of the Word of God relates to Godliness and purity. The Word of God is given to purify us, sanctify us, keep us from sin, and make us holy. Psalm 119:9-11 probably best captures this function of the scripture: "How shall a young man keep his way pure? By keeping it according to Thy word. With all my heart I have sought Thee; do not let me wander from Thy commandments. Thy word I have treasured in my heart that I may not sin against Thee."

Young Christians are often encouraged to memorize this text because it addresses this function in the context the discipline of memorizing the Word of God. "Thy Word have I hid in my heart **that** I might not sin against thee." The Word of God **will keep us from sin,** or **sin will keep us from** the Word of God. In verse 128 of the same chapter, we read: "Therefore I esteem right concerning everything. I hate every false way." As we feed on and understand the entirety of the Word of God, we begin to hate falsehood because we see the devastating consequences of sin."

God speaking to Jeremiah in condemning the false prophets and teachers of his day said, "If they had stood in my counsel then they would have announced my words to my people and they would have turned them turn back from their evil way and from the evil of their deeds" (Jer 23:22). Comparing rebellion to chaff which is burned and rock which is shattered he says, "Is not my Word like fire declares the Lord and like a hammer that shatters a rock (Jer. 23:29).

Jesus prayed that we might be kept from the world when he said, "Sanctify them in thy truth. Your Word is truth" (John 17:17). It is through the Word of God that the Spirit of God sanctifies us and keeps us from the corruption of the world. Not only does it keep us from corruption but the Word of God itself imparts holiness. In fact, the divine nature of God is imparted as we claim the promises that he has given. In 2Peter 1:4, we read that God has given us great and precious "promises that we might become partakers of the divine nature having escaped the corruption that is in the world because of lust."

> Throughout church history those who have distinguished themselves in the kingdom of God have invariably embraced the priority of the Word of God.

One of the ways the new covenant is superior to the old is that under the new, the law of God is engraved not on stone but on the tables of the heart by the Holy Spirit. "But this is the covenant that I will make with the house of Israel after those days, says the Lord: I will put My law in their inward parts (minds), and write it on their hearts; and I will be their God, and they shall be My people" (Jer 31:33).

The Scriptures in History—From Hearing to Seeing

Throughout church history those who have distinguished themselves in the kingdom of God have invariably embraced the priority of the Word of God. In the early centuries the church fathers compiled so many commentaries on the scriptures, it has been suggested that if we were to lose all copies of the scripture, we could reconstruct them from their writings. Origen, without the aid of a computer produced a critical edition of the OT in which he placed six texts in parallel columns. Entitled the Hexapla (six-fold), it included the Hebrew, a Greek transliteration, Aquila (a very literalistic translation of the Hebrew into Greek), Symmachus (an Ebionite who translated the OT freely into Greek-influenced Jerome's Vulgate), LXX, and Theodotion (a revision of LXX in the direction of the Hebrew, widely used by the Church Fathers of the 3rd and 4th centuries).[136] Chrysostom, the golden tongued expositor, produced volumes of commentaries and sermons on the scriptures, relating them to the state, the poor, and the masses.

Movement away from the scriptures as the word of God may be traced to the overwhelming impact of Greek philosophy on the early church. "For Jews, 'faith comes from what is heard' (Romans 10:17). *Dabar,* Hebrew for "word," refers particularly to the spoken word. *Logos*, Greek for word, primarily alludes to knowledge – through seeing." [137] This philosophical/cultural movement enabled the church to relate to the Gentile world and ultimately to a visually oriented culture as opposed to the Hebrew aural or word-oriented culture.[138]

During the Middle Ages, the movement toward visual imagery greatly increased. Church buildings themselves took on the function of relating the greatness and majesty of the kingdom of God. Ornate vestments, regal processions, and Latin liturgies, in the midst of religious art separated an increasingly illiterate population from the word of God while drawing them to a form of Godliness preoccupied with the ongoing sacrifice of the Mass and endless sacraments. The Monastic movement in this period represents the only pathway to the scriptures.[139]

Unfortunately, devotion centered on the Psalms and the gospels to the neglect of the epistles and the primary languages. "In general, medieval Biblical scholars were content to collect and synthesize the traditional explanations of theologians as far back as Origen. ... They produced massive volumes of dogma and morality which claimed to explain scripture but had hardly any connection with the Biblical text."[140] On the positive side, many of these monasteries became centers of spirituality and mission.

Seeing and Hearing

The Protestant Reformation was rooted in a rediscovery of the centrality of the scriptures to the life of the church: The word prevailed over the image, the ear over the eye, the sacraments were drastically reduced particularly in the Calvinist tradition and made subordinate to preaching; as a matter of fact, the sacrament was for Calvin yet another word, a verbum visible, a visible word. In many protestant churches the liturgical center was rearranged; the altar had to make way for the pulpit which was granted center stage.[141]

> The Protestant Reformation was rooted in a rediscovery of the centrality of the scriptures to the life of the church

Unfortunately, the early years of the Reformation, though marked by eloquent expositors such as Luther, Calvin, and Zwingli, were riddled with violent conflict culminating in Europe's Thirty Years War from 1618 to 1648. This reflects not only religious conviction but the intermingling of church and state. Radical reformers who made up the Anabaptist movement argued that "the authority of scripture was to be interpreted not by dogmatic tradition or by any ecclesiastical leader but by a consensus of the local gathering in which all could speak and listen critically."[142]

Tradition can be a powerful tool in the right context. Paul's exhortation to the Thessalonians was rooted in the "tradition" of Paul's personal life of sacrifice.[143] On the other hand tradition may contradict the teaching of scripture and the apostolic model in which case it must be resisted sometimes at great cost as it was in the life of the Anabaptists. This freeing the scriptures from ecclesiastical error was Jesus' concern in confronting the scribes and Pharisees who "for the sake of tradition invalidated the word of God" (Matthew 15:6).

The Anabaptists second great contribution was insistence on the separation of church and state. "They claimed they were free, unforced, uncompelled people. Faith is a free gift of God and "the authorities exceed their competence when they champion the word of God 'with a fist.'"[144] The Puritans of New England intended to create a state governed entirely by the scriptures. It was only as a result of conflict and compromise over many years that the ideals of leaders in Pennsylvania and Rhode Island outlived those of the Puritans in Massachusetts.[145]

The Anabaptists understanding of separation from society itself led them to view all of society as a mission field recovering the preeminence of the great commission as a guiding text of scripture.[146] "The Anabaptists also believed that the church was distinct from society, even if society claimed to be Christian. Christ's true followers were a pilgrim people, and his church was an association of perpetual aliens."[147]

The growth and expansion of the Protestant church has been intimately linked with the translation and distribution of the scriptures: In 1900, there were 517 languages into which at least one book of the Bible had been translated; at the beginning of 1975 the figure had reached 1577, and by 1990 it was almost 2000. The total number of complete Bible translations was 118 in 1900; today it is 310. At the same time there has been a great upsurge of new translations in languages which

The Apostle's Doctrine, The Word Of God

have long had versions of the Bible. There have been over 45 new versions of the New Testament in English and 16 in French in the 20th Century.[148]

Most of this work has come apart from any state or denominational influence. The Nineteenth Century brought an explosion in voluntary missionary societies as the conviction of the responsibility to spread the gospel came upon individual Christians. In 1792, William Carey wrote, *"An Enquiry into the Obligations of Christians to use Means for the Conversion of the Heathens,"*[149] in which he asked; "What would a trading company do?" He proposed the formation of a company of "serious Christians, layman, and ministers" to collect and analyze the situation, raise funds, and recruit suitable candidates.

In 1934 Cameron Townsend founded the Wycliffe Translators, which has grown to one of the largest societies in the world today with over 4500 missionaries. They have translated over 1200 languages, and in most cases produced the languages into a written form for the first time. The missionary work of translation has contributed to a deeper understanding of the nature of translation and our understanding of the scriptures themselves. There is today much greater freedom for the translator whose goal is to capture the natural equivalent of the original. This has in turn placed the Scriptures in the hands of the people. Churches are now joining the movement and the Second Vatican Council (1961-65) greatly encouraged the wide dissemination and study of the Bible.[150] The 20th century was marked by transitions in the evangelical world paralleling the rapid change in our high-tech world. Though Bible translation exploded as a result of computer assisted linguistics, the written word has yielded on many fronts to the visual as it did in the early centuries. One of the most successful enterprises in world evangelism in this century has been the *Jesus Film* with over six billion cumulative viewings.[151] *The Passion of the Christ* [152] was seen by millions in a matter of months and will undoubtedly find new outlets in coming years. Computer Bible programs not only facilitate scholarly research but lend high-tech capabilities to the local pastor in sermon preparation and delivery and in worship. Most of these innovations touch the masses as well as the individual on a deeply personal level. Even in mega churches the desire for the personal and intimate remains a central concern.

Dawson Trotman and The Navigators

One of the organizations which have maintained not only the intimate one-to-one focus on individuals but the centrality of the word while utilizing innovative imagery in association with scripture is the Navigators. Incorporated in 1943, the work was begun in 1933 by Dawson Trotman. After developing his work with high school students, Trotman taught a young sailor, Les Spencer, the basic principles of discipleship, spending time with him in prayer, Bible study, and scripture memory—one of the trademarks of the Navigators. Recognizing the changes in his life, Les brought a fellow sailor to "Daws", as he was affectionately known by his friends. When Les asked him to teach his friend what he had taught him, Trotman responded, "You teach him."

So, began the Navigators. Eventually 125 men on that ship, the U.S.S. *West Virginia,* were growing and actively sharing their faith. By the end of WW II thousands of men on ships and naval bases around the world were learning and sharing Navigator principles of discipleship. As these sailors went on to

The Apostle's Doctrine, The Word Of God

college on the GI bill, Navigators expanded to campus ministry. "Today, tens of thousands of people worldwide are coming to know and grow in Jesus Christ through the various ministries of The Navigators. Internationally, more than 4,000 Navigator staff of 64 nationalities serve in more than 100 countries."[153] Millions of people around the world have been touched often without any large meetings or open preaching—but through one-to-one discipleship and the Word of God.

Trotman excelled at developing visual tools to facilitate learning, retention and transmission of scripture while keeping his focus on the personal discipleship of the individual. Two illustrations developed in the early days of his ministry were the "Hand"[154] and the "Wheel."[155]. The wheel pictures the obedient Christian life on the rim linked to the center hub (Jesus) by four spokes: the Word of God, prayer, fellowship, and witnessing. Each topic is linked to one or two key scripture texts. The hand illustration pictures the Bible being gripped between the thumb which represents meditation (Josh 1:8) and each of the four fingers which represent a progressively strengthening grasp of the Word of God. The little finger represents hearing, the ring finger reading, the middle finger studying, and the index finger memorization. The TMS Topical Memory System began as a B Ration (**B** for Bible) pack of 49 cards evolving into 108 verses-3 verses on 36 topics which were memorized-"word perfect."[156]

Beyond the techniques though, Trotman had a passion for people and an amazing ability to motivate, confront, and encourage in the Word of God. When world-wide Evangelist, Billy Graham, needed someone to develop a follow-up program for his budding evangelistic crusades he turned to Dawson Trotman. By that time the Navigators had become an international ministry, but Trotman committed vast time and staff to the development to training materials and the counselor training and discipleship work which was to play such a part in the Billy Graham crusades.

Dawson Trotman drowned at age 50 in a boating accident after he saved the life of a young woman who could not swim. Billie Graham preached his funeral at the Navigators headquarters in Glen Eyrie outside Colorado Springs. Betty Lee Skinner recalls Graham's comments that day: He began, "Dawson loved the Word of God. I think more than anybody else he taught me to love it."[157]

When Graham recounted his early contacts with his friend, it evoked ripples of laughter across the crowd, in no way incongruous with the spirit of the occasion. He told of the time at Wheaton when Daws asked the eager freshman what the Lord had given him from the Word in his devotions that morning. "Well, I hadn't had my devotions. I hadn't been with him five minutes until he was challenging my life and probing to the depths of my life," he marveled. "Many times, we bared our souls to each other as only men do who have fullest confidence in each other. And I sought his counsel often. I haven't made a major decision in the last few years that I didn't seek his counsel."[158]

Next, and this is very important, Dawson was the *master of the soft rebuke*. He quoted that verse in Proverbs 27:6, *Faithful are the wounds of a friend* … He would come to you and say, "You know, I believe this ought to be in your life. You're not keeping up with your memory work; you're not keeping up with your prayer life." He had courage and did it in a sweet,

> Jesus said, "If you continue in my word, then you are truly my disciples" (John 8:31).

The Apostle's Doctrine, The Word Of God

humble way and quoted so many Scriptures you knew it came from God. He could rebuke you and make you love it. I learned something from him that way ... "I think he touched more lives than any man I have ever known."[159]

Jesus said, "If you continue in my word, then you are truly my disciples" (John 8:31). This continuance is the proof of an internal work of God. David could write, "Oh how I love thy law. It is my meditation all the day" (Ps 119:97); and in the same Psalm, cry out, "Oh that my ways may be steadfast in keeping your statutes. Then I shall not be put to shame having my eyes fixed on all your commandments. With my whole heart I seek you. Let me not wander from your commandments" (Ps 119: 5, 6, 10). Though it is the responsibility of each individual to continue in the word, those who continue humbly confess that it is not their effort but the grace of God within them.

"But to this one will I look – to him who is humble and contrite in spirit and who trembles at my word" (Isa 66:2). The humble heart immediately yields to the command of God and is responsive to it whereas the proud heart resists God, turns away, and disobeys. Zedekiah, "did what was evil in the sight of the Lord his God. He did not humble himself before Jeremiah the prophet, who spoke from the mouth of the Lord" (2Chron 36:12). [160] One of the surest signs of humility in the heart is joyful obedience in the life. An inner life of love for God, humility, obedience, and faith will be characterized externally first by a devotion to God's Word which serves as a light to our path and a lamp to our way (Ps 119:105). As we walk in this light John writes, we have **fellowship** with God and with one another. In the next chapter we consider the fellowship which characterized the early church and many disciples who historically have lived from the inside out.

CHAPTER 7

FELLOWSHIP, PARTNERSHIP WITH GOD AND MAN

"Let him who cannot be alone beware of community. He will only do harm to himself and to the community. But the reverse is also true; let him who is not in community beware of being alone. Into the community you were called, the call was not meant for you alone; in the community of the called you bear your cross, you struggle, and pray. You are not alone, even in death, and on the Last Day you will be only one member of the great congregation of Jesus Christ. If you scorn the fellowship of the brethren, you reject the call of Jesus Christ, and thus your solitude can only be hurtful to you."[161]

The early church devoted itself to four activities: the apostle's doctrine (the word of God), fellowship, breaking of bread, and prayer. These are marks of authentic Christianity. They give us a snapshot of the church. Just as love, humility, faith, and obedience are interconnected elements of the unseen character, these are interconnected activities of the visible church.

Fellowship, Partnership With God And Man

Devotion to the Word should result in devotion to fellowship since the Jesus commands us to love one another (Jn 15:12, 17). The Word commands love of one's neighbor. However sometimes we fool ourselves into thinking that because we read it—we have it.

Fellowship with others in the body of Christ is a function of our fellowship with God. Our fellowship is with the Father, and as we walk in the light, we have fellowship with one another. We are saved as individuals, but we are saved only as we are joined to Christ, and since he is joined to the rest of his body—so we are joined. We are called in one body, baptized into one body, made to drink of one Spirit. (I Cor 12:13) Though, in this sense, fellowship defines the church, because of the progressive nature of our salvation we must devote ourselves to fellowship.

We are prone to confuse understanding with obedience. Fellowship requires that we walk in the light, not just look at it. The Word likewise commands breaking of bread and prayer which deepen our experience in the Word and in fellowship. Yet none of these activities define the Christian faith or the authentic Christian church as do the unseen graces of love, humility, faith, and obedience.[162] It is the life of Christ lived out through His body which defines Christianity. "The Church's role in the world is not a series of independent items on an action checklist. Instead, the church's role (what it *does*) is dependent on its character (what it is) as a community of believers."[163] We could go further to say that the church is the loving, humble, obedient believers who are committed/devoted to the word of God, fellowship (or

> Fellowship with others in the body of Christ is a function of our fellowship with God.

community), breaking of bread, and prayer. Fellowship is the natural outworking of love, humility, obedience, and faith. But before we examine this relationship, we must define fellowship.

Koinonia at Philippi

Fellowship (*koinonia*) in the New Testament is defined by **sharing** on three levels: **sharing** in an endeavor, sacrifice, or partnership; **sharing** our resources usually food and finances; and finally **sharing in suffering and glory**.[164] The book of Philippians is the best commentary on authentic Christian fellowship. Only let your manner of life be worthy of the gospel of Christ so that whether I come and see you or am absent I may hear of you that you are standing firm in one spirit, with one mind, striving side by side for the faith of the gospel" (Phil 1:27 ESV).

> Fellowship (koinonia) in the New Testament is defined by sharing on three levels

The life worthy of the gospel of Christ is a life of unity, both in standing firm and striving side by side for the faith of the gospel. This striving "side by side" is a description of true fellowship, not a casual social interaction, but a costly endeavor which anticipates conflict. "Not frightened by your opponents... For it has been granted to you for the sake of Christ that you should not only believe on him but also suffer for his sake engaged in the same conflict that you saw I had and now hear that I still have" (Phil 1:29-30 ESV).

> A life of fellowship is a life of engagement.

Fellowship, Partnership With God And Man

A life of fellowship is a life of engagement. It is sharing in conflict and in suffering. The conflict here results from the proclamation of the gospel. There is an anticipated rejection of this message, not a casual rejection but a violent rejection. Jesus was sent into a world, which would reject and crucify Him. "So, it was granted to us, not only to believe, but also to suffer for His sake" —engaged in conflict. Fellowship in this context is not a fringe benefit. As we share abundantly in Christ's sufferings, so we share abundantly in comfort (2Cor 1:7). Both these words "share", are from the root word *koinonia.* In describing his ultimate purpose of knowing Christ, Paul includes knowing the power of his resurrection and the "fellowship of suffering" (Phil 3:10). As we share in His sufferings we partake of His glory (1Peter 4:13, 1Peter 5:1). "If there is any encouragement in Christ, any comfort from love, any participation (koinonia – sharing in the spirit), any affection and sympathy, complete my joy by being of the same mind, and having the same love, being in full accord and of one mind. Do nothing from rivalry or conceit, but in humility, count others more significant than yourself." (Phil 2:1-3 ESV).

This passage beautifully summarizes the idea that external behavior is motivated by an inner work of the Holy Spirit which entails love and humility. Obedience appears just a few verses later in verse 8. Christ's obedience is an act of faith in God's promise of exaltation in verses 9-11.

Paul, Timothy, and Epaphroditus all serve as models of this life of fellowship. Christ is our supreme example (Phil 2:1-11). The Philippian church should imitate Christ and the apostle Paul as they share in the mission (Phil 2:12-18). Timothy and Epaphroditus are Paul's fellow workers and fellow soldiers who served with him in the gospel, the work of Christ, risking their lives in the service (Phil 2:19- 30 ESV). They are co-workers who share in a common vision, a common activity, and a common endeavor. Paul claims there is no one like Timothy who is genuinely concerned for their welfare, whereas other supposed helpers, "seek their own interests, not those of Jesus Christ." Timothy "has served with me in the gospel." This is *koinonia.*

Paul contrasts the gain that he had from a legalistic conformity to the law with the gain that he had in Christ. He then shares his goal, "That I may know Him and the power of His resurrection and the fellowship of His sufferings, being conformed to His death in order that I may attain the resurrection from the dead" (Phil 3:10-11). Again, this "sharing in His sufferings" is the word "*koinonia.*" In the purest sense when we share in the benefits of the gospel, we share in the death and resurrection of Christ. As Christ partook of death for us, so too, in our partaking of Christ, we partake of the death and the life of Christ. We die to sin, and we live to God. Our ongoing life may be seen in terms of fellowship or sharing in the struggle and the journey.

"Not that I have already attained this or am perfect, but I press on to make it my own because Christ Jesus has made me his own. Brothers I do not consider it that I have made it my own, but one thing I do, forgetting what lies behind and straining forward to what lies ahead, I press on toward the goal for the prize of the upward call of God in Christ Jesus. Let those of us who are mature think this way. And if in anything you think otherwise, God will reveal that also to you. Only let us hold true to what we have obtained. Brothers, join in imitating me and keep your eyes on those who walk according to the example you have in us" (Phil 3:12-17 ESV).

Fellowship, Partnership With God And Man

This is a description of fellowship or *sharing* in the gospel. Paul describes Euodia and Syntyche as those who labored side by side with him in the gospel together with Clement and the rest of his fellow workers. This chapter concludes with the reminder that no church joined partnership in the sense of giving and receiving except the Philippians: "no church shared with me in the matter of giving and receiving but you alone" (Phil 4:15). This is the most common use of the word in the New Testament.[165] Christians not only share in gain, but they also shared in a loss of property.

> Koinonia, far beyond a church picnic, should rightly be understood as a life-encompassing journey

"But remember the former days, when, after being enlightened, you endured a great conflict of sufferings, partly, by being made a public spectacle through reproaches and tribulations, and partly by becoming sharers with those who were so treated. For you showed sympathy to the prisoners, and accepted joyfully the seizure of your property, knowing that you have for yourselves a better possession and an abiding one. Therefore, do not throw away your confidence, which has a great reward" (Heb 10:32-35).

Koinonia-A Life Encompassing Journey

Koinonia, far beyond a church picnic, should rightly be understood as a life-encompassing journey which demands all our resources and ends only as we share Christ's death, resurrection, and glorification. It is this understanding of fellowship which has led to some of the most amazing expressions of Christianity in the history of the church. In the early church, this concept of sacrificial sharing in suffering had a profound impact on the outside world. Lucian of Samosata told of how a charlatan Proteus Peregrinus was befriended by Christians during outbreaks of plagues at Alexandria. Christians tended the sick and buried the dead when nearly everyone else had fled. The Christian lifestyle was a very powerful influence in a society where kindness, honesty, and personal purity were rare.[166] Unfortunately, the struggle to share fellowship with Christ has sometimes been separated from sharing the sufferings of those in the world.

To separate themselves from the corruptions of the world and partake more of Christ's holiness, communal Monasticism began establishing itself in the early 4th century. In the first three centuries martyrdom was the mark of extreme devotion to Christ. With the legalization of Christianity, martyrdom ceased and monasticism came to replace it. In some ways, this movement separated the best of the church from the culture. However, the element of separation is often overstated. Monastic communities throughout the Middle Ages, became centers of transformation and preservation of culture.[167] This blossomed under Basal and Augustine who understood the "all consuming" nature of the call to fellowship with the living God. They understood the responsibility of sharing in transforming the world. Monastic communities among the Celts in the late 5th and early 6th century, and those under Benedict, incorporated prayer, work, and scholarship. At the heart of these communities was a vision of *koinonia*. The Middle Ages are marked by a depth of participation and communal life both in the Monastery and the mendicant orders of Francis and Dominic who truly sought to remain in the world yet not of it

Fellowship, Partnership With God And Man

It should be obvious that fellowship, understood as encompassing these three components (the gospel endeavor, finances, and suffering and glory) can proceed only from hearts of love, humility, obedience, and faith. Love seeks not its own but another's good (1Cor 13). Our love for Christ moves us to share his task of redeeming the world by joining him in a sacrifice of our lives (Rom 12:1). Love moves us to lay down our lives for the brethren (1John 3:16, Heb 10:32-34). In humility of mind, we are to consider others before ourselves as a manifestation of our fellowship in the spirit (Phil 2:1-7). Jesus' death for us is an act of obedience, and our obedience mirrors His (Phil 2:8-17). Costly fellowship on this level is possible only by faith (Heb 10:32-39, 2Pet 1-13).

> Fellowship is the work of maintaining and attaining unity.

This broad understanding of fellowship as a participation in the gospel in every aspect of life will keep us from an artificial holiness.

The Reformation, while dividing the unity of the body of Christ, brought with it new communities which, by virtue of their separation from the Catholic Church, required a new commitment to one another as a matter of survival. Fellowship requires unity, two cannot walk together unless they are agreed. Paul mentions two types of unity in his letter to the Ephesians. There is a unity of the Spirit which we are to **maintain** (Eph 4:3). This unity is a result of walking in the realm of the Spirit. We may enjoy this even if we disagree in some points of doctrine. Secondly, there is a unity of the faith and knowledge of the Son of God which we are to **attain** (Eph 4:13). In this

143

case we grow together as our beliefs and understandings match. Fellowship is the work of **maintaining** and **attaining** unity.

In the case of the Magisterial Reformers, Luther, Calvin, and Zwingli, their communities evolved into political states. When those involved were united in love for Christ, their fellowship bore the true marks of the early church. But as political entities, they suffered from the Constantinian problem of diluted Christianity. The Anabaptists, or radical reformers, sought to develop communities of faith marked by a separation from the world and its power structures. They were persecuted both by Catholics and Reformers since they seemed to abandon the state. This group under Menno Simons blossomed into the Mennonite movement. And their understanding of separation of Church and State eventually took root in the New World.

Pietists, Moravians, and Methodists

One of the greatest expressions of fellowship evolved out of the Pietist movement in Germany about 100 years after the reformation. While Calvin and his followers emphasized not only justification by faith but also an ongoing sanctification, Luther's followers in Germany descended into a dead orthodoxy which lost the heart of devotion to Christ. Philip Jakob Spener, after receiving his doctorate, became a pastor in Frankfurt. Alarmed at the lack of spirituality of his students he penned *Pia Desideria*,[168] (Pious Longings) in 1675. This work called on all Christians to assume responsibility for a life of devotion and suggested "colleges of piety" or small groups to facilitate this goal. August Francke, a professor at the University of Halle, which became a center for training missionaries, was Spener's greatest follower. Thousands embraced the Pietist movement

Fellowship, Partnership With God And Man

joining the small groups which would eventually leave a mark on the entire Lutheran tradition.

The small groups may have reached their zenith in the community we remember as Herrnhut "The Lord's Watch". In 1722, Count Zinzendorf, who wrote, "There can be no Christianity without community," offered a company of Moravians refuge on his estate. Zinzendorf, whose godfather was Spener, had been raised in a devout Pietist home and studied under Franke at Halle. He had been deeply spiritual from his childhood captivated by the love of Christ and the fellowship of his suffering. He longed to see the unity that this could bring to the entire Christian church. These Moravians were descendants of the Unitas Fratrum (The unity of the brethren) whose joy in Christ was centered in their fellowship with all children of God across every congregation.

> John Wesley was convinced that changing the world was possible only by making disciples, and it was in the context of small groups that this must be done.

The Herrnhut community became a model of Christian Fellowship. Commenting on his visit there, John Wesley wrote, "I would gladly have spent my life here; O when shall this Christianity cover the earth 'as the waters cover the sea'?" [169] The community at Herrnhut launched the modern mission's movement, and it was because of his contact with Moravian missionaries that John Wesley came to his understanding of true spirituality and fellowship with Christ.

Living Inside Out

Wesley: Fellowship as Societies

John Wesley was convinced that changing the world was possible only by making disciples, and it was in the context of small groups that this must be done. His convictions were developed as a student at Oxford in the small group known as "the Holy Club". "The club's rules called for strict personal discipline, a rigorous devotional life, and significant charitable work among the poor."[170] As a traveling evangelist, Wesley established the Methodist societies to help implement the disciple making process.

"Wesley's concept of discipleship can be broken down into four supporting convictions:

(1) the necessity of discipleship,

(2) the necessity of small groups for discipleship,

(3) the necessity of lay leadership for discipleship and,

(4) the necessity of making holiness and service the double goal of discipleship."[171]

Wesley's goals for the "classes", the most basic small group, was to encourage godliness, to pray for each other, to exhort one another, and to "watch over one another in love, that they may help each other to work out their salvation."[172] There was confession of sin and accountability for personal spiritual development with a view to holiness. They attended to the needs of the poor and were disciplined for sinful conduct.

Fellowship, Partnership With God And Man

Societies beyond the Methodist model flourished in England and in America in the 1800s. These societies reveal the enthusiasm which can take place as individuals fellowship purposefully sacrificing personal agendas. They also foreshadow the dangers of misguided "fellowship".

"We are all a little wild here with numberless projects of social reform, Ralph Waldo Emerson confessed to Thomas Carlyle in 1840. Not a reading man but he has a draft of *A New Community* in his waist coat pocket. Emerson was attempting to convey the extent to which Americans were rejecting conventional, social arrangements and joining missionary-like crusades to regenerate the social order. Possessing a heavy confidence that much could be done to transform human character, Americans organized scores of reform societies in fields such as anti-slavery, temperance, peace, women's rights, missions, education, and penal reform. More than 100 communitarian experiments emerged from these endeavors."[173]

> These Mission Societies shortly transformed the way the gospel was taken to the world.

Having recognized the failure of denominationalism, and division over forms of church government, the establishment of Mission societies beyond the confines of Methodism burst on the scene in the 19th century. These Mission Societies shortly transformed the way the gospel was taken to the world. These voluntary societies could circumvent the divisions denominations had created. In 1795, The London Missionary Society proclaimed its "fundamental principle that our desire is not to send Presbyterian, Independency, Episcopacy, or another form of church government but the glorious, blessed God to the

Heathen."[174] The American missionary, Rufus Anderson, wrote in 1834, "It was not until the present century, the Evangelical churches of Christendom were ever really organized with a view to conversion of the world. They became organized by means of the voluntary society."[175]

The denominations eventually caught on to the explosion of interdenominational societies and developed in turn denominational agencies focused on evangelism. In 1818, the Methodist conference brought together the auxiliaries in a Methodist Missionary Society so that eventually every member of the Methodist church was automatically a member of the Society. In 1810, the first society specifically designed for worldwide missions was founded: The American Board of Commissioners for Foreign Missionaries.

Mission societies were followed by tract societies concerned about the unavailability of scripture, and scripture portions in various languages and the Bible Societies followed with a commitment to take the scripture to the entire world. Our present-day movements of Campus Crusade, Intervarsity Christian Fellowship, the Billy Graham Evangelistic Association, are all extensions of this movement of societies rooted in the concept of *koinonia* as a partnership–an endeavor–a sharing in the accomplishment of a goal. This is a goal that involves a financial commitment, sharing in the death resurrection and glorification of Christ, in the benefits and proclamation of the gospel, and lastly in sharing in the suffering that the proclamation of the gospel will bring.

Bonhoeffer: Truth and Consequences of Fellowship

Though Wesley's Methodism is undoubtedly the most successful organizational model of fellowship, in our modern day, no one has contributed more to the understanding of fellowship than Dietrich Bonhoeffer, whose writings and testimony point out the dangers of fellowship with the world and the cost of true fellowship with Christ. "The fellowship between Jesus and His disciples covered every aspect of their daily lives. Within the fellowship of Christ's disciples, the life of each individual was part of the life of the brotherhood."[176]

"Of the many pilots who have sought to steer the church though similar storms, German theologian and pastor Dietrich Bonhoeffer was one of the most successful. In the Hitler-crazed Germany of the 1930's, when nationalism became vicious and the German Christian churches bought a party card, Bonhoeffer turned to the resources of genuine Christian community to guide the church. In ways that he could not foresee, he also laid down a theology of Christian fellowship that can help us combat both the selfism and the tribalism of the post-modern world."[177]

Having completed his doctoral work in 1927 at the University of Berlin, Bonhoeffer spent a year in 1930 at Union Theological Seminary in New York. Concerned by the National Socialism overtaking his nation, he returned to Germany after just a year. Shortly after Hitler took power, Bonhoeffer addressed the nation over public radio warning, "A leader who makes an idol of himself and his office mocks God."[178] The station lost power before the lecture was completed. The Reich soon controlled the church, arresting Lutheran pastors who opposed the German/Christian movement.[179] By 1935, Bonhoeffer was conducting an underground seminary as a part of a resistance movement, writing: "The students must learn how to lead a communal life in daily and strict obedience to the will of Christ Jesus and the humblest and highest service one Christian brother can perform for another, they must learn to recognize the strength and liberation to be found in brotherly service and communal life in a Christian community."[180]

Bonhoeffer is best remembered for his works, *The Cost of Discipleship* and *Life Together*,[181] which address the concept of community. According to Mark Shaw, Life *Together* can be summarized in six principles.

(1) "In a hostile world the gift of Christian community is a great treasure from God, not to be despised.

(2) In a self-reliant age, Christian community must be mediated by Christ alone.

(3) In a world addicted to ideology, Christian community must not be based on an ideal of community.

(4) In a humanistic age, Christian community must not be based on human love.

(5) In an age of selfism and tribalism, the only individualism that is safe is in Christian community, and the only Christian community that is safe is that which allows individualism.

(6) In an arrogant age, the Christian community must humbly practice the disciplines that will make it strong in Christ."[182]

Fellowship, Partnership With God And Man

The fourth point is especially important in delineating true and false fellowship.

"In the community of the spirit, there burns the bright love of brotherly service, *agape*; in human community of spirit, there glows the dark love of.... *eros*. In the former there is ordered, brotherly service, in the latter disordered desire for pleasure; in the former humble subjection to the brethren, in the latter humble yet haughty subjection of brother to one's own desire."[183] This fellowship is not only governed by a subjective love but by the objective Word of God.

> Bonhoeffer calls us to biblical fellowship which loves sacrificially; and boldly confronts a culture which too often marginalizes the helpless.

"In the community of the spirit, the Word of God alone rules; in the human community of spirit, there rules, along with the Word, the man who is furnished with exceptional powers, experience, and magical, suggestive capacities. There God's Word alone is binding; here, besides the Word, men bind others to themselves. There all power, honor, and dominion are surrendered to the Holy Spirit; here the spheres of power and influence of a personal nature are sought and cultivated."[184]

Bonhoeffer calls us to biblical fellowship which loves sacrificially; and boldly confronts a culture which too often marginalizes the helpless. He was actively involved in rescuing Jewish people throughout the nation and was eventually arrested on that charge (though he had also been engaged in a plot to assassinate Hitler). He wrote:

"Cheap grace is the preaching of forgiveness without requiring repentance, baptism without church discipline, communion without confession, absolution without personal

Living Inside Out

confession. Cheap grace is grace without discipleship, grace without the cross, grace without Jesus Christ, living and incarnate."[185]

Bonhoeffer was placed in an extermination camp and hanged with six others on April 9, 1945, just one month before Germany surrendered.

Fellowship then, is an outflow of love, humility, faith, and obedience which characterizes the true Christian church. It is a sacrificial partnership in which the saints gather together with a united purpose of glorifying God, supporting one another, and boldly proclaiming the Gospel of Christ to a dying world. This is possible only by the power of the Holy Spirit enabling the members to lay down their lives one for another.

> Fellowship then, is an outflow of love, humility, faith, and obedience which characterizes the true Christian church.

In commenting on Acts 2:42, Bonhoeffer writes: "It is instructive to note that fellowship–*Koinonia*–is mentioned between word and sacrament. This is no accident for fellowship always springs from the word and finds its goal and completion in the Lord's Supper. The whole common life of the Christian fellowship oscillates between word and sacrament. It begins and ends in worship. It looks forward in expectation to the final banquet in the kingdom of God. When the community has such a source and goal, it is a perfect communion of fellowship even material goods fall into their appointed place. In freedom, joy, and the power of the Holy Spirit, a pattern of common life is produced where 'neither was there any among them that lacked.'"[186]

Fellowship, Partnership With God And Man

In the next chapter we will look in-depth at the Lord's Supper or the 'breaking of bread,' its history, interpretation, and priority since, "The fellowship of the Lord's Supper is the superlative fulfillment of Christian fellowship."[187]

CHAPTER 8

COMMUNION, SHARING IN LIFE AND DEATH

Communion, also known as the Breaking of Bread, or the Lord's Supper, is the third activity to which the early church in Acts 2 "devoted" itself. According to the dictionary, "devoted" means loyal, faithful, true, staunch, steadfast, constant, committed, dedicated, devout; fond, loving, affectionate, caring, and admiring. "Devoted" is hardly the way most contemporary American Christians would describe their relationship with Communion. One of the reasons for this disconnect may be that the early church saw the celebration of the Lord's Supper as the primary context for corporate worship. Luke writes that the church at Ephesus gathered on the first day of the week, "to break bread" (Acts 20:7). That was their purpose in gathering. And this is the only reference in the New Testament as to the frequency for meeting.

Paul rebuked the church at Corinth because of their disorderly conduct with the words, "when you meet together, it is not to eat the Lord's Supper" (1Cor. 11:20-33), that is, your purpose

Communion, Sharing In Life And Death

in gathering should be to eat the Lords Supper, but unfortunately, something else is happening. THE REMEMBRANCE OF THE LORD was not central to their supper.

Communion is not simply a dinner to satisfy hunger but a sharing of bread and wine to remind us of Christ—His life, death, and resurrection. It is a celebration of the fact that we now have spiritual life in Him just as we have physical life through the food we eat. When we remember Him, **we remember His love** for us which led him to leave heaven and take up a human body, share our trials, and ultimately bear our cross. **We remember His humility** in becoming a servant **and His obedience even to death. We remember His holiness** and His Majesty, His power to subject all things to Himself. And ultimately, **we remember Him as the author and finisher of our faith.** All the core elements of the heart we studied in chapters 1-4 **are encompassed in Him.** Our remembrance is a participation in His body (incarnation/life) and blood (death), in His purpose for our lives.

> Our remembrance is a participation in His body (incarnation/life) and blood (death), in His purpose for our lives.

Paul rebukes the Corinthians because they have gathered to eat in an unworthy manner first in not examining themselves beforehand to see that they have truly turned from the world to Christ and second in taking the emblems in the context of a feast for the body and not the soul. Any time we engage in external activities, no matter how good, without faith and love, we incur judgement, and we reveal hearts of rebellion and unholiness. Isaiah writes God hates it! Isaiah 1:11-20.

Living Inside Out

The relationship between eating, and praising, remembering and worship is beautifully captured in Ps 22:25-29. "All the ends of the earth will <u>remember</u> and turn to the Lord, and all the families of the nations will <u>worship </u>before Thee" (Psa 22:27).

This chapter will explore the Hebrew roots of the Lord's Supper in the Passover Seder,[188] the separation of the Church from Judaism in the first centuries with the resulting loss of our Hebrew heritage, the centrality of the Sacrament in the Middle Ages, the reinterpretation of the ordinance during the Reformation, and the subsequent marginalization of the Lord's Supper in ensuing centuries.

Hebrew Roots: The Lord's Supper in the Jewish Passover

When the hour had come, He reclined at table and the apostles with Him and He said to them, 'I have earnestly desired to eat this Passover with you before I suffer. For I say to you I shall not eat it until it is fulfilled in the Kingdom of God" (Luke 22:14-16). We can better understand this as Americans if we imagine it as a combination of New Year's Day, the Fourth of July, and Thanksgiving Day all rolled into one.

Jesus and His disciples came together to celebrate God's hand in the Creation of the Nation of Israel, their miraculous deliverance from captivity, the pouring out of plagues upon the Egyptians, and the deliverance of the firstborn sons. They came to eat a feast of lamb, unleavened bread, bitter herbs, and wine. It was a celebration of the greatest gift they could ever be given. It was a gift of freedom and deliverance. It was also a celebration of life from the dead. The Jewish people had been slaves for four hundred years in Egypt with no hope from any quarter. God with a mighty hand and an outstretched arm delivered them and brought them forth through the desert to the land of Israel.

It happened in the spring of the year which then became the first day of their new life and the first day of the year. The season itself in the spring rains and budding trees joined with them in their celebration of life. Not only was it a remembrance of God's mighty hand but it came to be a symbol of God's ability to deliver them from any foe, take them through any desert, give them light in any darkness, heal them from all their diseases, free them from their labor, and usher them into an age of prosperity and blessing. The feast was a time of expectation, a time when Messianic hope blossomed in their hearts. It's no wonder they wanted to remember it.

> The feast was a time of expectation, a time when Messianic hope blossomed in their hearts. It's no wonder they wanted to remember it.

Jesus told his disciples, "I have earnestly desired to eat **this Passover** with you before I suffer." Then He added, "For I tell you I will not eat it again until it is fulfilled in the Kingdom of God." For the disciples seated around the table with Jesus that evening, it would have meant two things. First, since it was to be eaten every year, Jesus could have only meant that the Kingdom of God would be established within another year. They had not considered the possibility that he would die and be resurrected before the next Passover then eat it again on his return. Secondly, it would have sparked an immediate question as to the meaning of "fulfilled." The Feast was primarily a celebration of an historical event that looked forward to God's continuing deliverance of His people.[189]

Living Inside Out

To speak in terms of it being "fulfilled," must have prompted multiple questions in their minds. During this dinner, Jesus would have expounded numerous texts. He would have partaken of numerous symbolic elements in the meal, but he assigned new meaning to two in particular – the bread and the cup after supper. These two elements were eventually separated from the context of the Passover meal and elevated to a sacramental status in the Christian church. Before discussion of these two elements in particular, it is important to understand the Passover itself in its original context and as it evolved to the time of Jesus.

The Original Passover

The original Passover, as described in Exodus 12, was eaten in the land of Egypt when the Jewish people were under the hand of Pharaoh. This Passover dinner was eaten in haste, with their sandals on their feet, their staffs in their hands, in anticipation of the exodus from Egypt. They were instructed to take a lamb for each house, kill it, catch its blood, strike the blood on the door posts and the lentils of the house, and eat it inside the house. The lamb was to be eaten with bitter herbs, roasted with fire—not boiled, and all that was not eaten was to be burned up.

As the family was in the house eating the lamb, the Angel of the Lord passed through the land, and as he saw the blood on the door posts, He would pass over or hover over the door. Literally this is "to pass over" (*Pessach*). He was not to skip that house but to hover over it and protect it so that the destroying angel could not come in to kill the firstborn. God Himself would Passover that household to protect it from death.[190]

Communion, Sharing In Life And Death

In the years to come, the father of each Jewish household would relate this story of how the Lord had passed over their households and protected them. "With a mighty hand and an outstretched arm, God delivered the children of Israel." They went forth guided by a pillar of fire. God led them to the Red Sea where He parted the waters which swallowed up the Egyptian army pursuing them. When Israel looked the next morning, not one of their enemies remained alive. Israel saw, feared, and believed.

They were then instructed to keep the Passover as a memorial feast. This memorial feast was to be kept as a Shabbat. They were to eat it reclining. They were to eat the lamb roasted with fire, but its bones were not to be broken. It was to be eaten with bitter herbs and unleavened bread. In the original Passover, they left in haste and there was no time for the bread to rise. But the memorial feast became a symbol of their rest and exaltation. They were no longer to eat as slaves but as free men, reclining and recounting the story in detail.[191] This was one of three pilgrimage feasts each year requiring all males to appear in Jerusalem. Recurring apostasy, the destruction of the temple and the subsequent 70-year Babylonian Captivity brought additional modifications. Particular Psalms were added over the centuries.

By the first century, the Seder,[192] or order of the service developed and became standard tradition. At that point the story was to begin with the call of Abraham in Ur of the Chaldees when God promised to give him a land and make of him a great nation. He would bless Abraham, and those who blessed him and curse those who cursed him.

The story then traced the lives of the patriarchs, Isaac, Jacob, and Joseph with the promise being repeated to the time of

Living Inside Out

Moses when a pharaoh arose who said, "I will cast every male Hebrew child into the Nile to die by drowning." This Pharaoh who cursed the children of Israel was visited with a series of curses or plagues which culminated in the tenth and final curse. The Passover was marked by the death of the first born of those unprotected from the Angel of Death, and ultimately the drowning of the entire Egyptian army in the depths of the Red Sea. The whole Passover story begins and ends with the fulfillment of God's promise to Abraham and his seed, "the one who curses you will be cursed, and the one who blesses you will be blessed."

> The whole Passover story begins and ends with the fulfillment of God's promise to Abraham and his seed, "the one who curses you will be cursed, and the one who blesses you will be blessed."

By the time of Jesus, the Seder would have included the lighting of Passover candles similar to the Shabbat candles, and the sharing of four glasses of wine which were taken in the course of the Passover narrative. The first cup is called the "cup of sanctification;" the second is the "cup of plagues;" the third cup, taken just after the meal, is the "cup of redemption;" and the final cup is the cup of *Hallel* or praise, to be taken in the midst of a series of songs.

A piece of the unleavened bread[193] is taken in the first part of the dinner, broken, wrapped in a linen napkin, and put away until the end of the meal at which time it is taken out again and shared just prior to the third cup—the cup of redemption. During the meal, in addition to the historical narrative of Abraham, Isaac, Jacob, Joseph, and Moses, Psalms 113 to

Communion, Sharing In Life And Death

115 are read early in the meal, and Psalms 116 to 118 are read toward the end of the meal.

Messianic Jewish and Christian scholars today who have followed the development of Passover are in agreement that the elements that Jesus used in the Last Supper were the unleavened bread taken at the end of the Passover meal and the third cup of wine (the cup of redemption), of Passover meal.[194] He would then have taken the cup of Hallel, the final cup of Blessing, and sung Psalm 118 with the disciples prior to entering Gethsemane.[195] This is a striking Psalm from a Messianic perspective concluding with the words:

> Jesus was about to fulfill the Passover in His own death as the Passover lamb.

"This is the day that the Lord has made. I will rejoice and be glad in it…. Bind the festival sacrifice with cords to the horns of the altar…. You are God and I will praise you. You are my God, and I will exalt you... This is the Lords doing and it is marvelous in our sight… I will not die but live and tell of the works of the Lord" (Psalm 118:24, 27, 28, 23, 17).

The imagery of binding to the altar recalls the binding of Isaac as well as the nailing of God's son, Jesus, to the cross. Deliverance from death to tell of the works of the Lord may well be a prophetic reference to the resurrection of Christ. It is no wonder that Jesus would say to his disciples, "I have longed to eat this Passover with you before I suffer, for I will not eat again until it is fulfilled in the Kingdom of God." Jesus was about to fulfill the Passover in His own death as the Passover lamb. John the Baptist had prophesied of Jesus, "Behold the lamb of God who takes away the sin of the world."

Living Inside Out

In the Passover meal with the disciples, Jesus would have had the opportunity to review the call of Abraham, the faithfulness of God to Isaac, Jacob, and Joseph, to review the binding of Isaac which is a prominent part of the Passover story, and the provision of the lamb as a substitute for the beloved son. He would have reviewed the story of Joseph, the plots of Joseph's brothers, and the ultimate triumph of God's chosen one both in his personal deliverance, his deliverance of the Gentiles, and his ruling over his brothers. So the Passover narrative is a story of victory out of defeat. It is a story of the vindication of God's elect. It is a repeated chronicle of God's faithfulness and His sovereign execution of His plan in spite of the belligerent resistance of man.[196]

> The cup of redemption—the third cup taken after the meal—which spoke of the blood of the Passover lamb—found its ultimate fulfillment in the blood of the Messiah.

The taking of the bread and the cup was given a special significance when Jesus said, "This bread;" which at the time of the first century not only reminded Him of the manna from Heaven but also of the Passover lamb itself. It was symbolic of His own body which was given for them. The cup of redemption—the third cup taken after the meal—which spoke of the blood of the Passover lamb—found its ultimate fulfillment in the blood of the Messiah.

This was no mere addendum but a reinterpretation of crucial elements of the ancient Passover. It is no wonder then that early Christians continued to celebrate the Passover and to see in it—the fulfillment of a second Passover that delivered them not from bondage in Egypt but from bondage to sin

Communion, Sharing In Life And Death

which enslaves not only the Jewish people but every human being. Reference is made to crucial elements of the Passover throughout the New Testament. The Passover marks the beginning of the "new life, and the new year" (Exo 12:2), just as receiving of Messiah as Lord marks the beginning of a new life for every believer (2Cor 5:17).

Prior to the taking of the Passover meal the Jewish people were instructed to search their homes and to purge out the leaven (yeast) (Exo 12:15). Paul refers to this tradition (1Cor 5:7-8) when he exhorts the Corinthians to a holy life. He says, "You are in fact unleavened. Christ our Passover is sacrificed for us, therefore let us keep the Feast not with the leaven of malice and wickedness but with the unleavened bread of sincerity and truth." His reference is to the purging of the leaven at the Feast of Unleavened Bread which continues for seven days following the Feast of Passover. The leaven is purged prior to the evening of Passover and the people eat only unleavened bread for the following week.

> Christ our Passover is sacrificed for us, therefore let us keep the Feast not with the leaven of malice and wickedness but with the unleavened bread of sincerity and truth.

Paul takes this as a picture of the holiness of the Corinthian church and the church in general. He then challenges the church to a life of moral purity based upon this very ceremony. This concept must have been common knowledge, not only in the Jewish synagogue, but also to the Gentiles at Corinth in the first century. The lamb slain for the first born in Exodus 12:5-6 is a type of Christ slain for each of us (1Cor 5:7).[197] The blood of the lamb applied to the lentil and door post is a picture of

Living Inside Out

the blood applied to our own heart. The feasting on the lamb in the house over which God hovers is a wonderful picture of our abiding in Christ in John 15.

Paul says, "As often as we eat this bread and drink this cup, we 'proclaim' the Lord's death" in the same way that the taking of the Passover meal proclaims Gods redemptive hand to the children of Israel.[198] All of these wonderful truths were the meditation of the early Christian community—every time they took the bread and the wine of Passover in their weekly communion service. Unfortunately, the first century saw a hardening of the Jewish leadership opposed to the minority Messianic movement which was entirely Jewish in the early years.[199] With the conversion of Cornelius, a door was opened for the Gentiles as promised to Abraham: "In you all the families of the earth shall be blessed." This expectation is repeated throughout the Seder,[200] but no addition to any family is without its surprises, both joys and heartaches.

Separation of Jews and the Gentiles in the First Centuries

With the massive influx of Gentiles into the Christian community, its Jewish foundation was shaken. This was a result of multiple political, social, and theological forces. In the early church, a Judaizing force which sought to impose circumcision and the Mosaic Law on Gentiles as a prerequisite for conversion was a constant problem even from apostolic times.[201] Though it's clear that the Jewish community retained its identity, the defining of their Jewish heritage was problematic. Paul, even in the face of his strong condemnation of the Judaizers, kept the feasts and considered himself a Hebrew of Hebrews (Phil. 3:5, II Cor 11:22).

Communion, Sharing In Life And Death

Peter and Paul had numerous controversies as recounted in Galatians and Acts. The Epistle to the Hebrews addresses Messianic Jews who are in danger of reverting to their traditions in denial of their newly found faith. The author of Hebrews argues this is not new at all but is a faith common to all of the heroes of the Torah (Hebrews 11). The book of Matthew was probably not written to persuade Jews to **come to** Christ but rather to reassure those who **had** come to Messiah of the consistency of their decision and of the biblical foundation upon which their faith in Messiah rested.[202]

Multiple forces continued to divide the Jewish and Christian communities and to marginalize Jewish Christians. Prior to the destruction of Jerusalem in 70 AD as Roman legions approached the city, many Messianic Jews fled to Pella east of the Jordan in response to Jesus' words in the Olivet discourse. Rather than acknowledge the prophetic character of the warning, the scattered Jewish community regathered at Jabneh and condemned the Messianics—barring them from the synagogues. During the second Jewish revolt in 132AD, over ten thousand Messianic believers were killed by Bar Kochaba's followers because of their refusal to acknowledge him as Messiah and to take up arms in support of this revolt. With the suppression of this rebellion by Rome, Jews were driven from the city of Jerusalem, and Messianic Christians found it politically beneficial not to associate with or identify themselves as Jews in the Roman world.[203]

The temple tax levied earlier on Jews was continued and placed in Roman coffers. If Christians could persuade Romans that they were in fact separate from the Jewish population this could prove an economic advantage as well. Formal actions deepened the division between the Jewish and Christian communities. This included the addition of *Notzrim* (Christians) to the *Birkat Ha-Minim* or the heretic benediction which is a part of the *Amdah*—the standing prayer of the Jewish community; the change of the Sabbath to the Lord's Day; and eventually the second Jewish revolt of 132AD to 135AD.[204]

With the massive influx of Gentiles to the Church in the second and third centuries and the widening rift between Messianic and non-Messianic Jews, the church took on a distinctly Gentile character. As the Jewish community had attacked Christians, now the Christian community would attack Jews. The first attack would come with a takeover of the Scriptures themselves and the promises of God which define Israel. It is Origen's (185-254 AD) system of interpretation that replaces Israel with the church.[205]

"It is no exaggeration to say that for Origen the whole of the debate between the church and synagogue can be reduced to the one question of the interpretation of scripture. The difference between Judaism and Christianity is that Christians perceive the mysteries which are only hinted at, whereas Jews are capable only of a strict literal reading of the text. It may be thought remarkable that Origen of all people who was well acquainted with Jewish exegesis and all of its aspects should have perpetuated this myth of "Jewish literalism," but perpetuate he certainly did."[206]

Anyone who did not accept Origen's allegorical system of interpretation was nothing more than a "*Jew*" and really did not belong in the Church. Origen wrote: "If anyone wishes to hear and understand these words literally, he ought to gather with the Jews rather than the Christians. But if he wishes to be a Christian, the disciple of Paul, let him hear Paul saying, 'The

Communion, Sharing In Life And Death

law is spiritual' and declaring that these words are allegorical when the law speaks of Abraham and his wife and his sons."[207]

Origen's teachings ultimately demanded an anti-Judaic outlook. He disinherits the Jews and sets the church in their place. The scriptures that promise judgment on Jews or Jacob are still to be understood in a literal sense, but those scriptures that promise blessing on Israel were henceforth only to be understood as referring to the church.[208]

The Early Church Fathers exhibited a growing tendency to distance themselves from Judaism and in doing so became increasingly indiscriminate in their overall condemnation of everything Jewish. Justin Martyr in 160AD went so far as to argue, "The scriptures are not yours but ours"[209] "God blesses this people (Christians), He calls them Israel, and He declares them to be His inheritance. So why is it that you (Jews) do not repent of the deception you practice on yourselves, as if you alone were Israel."[210] "The Jews have justly rejected the Son of God and cast Him out of the vineyard when they slew Him. Therefore, God has justly rejected them."[211] "They (Jews) are disinherited from the grace of God."[212] In the first three centuries the works of Cyprian (*Three Books of Testimonies Against the Je*ws), Hippolytus (*Expository Treatise Against the Jews*), Tertullian (*Against the Jews*), Irenaeus, and others are among those of special note.[213]

By the 4th century John Chrysostom unleashed a series of *Eight Homilies Against the Jews.*[214] Eusebius continued in the fourth century that the promises of the Hebrew Scriptures were for the Christians but not for the Jews, but the curses were for the Jews. This was the beginning of a *Replacement Theology*[215] which basically saw the church as replacing Israel. By the time of Eusebius, who was a friend of Constantine, and

Living Inside Out

wrote in large part to affirm the church-state relationship that Constantine established, the movement to separate the church from Israel or rather to see the church as the New Israel, distinct from its corrupted Jewish influence, was well underway.[216]

Centrality of the Sacraments in the Middle Ages

We have seen now how the church became separated from its Jewish roots in the first three centuries and lost the cultural context out of which the new covenant arises. With secularization of the church during the age of Constantine, baptized multitudes were brought into the visible church. Constantine, "built buildings which were called churches; and people who were not the church began to fill them. They *went* to church but did not seek to *be* the church."[217] The foundation was laid for the errors that would ensue in the next thousand years wherein completely new interpretations were imposed upon the meaning of the Lord's Supper.

The Lord's Supper changed from a memorial celebration in the homes of the common people affirming God's faithfulness in delivering His people not only from bondage in Egypt, but also from bondage to sin into the glorious liberty of the sons of God; to a sacrament in the hands of a priest in a cathedral affirming the mystical presence of God suffering and dying in the offering of the mass. The meal originally intended to employ the common elements of bread and wine as a memorial and proclamation of

> Over the period of a thousand years The Lord's Supper moved from a simple memorial celebration rooted in the Passover to a mystical rite rooted in Greek philosophy.

the Spiritual bread from heaven was reinterpreted to confer a particular grace in the hands of a clerical hierarchy!

How could this happen? Over the period of a thousand years The Lord's Supper moved from a simple memorial celebration rooted in the Passover to a mystical rite rooted in Greek philosophy. Jesus emphasized a link between physical and spiritual deliverance. Passover celebrated God's mighty hand of deliverance in Egypt which was extended again in the person of His son. The New Testament linked the picture of physical deliverance from Egypt: the Passover Seder; and the picture of spiritual deliverance in Jesus's incarnation, crucifixion, and resurrection. The elements of bread and wine were each a picture of the finished work emphasizing the grace of God.

However, as the church became separated from its Jewish roots, it also became enamored with Greek philosophical concepts of salvation. The church soon became preoccupied with the link between the illustration and the reality. Having dismissed the Jews as concrete, physical, and spiritually blind, the church became preoccupied with the spiritual reality behind the physical sign. Over time the symbols "mysteriously" became the thing symbolized. The mystery of the incarnation symbolized in the bread and wine soon became the actual bread and wine becoming Christ! These newly defined symbols were mystically infused with the power to impart grace!

Though at first, the symbols were limited to bread, wine, and water (baptism), they eventually multiplied to include confirmation, penance, ordination, and even marriage. Augustine expanded the list to thirty different sacraments.[218] This preoccupation with the link between the symbols, the thing symbolized, and spiritual salvation became a system we know as sacramentalism. It evolved over a period of a thousand years amidst constant debate.[219] "The idea is clearly that the Eucharist does not merely *signify* eternal life but is somehow instrumental in effecting it."[220]

By the end of the Middle Ages, the system had come to dominate. "The Counsel of Trent reacting to the Protestant approaches to the sacraments responded by defending the position outlined by Peter Lombard. 'If anyone says that the sacraments of the new law were not all instituted by our Lord Jesus Christ, or that there are more or less than seven, namely, baptism, confirmation, Eucharist, penance, extreme unction, ordination, and marriage, or that any one of these seven is not truly and intrinsically a sacrament, let them be condemned.[221]

The Middle Ages represents a time in the history of the church when we may truly say, "They were devoted to the breaking of bread." The problem is, that the breaking of bread had come to have an entirely new meaning removed from its Jewish context and placed at the center of a system Luther would describe as *"The Babylonian Captivity of the Church."*[222] The language of worship too became a barrier to understanding.[223] In the western world, by the fourth century, Latin replaced Greek as a language of worship. With the loss of a population literate in Latin, later centuries would find congregations attended upon symbols and ceremonies quickly elevating the Lord's Supper to a place of mystical spirituality. It is no wonder that the appearance of the Scriptures in the language of the common people was essential to a confrontation of the whole system which had developed over the previous 1000 years.

Reinterpretation of the Lord's Supper in The Reformation

During the Middle Ages, the development of sacramental Christianity became consumed with the ongoing death of Christ repeatedly offered in sacrifice throughout the day, year after year, and century after century in expectation of the dispensing of grace both for the living and the dead. Luther's protest of indulgences and their misrepresentation is often seen as the igniting spark of the Reformation, however numerous elements associated with sacramentalism and with the entrenched separation of the church from its ancient Jewish roots including a devotion to the Scriptural fueled the revolution.[224]

Unfortunately, the Reformer's debates about the nature of the Communion service and the elements of bread and wine seldom turned on first century understandings of the Jewish Passover celebration or of Jesus' thoroughly Hebraic teaching style throughout the gospels.[225] Menno Simons, father of the Mennonites, does argue specifically from the Passover.[226] But the reformers are, for the most part, still struggling to free themselves from the errors of sacramentalism in a western (Greek and Latin) playing field.[227]

"John Calvin regarded only baptism and communion as sacraments. Baptism was the individual's initiation into the new community of Christ. Calvin rejected Zwingli's idea that the sacrament of communion was merely a symbol. But he also warned against a magical belief in the real presence of Christ in the sacrament."[228] Zwingli wrote that in serving the Lord's Supper, the intended action should be announced intelligibly and in German so that the common people could understand it. The bread would be carried about by "designated servers

Living Inside Out

on wooden platters so as to avoid pomp." He concludes this by saying, "We shall use this order so long as it pleases our churches four times a year, Easter, Pentecost, autumn, and Christmas."[229]

While the Reformers themselves maintained a high view of the sacrament of Communion, their wrath at the abuse of the sacrament combined with their differences as to the true meaning and uses of it led to the next generation's marginalization of the event. It is difficult today to grasp the almost magical belief in the presence of Christ in the sacrament that Calvin warned against. The Reformers were reacting to such abuses as "sacramental gazing." Often in the Middle Ages, the laity only received the Mass once a year. During the rest of the year, they engaged in this "sacramental gazing" which was simply the reverent observation as it was lifted by the priest to undergo "transubstantiation" (the magical transformation of the elements into the actual body and blood of Christ).[230]

A growing hunger for true spirituality in the late Middle Ages exemplified by Thomas A.'Kempus, contributed to reform. His work *The Imitation of Christ* has been popular over the centuries both with Protestants and Catholics because it focuses so clearly on the essence of the imitation of Christ. The fourth major division of his work centers on the Holy Communion. His focus is never on transubstantiation, elevation, or other questionable doctrines but on the heart of the individual receiving the sacrament. In chapter one of this final section entitled *The Emblems of Christ Received with Reverence;* he contrasts his own preparation with that of Solomon and David as they came to worship God.

"How short a time I spend when I am preparing myself to receive the communion. Seldom am I wholly collected. Very

Communion, Sharing In Life And Death

seldom am I cleansed from all distraction. The most devout King David danced before the ark of God with all of his might, calling to mind the benefits bestowed in time past upon his forefathers. He made instruments of various kinds. He set forth Psalms and appointed them to be chanted with joy. Our lukewarm attitude and negligence are exceedingly to be lamented and pitied. Though we are not drawn with greater affection to Christ in whom lies all the hope of those who are to be saved for He Himself is our sanctification and our redemption" (1Cor 1:30).[231]

Again, this is the tone of the entire section: "Diligently examine your conscience to the utmost of your power, purify and make it clear, with true contrition, and humble confession, so you may have no burden nor know anything that may breed remorse of conscience and hinder your drawing near (to Christ). Confess to God in the secret of your heart all the wretchedness of your evil passions."[232]

The Reformation represents a time of correction for the church—a time to reexamine an essential practice of the sharing of bread and wine in remembrance of the work of Christ with the goal of deepening love, humility, faith, and obedience before God. Protestant reformers and Catholic counter-reformers especially among the mystics would seize this age to draw near to God. Others became embroiled in debating transubstantiation and indulgences. Sadly, the right of kings to decree to their subjects their particular interpretation would lead Europe into bloody conflict. The aftermath of this conflict resulted in the marginalization of the Lord's Supper in the next generation.

Marginalization in the 18th to 20th Centuries

Following the turmoil of the Reformation and the so-called Wars of Religion,[233] the major debates over the nature of baptism and the sacrament of the Lord's Supper turned to the reality of our spiritual relationship with God and the independence of the congregations from governmental and denominational control. The Age of Reason or the Enlightenment would be accompanied by an age of renewal and personal piety which would in turn lead to The Great Awakening. This was a period of personal, religious experience which was in a large part removed from spirituality associated with the sacraments. The Awakening was rooted in reason and piety. Attention was turned to the nature of spiritual awakening as it manifested itself in personal piety and "experimental religion" as it came to be known in the colonies.

Jonathan Edwards, in his *Faithful Narrative of the Surprising Work of God* (1739), describes a transition which took place in a small community in the Connecticut River valley in 1735. At the beginning of his ministry in 1733, Edwards describes the people as "very insensensible" (sic insensitive) of the things of religion. But by 1735, "There was scarcely a single person in the town, old or young, left unconcerned about the great things of the eternal world."[234] Edwards was ultimately dismissed from his pastorate in 1750 after a long controversy about admitting unbelievers to the church's ordinances—especially the Lord's

Communion, Sharing In Life And Death

Supper. What is remarkable here is that the Lord's Supper had become for the American church a social community activity distinctly separated from the true grace of God and salvation which were received in a spiritual visitation of God, quite apart from any sacrament.

Scottish Holy Fairs

Perhaps the most remarkable celebrations of the Lord's Supper of their time served to show why the sacrament itself became marginalized. These events are little known to most modern-day Christians, but in fact, set the stage for modern American revivalism.[235] The Scottish reformers combined a strong anti-Roman Catholic mindset with a dislike for the English and a rejection of their king and his Anglican Church. "Scottish Protestants like the Catholics before them continued to see the Eucharist (the Lord's Supper) as the most

> Perhaps the most remarkable celebrations of the Lord's Supper of their time served to show why the sacrament itself became marginalized.

solemn and august act of Christian worship."[236] On one hand, they sought to remove vestiges of Roman Catholic religious life eliminating many of the sacramental festivals and holy days reducing the celebration of the Eucharist to an annual occasion. In doing so, the celebration of the sacrament became a yearly festival and a focal point for the Scottish Presbyterians.

They reclaimed the cup from Rome and rejecting the English king's Five Articles[237], they sat together to celebrate the Lord's Supper at a common table. Exactly what happened? Preparation for the festival focused on five steps including self-examination, personal covenant, prayer, meditation, and devotional readings to prepare oneself for the celebration of the sacrament.[238] On Sunday the week before the celebration, teachings on the Lord's Supper and the dangers of partaking in an unworthy manner were expounded. On the Wednesday prior to communion, sins were reviewed and condemned, and the Ten Commandments were expounded. Saturday service focused on the dying love of Christ. Having been questioned by their leaders on Sunday, tokens were issued to those who had made the necessary preparations and were planning to come forth and be seated at the tables to receive the elements.[239]

These fairs, festivals, and sacramental celebrations occurred at various locations from May to October and people would travel from place to place to experience and re-experience the excitement. If it did not happen in one community, then perhaps it would at the next community, and so it went. The expectations for renewal, if not always for ecstatic experiences, were regularly met. One man recalled his experience at the sacramental table: "I saw divine justice stretching out its hand to take hold of me and Christ as it were stepping entwist justice and me showing His wounds and what He had suffered for me in satisfying Justice and saying, 'I have satisfied you for his sins, upon which the hand of Justice could not touch me. And recovering out of the trance, I felt my soul filled with great joy and comfort and thankfulness to God.[240]

These ecstatic experiences were quite prevalent as noted in many journals from the era. Often the visions focused on the symbol of Christ as Bridegroom describing the experience of Christ's love enjoyed and encountered at the table.[241] What came of these Holy Fairs? Schmidt traces three influences that marginalized these celebrations. First enlightenment thinking

Communion, Sharing In Life And Death

cast these celebrations as excessive and unenlightened. Robert Burns wrote his cutting poem *Holy Fair,* presenting only the worst of the excesses of such occasion. The upper classes began looking on the Holy Fairs as revealing the ignorance and fanaticism of the lower class of the people in Scotland.[242]

Theologians had long debated the excesses of the events while some wanted more frequent and localized expression of the sacrament. arguing that "continual vitality and sustained disciplines were the hallmarks of genuine Christian piety and frequent communion would nurture such spirituality."[243] However the great revivals in places such as Shotts, Cambuslang,[244] and Cane Ridge in Kentucky would have lasting impact.

Cane Ridge

By the time of Cane Ridge,[245] the Scottish Presbyterian sacramental tradition was over two centuries old. "Cane Ridge has a special epochal position in American religious history. From August 6-12, 1801, in the first summer of a new century thousands of people gathered in and around the small Cane Ridge meeting house in Bourbon County in central Kentucky to prepare for and to celebrate the Lord's Supper. Never before in Americana had so many people attended this type of sacramental occasion". The gathering there was not as large as many of those throughout Scotland, but it was the largest in the New World, and "in many respects it presaged the end of that tradition."[246] Reformed Christianity had recovered the

> The Reformers recovered the centrality of faith and the use of the sacraments as an affirmation of their faith, obedience, and holiness.

centrality of faith by which one is united to God through Christ in a love relationship which produces holiness from the inside out.[247] In the Medieval church, sacramental obedience had at least obscured faith if not replaced it. The Reformers recovered the centrality of faith and the use of the sacraments as an affirmation of their faith, obedience, and holiness. By the eighteenth century "evangelical" was coming to mean a focus on a crisis conversion—a second birth.

Becoming born again was a deeply emotional spiritual experience as contrasted to the more methodical, ritualized process of church membership. While the early Methodists were moving toward the emotional and the Anglicans toward ritual, Presbyterians were trying to maintain somewhat of a middle road. The yearly sacrament represented a ritual with significant emotion. It was estimated that nearly two thousand Presbyterians planned to attend Cane Ridge. There were eighteen Presbyterian ministers present with numerous Methodists and Baptists who attended. Though only ministers preached and prepared sermons, literally hundreds of people served as exhorters at Cane Ridge. With the exception of speaking in tongues, the scene would rival any modern-day Pentecostal meeting![248]

The significance of Cane Ridge is the aftermath: the Presbyterian Church would become divided[249] and the Restoration churches (the Disciples of Christ, Christian, Churches of Christ, and the new Cumberland Presbyterian Church) would emerge. Beyond the denominational changes came changes in the role of Communion.

Clearly the communion service was not as central, and not so tied to conversion. Among Methodists and Baptists, although their conferences and association meetings usually climaxed in

Communion, Sharing In Life And Death

a communion service, it seems reasonably clear that by the time of Cane Ridge, the sacrament was already losing significance for almost all evangelicals, and that new revival techniques, some already in evidence at Cane Ridge, hastened this erosion. This is why I said, at the beginning, that Cane Ridge was not only the greatest Scottish communion in America but in a symbolic sense also one of the last.[250]

Implications for the 21st Century

The development of biblical archaeology and renewed interest in the Jewish roots of the Christian faith together with the reestablishment of the state of Israel, the blossoming of the Messianic Jewish community, and the explosive growth of radical Islam at the close of the 20th century, provided a new context for interpreting Passover and the Lord's Supper. The church must no longer see itself as the "New Israel" but as an expanded Israel.[251] It must take its place as a guest in the house of Israel "Gentile believers should start acting like Ruth and not like Orpah."[252] The Christian church does not keep the Passover as the Jewish people are commanded to keep the Passover. But they celebrate the Lord's Supper in memory and proclamation of the death, burial, and resurrection of the Messiah—the Passover Lamb of God who will restore the Kingdom to, and reign over, Israel.

In our post-modern world, cultural context is fundamental. Stories define our culture and truth. The Passover story gives historical context to the Lord's Supper while allowing it to be reinterpreted in a Christian milieu. The story itself is defining and empowering. Renewed interest in orthodox Christianity and Catholicism in America allows today's post-modern

179

generations to contextualize their religious experience—to root it in history and community. Unfortunately, many Christians have stopped short of the true Jewish historical context and community in Passover. The rediscovery of the Jewish Roots of the Lord's Supper in Passover serves as a cultural context for the Evangelical community and a common ground for dialog across the denominational divisions in Christianity.

> The rediscovery of the Jewish Roots of the Lord's Supper in Passover serves as a cultural context for the Evangelical community and a common ground for dialog across the denominational divisions in Christianity.

Two movements have paved the way in the twentieth century for the recovery of the celebration of the Lord's Supper as an aid to, and expression of, true spirituality. Both are somewhat marginal groups and are related to one another only indirectly. The first is the Plymouth Brethren[253] movement associated with J.N. Darby and later with Prophecy conferences with C.I Scofield and the doctrine of dispensationalism. The founders were mainly Anglican Evangelicals known as Plymouth Brethren because they originated in Plymouth, England.

Strongly, academic, Calvinistic, and evangelical, it is estimated that one percent of the Brethren became missionaries in the early years. Their early leaders, concerned by denominationalism and secularism in the church, sought to establish a simple communion service in which the Priesthood of believers would be expressed by the leading of the Spirit in a shared remembrance around the common elements of bread and wine. Under the Plymouth Brethren model, priesthood is exercised

Communion, Sharing In Life And Death

in two directions: upward to God in worship and outward to men in proclamation.[254]

Their (Plymouth Brethren) weekly communion service is characterized by an open forum in which all are free to offer a prayer or expound a text relating to the elements in the rememb rance of Christ. This meeting is the central focus for the church and is never seen as an addendum to the sermon or prayer meeting; rather, it

> Their (Plymouth Brethren) weekly communion service is characterized by an open forum in which all are free to offer a prayer or expound a text relating to the elements in the remembrance of Christ.

is the fundamental context for worship.[255] It is this format and priority which has the potential to transform our present marginalization of the Supper. Unfortunately, the actual services are lacking the contemporary musical element of worship associated with much of evangelicalism. Most often, the hymns are taken from hundred-year-old hymnals and sung acapella!

The Brethren are commonly associated with the development of the doctrine of dispensationalism which emphasizes the church's distinction from the nation of Israel: the church with a heavenly home as opposed to earthly Israel.[256] This element of teaching has been embraced by a large segment of the Evangelical community and has played a foundational role in the development of the Jewish Messianic movement which is the second movement contributing to the recovery of the centrality of the sacrament. Unlike the Brethren, worship in this movement is very contemporary often embracing various Charismatic practices.

Living Inside Out

An extremely diverse movement, the Messianic or Jewish Roots movement has contributed to the recovery of the Jewish context of the sacrament of Holy Communion. Moshe Rosen, founder of the "Jews for Jesus" developed a presentation he entitled, *Christ in the Passover.*[257] As the premier Evangelical arm of the Messianic movement, the organization *Jews for Jesus,* continues to provide informative Passover presentation in groups and churches around the world to help Jewish and Gentile Christians recover their Jewish roots.

Daniel Juster is one of the leading theologians of the Messianic Movement. Among his writings is *Jewish Roots,*[258] rightly described as "the first comprehensive theology for Messianic Judaism."[259] Having served numerous terms as president of the MJAA (Messianic Jewish Association of America), Juster is now involved in forming Jewish speaking congregations within the land of Israel and coordinating numerous international Messianic ministries. In terms of the sacrament of Communion, Juster's primary contribution to Communion is in the recovery of the celebration of the feasts in a Jewish context.

> An extremely diverse movement, the Messianic or Jewish Roots movement has contributed to the recovery of the Jewish context of the sacrament of Holy Communion.

This return to the Passover roots has resulted in a deepening appreciation of the symbolism and nature of the sacraments and the uniting of the Jewish and Gentile elements of the church, bringing with it the potential to fulfill Paul's mandate as an apostle to the Gentiles." Inasmuch then as I am an apostle of Gentiles, I magnify my ministry, if (in hope that)

Communion, Sharing In Life And Death

somehow, I might move to jealousy my fellow countrymen and save some of them. For if their rejection is the reconciliation of the world, what will their acceptance be but life from the dead (Rom 11:13-14)?

The unity of the church in its outward expression is seen first in its devotion to the Apostle's Doctrine as embodied in the NT and by implication its devotion to the Torah. It is seen secondly, in devotion to fellowship or sharing in the benefits and the propagation of the gospel of the good news of Christ. Unity is found thirdly in a devotion to the Breaking of Bread— the celebration of Christ as our Passover since it encapsulates and visually proclaims the fundamental realities of our new life in Christ. Lastly there will be a devotion to prayer, a sort of neurological system of the Church whereby the body communicates with the head and the head with the body. This is the subject of our final chapter.

CHAPTER 9

PRAYER, COMMUNICATION WITH GOD

Why Pray?

In the previous chapters, we learned the apostles devoted themselves to four activities: the apostles' teaching, fellowship, the breaking of bread, and prayer (Acts 2:42). Prayer was not a casual, haphazard, religious activity attached to their busy careers, but a sort of neurological system tying the body to the head in terms of communication. They were devoted to prayer because it was essential to the church and each individual believer. Prayer was on the same par with the apostle's teaching, fellowship, and with breaking of bread. Over the centuries prayer has been central to the strong healthy church just as prayerlessness has characterized the weak unhealthy church. By His Spirit, God leads us to pray according to His will. And by that same Spirit, He answers prayer working all things according to His will. This begs the question, why does God require we pray?

Prayer, Communication With God

Why involve us in any other activity: sharing the gospel, bearing a burden, planting a seed, building a house? The answer—prayer is God's plan. In the same way that the gospel is not proclaimed without a preacher, a field is not planted without a farmer, nor a house built without a carpenter, some things do not happen without prayer. We often have not **because** we ask not. God wills to act on behalf of those who ask. Countless miracles are recorded in the gospels on behalf of those who asked Jesus to act. And clearly, they would not have been done apart from the asking (Mk 7:24-30; 9:29).

> In the same way that the gospel is not proclaimed without a preacher, a field is not planted without a farmer, nor a house built without a carpenter, some things do not happen without prayer.

Just as any other activity may be done in the flesh or in the Spirit, as a requirement or a delight, skillfully or negligently, so it is with prayer. Richard Foster suggests that "in prayer we come home to the heart of God."[260] The Talmud[261] teaches that it is by praying we serve God with the heart in fulfillment of the command, "You shall serve the Lord your God with all your heart" (Deut 11:13). Prayer for Paul was "first and last": he exhorted Timothy, "First of all, then, I urge that supplications, prayers, intercessions, and thanksgivings be made for all people" (1 Tim 2:1 ESV). Then, having described the armor of the Christian, Paul concludes, "praying at all times in the Spirit, with all prayer and supplication. To that end keep

> Just as any other activity may be done in the flesh or in the Spirit, as a requirement or a delight, skillfully or negligently, so it is with prayer.

185

Living Inside Out

alert with all perseverance, making supplication for all the saints, and, also for me" (Eph 6:18 ESV).

How to Pray

Love

Prayer is essentially a statement of dependency on God. While man may find sufficiency in himself and comfort in his independence, his prayer is an abomination to God (Isaiah 1). But when the heart is broken and contrite and the life upright, prayer, is "God's delight." "The prayer of the upright is His delight" (Proverbs 15:8).

> But when the heart is broken and contrite and the life upright, prayer, is "God's delight.

Psalm 27 gives a glimpse into the prayer of the upright and the basic requirements for prayer. This Psalm is especially relevant because it identifies prayer as a priority in the life of King David. The **most important things or essentials** were addressed in the first section. In this Psalm, David says, "One thing I have asked of the Lord that I will seek after: that I may dwell in the house of the Lord all the days of my life, to gaze upon the beauty of the Lord, and to inquire in His temple. He will hide me in His shelter in the day of trouble. He will conceal me under the cover of His tent; He will lift me high upon a rock (Psalm 27:4-5 ESV)."

The one thing that David asked of God is "that he might dwell in His house," not just one day, but for the entirety of his life. His goal in being in the presence of God was "to gaze on the beauty of the Lord and to inquire in His temple." In the previous Psalm, we read, "Oh Lord, I love the habitation of your house and the place where your glory dwells" (Psalm 26:8). Prayer is essentially the overflow of a love relationship with God. This love includes humility, a longing for holiness, and a faith which produces prayer. We read this throughout the pages of church history both in the mouths of ancient and modern commentators. Richard Foster begins his classic work on prayer with the words of Augustine. "True, whole prayer is nothing but love."[262] Foster agrees: "My first counsel is simply a reminder that prayer is nothing more than an ongoing and growing love relationship with God the Father, Son, and the Holy Spirit."[263] "Prayer, this experience which begins so simply, has at its end a totally abandoned love to the Lord. Only one thing is required, Love."[264] To the question, "How does one serve (God) 'with all the heart'" (Deut 11:13), the Talmud answers: "By Praying."[265]

> Prayer is essentially the overflow of a love relationship with God.

Julian of Norwich (1344-1413) the English Mystic, lay dying in a monastery, at the young age of 30, when she prayed for a vision of Christ's passion. In response to her prayer, she heard the words, "I am the foundation of your praying." After lying gravely ill for several days, Julian recalls, "I wanted to live to love God better and longer, so that I might through the grace of that living have more knowledge and love of God than I might have even in Heaven!"[266] She did live and spent the rest of her life writing of the Love of God and the overflow of that love in prayer. Julian was not concerned so much with prayer as we often consider it: making our requests known to God; but rather asking for Him to make himself known to us.

Living Inside Out

"We are so preciously loved by God that we cannot even comprehend it. No created being can ever know how much and how sweetly and how tenderly God loves them. It is only with the help of his grace that we are able to preserve in spiritual contemplation, with endless wonder, and His high surpassing immeasurable love which our Lord reveals in His goodness for us ... The highest form of prayer is to the goodness of God. It comes down to us to meet our humblest needs. It gives life to our souls and makes them live and grow in grace and virtue… Therefore we may ask for our Lover to have all of Him that we desire. For it is our nature to long for Him and it is His nature to long for us. In this life we can never stop loving Him."[267]

Humility

Prayer flows not only from a love for God but from a humility before God. We humble ourselves by casting all our care on God (I Peter 5:6-7). As pastors call the nation to prayer, the text most often quoted is 2Chronicles 7:14. "If my people who are called by my name will humble themselves and pray, and seek my face, and turn from their wicked ways, then I will hear from Heaven, and forgive their sin, and heal their land." This promise was given to Solomon at the dedication of the first temple. It was actually an answer to his dedication prayer in chapter 6 where he asked repeatedly that God would, "Have regard to the prayer of your servant and to his plea, O Lord my God. Listen to the cry and to the prayer that your servant prays before you, that your eyes may be opened day and night toward this house, the place where you have promised to set your name, that you may listen to the prayer that your servant offers towards this place, and listen to the pleas of your servant and your people, Israel, when they pray toward this place" (2Chr 6:19-21).

He went on to make specific request that God would hear prayers for forgiveness (verses 22 and 23), for deliverance from their enemies (24-25), for deliverance from drought (26-28), and finally in verse 29 he prayed generally; "Whatever prayer, whatever plea is made by any man or by all of your people, each knowing his own affliction and his own sorrow, stretched out his hands towards this house, then hear from Heaven your dwelling place and forgive and render to each whose heart you know according to all of his ways" (2Chr 6: 29-30 ESV). Solomon expanded the request to include foreigners, not of the house of Israel, who come into the land and pray toward the house in verse 32. Finally in conclusion he asked: "If they return to Thee with all their heart and with all their soul in the land of their captivity, where they have been taken captive, and pray toward their land which Thou hast given to their fathers, and the city which Thou hast chosen, and toward the house which I have built for Thy name, then hear from heaven, from Thy dwelling place, their prayer and supplications, and maintain their cause, and forgive Thy people who have sinned against Thee" (2Chr 6:38-39).

In this the final request, the heart of humility is seen. They have repented with their mind and their heart and turned toward God. This is exactly what God desires. If the people "humble themselves and pray and seek my face and turn from their

Living Inside Out

wicked ways, I will hear from heaven, and forgive their sin, and heal their land."

If God is to hear prayer for any of those things, it must be offered in humility, brokenness, and repentance. This classic text has been echoed throughout the ages by many who have taught on prayer. When Jesus taught specifically on prayer, he did it in the context of individuals praying within the temple. His focus was not simply that they prayed toward the temple or that they came into the temple to pray. In fact, he notes that the tax collector was *standing far off* though obviously he had come to the temple to pray.

Jesus graphically illustrates the right and wrong attitude in prayer. He told this parable to some who trusted in themselves that they were righteous and regarded others with contempt: "Two men went up into the temple to pray, one a Pharisee, and the other a tax-gatherer. The Pharisee stood and was praying thus to himself, 'God, I thank Thee that I am not like other people: swindlers, unjust, adulterers, or even like this tax-gatherer. I fast twice a week; I pay tithes of all that I get.' But the tax-gatherer, standing some distance away, was even unwilling to lift up his eyes to heaven, but was beating his breast, saying, 'God, be merciful to me, the sinner!' I tell you this man went down to his house justified rather than the other; for everyone who exalts himself shall be humbled, but he who humbles himself shall be exalted" (Luke 18:10-14).

Here the context is prayer. The essential requirement is humility. The answer to the humble tax collector's prayer for mercy is that he will be justified and even exalted. "Luther exhorted, 'Prayer is not overcoming God's reluctance but taking hold of His willingness.'"[268]

"Prayer is not so much an act as it is an attitude—an attitude of **dependency**, dependency upon God. Prayer is a confession of creature weakness, yea, of helplessness. Prayer is the acknowledgement of our need and the spreading of it before God. We do not say that this is **all** there is in prayer, it is not: but it *is* the essential, the primary element in prayer.... Prayer is fundamentally an attitude of dependency upon God. Therefore, prayer is the very opposite of **dictating to** God... The one who really prays is **. . .** submissive to the Divine will. And the "Divine will" means that we are content for the Lord to supply our need according to the dictates of His own sovereign pleasure."[269]

Faith

The fuel of fervent prayer is faith. Jesus repeatedly declares that faith is an essential element. Following the withering of the fig tree, He emphasizes the power of faith to move mountains *and* concludes "and whatever you ask in prayer you will receive if you have faith" (Matthew 21:22ESV). James likewise emphasizes the role of faith when he writes, "But let him ask in faith with no doubting. For the one who doubts is like the wave of the sea that is driven and tossed by the wind. For that person must not suppose that he will receive anything from the Lord" (James 1:5-7 ESV). True faith rests in the person and promises of God. If we ask according to his will, we know we have the request because he has promised it. When we pray not knowing Gods will, we trust in God's character believing that he is good (2 Chron 20:12).

Obedience/Holiness

A heart of obedience is a heart that wants above anything else to accomplish the will of God. James again is very forthright. "You ask and do not receive because you ask wrongly to spend it on your passions. You adulterous people! Do you not know that friendship with the world is enmity with God" (James 4:3-4 ESV). A heart of disobedience and unfaithfulness nullifies our prayers. The Psalms address this concept time and time again as the prayers of the wicked and the prayers of the righteous are contrasted.[270] The prayer of the upright is His delight because it aligns with the heart of God. No matter how holy we are, we need more holiness, so this is a focus of prayer (1 Thes 3:13, 4:3-8,5:23).

> A heart of disobedience and unfaithfulness nullifies our prayers.

What to Pray?

Written Prayers

If prayer is essentially a matter of the heart and the requirements spiritual, of what importance are the words, especially in memorized or written prayers? The scriptures themselves record not only spontaneous prayers but many

> If prayer is essentially a matter of the heart and the requirements spiritual, of what importance are the words, especially in memorized or written prayers?

Psalms intended for corporate recitation. Prayer books abound. *The Valley of Vision* compiles the prayers of the Puritans who were actually opposed to written prayers arguing that all prayer should be extemporaneous. This collection was penned by those who heard and recorded the prayers. The Psalms, the many Pauline prayers, and the Lord's Prayer itself, set the precedent for written prayers. Alternatively, the scriptures teach that prayer is primarily the pouring out of the heart before God. It must not become mechanical but remain a vital expression of the soul's intimate needs and passions.

An Episcopal prayer book[271] reads, "I rise from my bed of sleep to praise your holy name, to live for you this day, to help you build your kingdom on the earth, and to find in you, eternal life." This Morning Prayer beautifully captures the balance of worship and work, of heavenly and earthly vision, and an eternal perspective on the temporal life. I have begun my day with this prayer for many years. "I rise from my bed of sleep," … a sleep that God has ordained to refresh us before we undertake the day before us. In the Jewish world the evening and the morning constitute the day. God had designed us not as independent, autonomous beings but as dependent creatures. We rest and receive our strength from Him. We "rise from our bed of sleep to praise His holy name." This is our first and foremost calling.

David said, "One thing have I asked of the Lord, that will I seek; that I may dwell in the house of the Lord all the days of my life to behold the beauty of the Lord and to meditate in His temple."[272] "The chief end of man is to glorify God and enjoy Him forever." [273] It is attitude of heart, placing God above all, to love the Lord with "all the heart and soul and mind and strength".[274] That glorifies God the most.

"To live for you this day," is a reminder not to live for our own lusts, for our own desires, for our own glory, but to live for the glory of God. We cannot live in the past, neither in the successes nor the failures, nor can we live in the future. But we can live moment by moment, hour by hour, day by day for our Lord and Savior and for Him alone.

"To help you build your kingdom on the earth," defines life in terms of God's kingdom. John MacArthur rightly replied to an interviewer who asked him what he felt was the most important factor in building his church. His spontaneous response was, "first, it is not **my** church, and I would never want to build *my* church since Jesus Christ Himself is building **His** church and I have been called to minister in that church."[275] The awareness that Christ is building His church, and "the gates of Hell will not prevail against it"[276] is a bulwark of hope and strength in the face of any obstacle. It is something that many Christians and even pastors forget in the business of their service. Beyond the everyday cares of eating and drinking, the Kingdom is "righteousness, peace, and joy in the Holy Spirit" (Romans 14:17). These are our primary concerns in every endeavor if we are truly seeking first the Kingdom of God.

The final element of this prayer, "To find in YOU eternal life," represents a broader understanding of the salvation experience than often occurs in Protestant circles today. There is such an emphasis on the assurance of future salvation rooted in the promise of God in John 3:15 ("Whoever believes in Him should not perish but have eternal life") that there is often a neglect of the ongoing deliverance discovered day by day as Christ saves us. John concludes his epistle "And we know that the Son of God has come and has given us understanding in order that we may know Him who is true, and that we are in Him who is true, in His Son Jesus Christ. He is the true God and eternal life" (1John 5:20 ESV).

Prayer, Communication With God

Eternal life is not simply a home in heaven but a quality of life that we enter now as we receive the Son, feed on the Son, and discover in Him true spiritual life. Following our physical death, this mortal puts on immortality. The life that we now know in Christ takes on a new dimension. Paul writes, we will 'know as we are known' when the perfect has come.[277] This prayer is a plea that we experience today in Christ all that we can of what is assured in eternity but veiled to many.

Praying the Names of God

The names of God represent milestones in the history of God's revelation of Himself to His people and serve as impetus to prayer. After preparing to offer his son Isaac as a sacrifice to God, a ram was provided as a substitute which Abraham took and offered, calling the place *Jehovah Jireh* "The Lord is my provider." God had provided for Himself a sacrifice which took the place of Abraham's beloved son Isaac.[278]

The English is a wonderful translation of the Hebrew and a transliteration of the Latin. The Hebrew *Yahweh Yireh* literally means "the Lord who sees to it." There is a play on God's and Abraham's seeing throughout the text. The Latin translation of this Jehovah *Jireh* employs the word

> The names of God represent milestones in the history of God's revelation of Himself to His people and serve as impetus to prayer.

vide from which we derive the word video. The English word "provides" is from the same Latin root which means "to see to it" or to "see beforehand;" foresee and make provision for the future. This is exactly what God had done and what the Hebrew

195

word entailed. God sees our future and he sees to our need. He provides for us.

Reviewing this at the beginning of each day prompts praise to God for meeting the believer's *grace need* in Christ and giving assurance that He will meet *every need* that will be faced for the day. "He who did not spare His own son but gave Him up for us all, how will He not with Him graciously give us all things" (Romans 8:32 ESV). It is difficult at times to move beyond this first thought delighting in God's abundant provision resulting in praise to Him that in Christ all things are mine.

The second Yahweh construction is in the book of Exodus where we read of God's promise to the children of Israel following the Passover deliverance, that He will heal them and put none of the diseases that afflicted the Egyptians as they serve Him and they keep his commandments.[279] He is *Jehovah Rapha*, the Lord who heals us. This healing includes not merely physical healing from common disease, but avoidance of all the ten plagues including the pollution of the water with blood, frogs, lice, flies, pestilence, boils, hail, locusts, darkness, and the death of the first born. This goes far beyond the question of "healing in the atonement", which has occupied those in Pentecostal and Charismatic circles. This healing extends to every part of creation. However, the focus in prayer is not upon the temporal realization of these healings which may from time to time be miraculously provided or allowed but upon the Healer Himself and the realization that God and not modern medicine or science is ultimately responsible for all healing and all restoration of creation.

The third occurrence of the Yahweh construction is in the seventeenth chapter of Exodus. Following the defeat of Amalek at the hand of Joshua; Moses built an altar and called

Prayer, Communication With God

it "the Lord my banner, *Yahweh-nissi.* " In the story of the battle, Joshua's victory occurred miraculously as Moses raised his hands to God. When his hands were raised, Joshua prevailed. When he lowered his hands, Amalek prevailed. Aaron and Hur stood at Moses' side and held his arms up until Amalek was overwhelmed.[280]

Much has been made of that victory and the battle with Amalek through ongoing generations because Amalek is a descendent of Esau – the man of the flesh. The descendants of Amalek include both Haman who attempted to destroy all the Jews in the time of Esther, and Herod who sought to kill Jesus at His birth. So, this title, the Lord our banner—the one who fights for us against Amalek and will continually have war with him in all generations—signifies the Lord's ongoing battle and victory over our flesh. The symbolism both of Joshua fighting and Moses lifting his hands in prayer serve to illustrate our struggle for sanctification.

> In thanksgiving, we thank God for a particular action, but in adoration our focus is on His very nature, his character, his being, and worship results.

God reveals Himself in acts of deliverance and those acts serve to remind us of His very nature. He not only **provides** a sacrifice, but He is **our provider**. He not only heals particular diseases, but He **is our healer**. He not only **defeats** our enemies, but He **is the warrior** who rejoices over us with shouts of joy. So it is with each of these names of God, a particular episode serves to illustrate an essential attribute of God's very being, so that we are moved from thanksgiving to adoration. In thanksgiving, we thank God for a particular action, but in adoration our focus is on His very nature, his character, his being, and worship results. Worship turns the focus from the deliverance to the deliverer.

Each of God's covenant names provide insight into His being and serves as an impetus to prayer. a list for further personal study is as follows: *El Elyon* (The Most High), *El Roi* (The strong one who sees), *Jehovah Shalom* (The Lord is peace), *Jehovah Sabbaoth* (The Lord of Hosts or The Lord Almighty), *Jehovah Tsidkenu* (The Lord our righteousness), *Jehovah El Gmolah* (The Lord God of recompense), *Jehovah Nakeh* (The Lord that smites), *Jehovah Shammah* (The Lord who is present).[281]

A. C. T. S.

Adoration, Confession, Thanksgiving, Supplication

This acronym is a popular contemporary tool for teaching, but the four categories are found in the Jewish *Siddur* (Prayer Book).[282] Adoration is occupation with God Himself. We see in the Lord's Prayer this example of beginning with adoration. "Our Father who art in heaven, hallowed be Thy name. Thy kingdom come. Thy will be done, on earth as it is in heaven" (Matt 6:9-10 KJV). "In one sense adoration is not a special form of prayer for all true prayer is saturated with it. It is the air in which prayer breathes, the sea in which prayer swims. In another sense, though, it is distinct from other kinds of prayer, for in adoration we enter the rarefied air of selfless devotion. We ask for nothing but to cherish Him. We seek nothing but his exaltation. We focus on nothing but His goodness".[283]

The second type of prayer is confession. It is the **C** in the acronym of A.C.T.S. This follows naturally as we behold God in His glory. The Hebrew word for to pray, *l'hit palel*, does not mean to ask or to petition God. It is derived from a stem *pll* that is closest in meaning to self-searching confessional prayer. It means to judge, therefore *l'hit palel*, (to pray) could also be translated as to judge oneself. Here lies a clue to the real purpose to engaging in prayer.[284]

We see ourselves in our fallen state. Confession means literally to agree with God. It means to say the same thing God says in respect to our sin. We are not to cover it but to expose it, to turn from it, and to be forgiven for it. "If we confess our sins, He is faithful and just to forgive us our sins and to cleanse us from all unrighteousness."[285]

Two of the greatest prayers of confession are Psalm 51 and 106. The confession of Ezra and his call for God's people to confess their sins, Ezra 9 and 10, are moving examples of the priority of confession. Over the history of the church, confession has taken many forms. A contemporary Protestant approach (to confession) may be to keep short accounts with God, confessing immediately, repenting, and going on with a focus being on the sufficiency of the work of Christ.

> Thankfulness in trials reveals a heart of faith knowing that God is in control and allows only those trials which are best for his children.

In the Middle Ages an elaborate system of confession required both attrition and contrition: sorrow for sin and its consequences, as well as sorrow for the sin as an offense against God. Prayer as confession is essential to holiness. It is important to keep a right balance in our confession: on one hand, examining ourselves carefully for hidden sin and at the

Living Inside Out

same time trusting confidently in the sufficiency of the work of Christ to cover even our greatest sins.

The third type of prayer, denoted by the **T**, is thanksgiving. It is this aspect of prayer that can turn even simple blessings or trials into the stimuli for spiritual growth. Paul reminds us to give thanks in all things and for all things. He begins most of his prayers with thanksgiving. Thankfulness is a habit to be seeded and cultivated. It flows from a heart of humility knowing that we receive far more than we ever deserve from the hand of our gracious Father.

Thankfulness in trials reveals a heart of faith knowing that God is in control and allows only those trials which are best for his children. He allows those things that are necessary for their growth. Thankfulness, since it is commanded, is a response of obedience. It must be learned and practiced from our earliest years. It is natural for children to ask, and ask, and ask, and, in the same way, it is natural for the immature Christian to focus more on want or need than on thanksgiving. It is important to teach children the importance of being thankful and expressing a heart of thankfulness to God as a priority of prayer.

The scripture is clear that we should make request with thanksgiving. It is this combination that best overcomes anxiety: "Be anxious for nothing but in everything by prayer and supplication with thanksgiving let your requests be made known to God." It is not simply the supplication but the asking with thankfulness which causes the peace of God to rule in our heart: "And the peace of God which surpasses all comprehension shall guard your hearts and your minds in Christ Jesus."[286]

The Psalms are a treasure of thanksgiving, especially Psalms 92, 95, 105 to 107 and 111 which begins, "I will give thanks to the Lord with all my heart (or my whole heart), in

Prayer, Communication With God

the company of the upright and in the assembly." How could we give less to the Lord who gave all for us?

S–Supplication is the essential meaning of the English word "prayer." It is to make request. The previous elements of prayer precede supplication because they address relationship, which is essential to our privilege of making supplication. As aliens and enemies of God, we have no grounds for supplication. In fact, "He who turns away his ear from listening to the law, even his prayer is an abomination" (Proverbs 28:9). Supplication is "simple prayer" according to Richard Foster.[287]

The Greek words for prayer are centered on the concept of supplication. Indeed, this is the essence of the words to **pray – to ask- to beseech God in prayer**. In prayer, there is a pouring out of our heart before the Creator, often in the form of worship, but also in asking something of God. The Lord's prayer has at its heart two concerns: first (verses 9-10), the

> It would be as foolish to think that we could dictate to the Heavenly Father as it would be to assume that any loving earthly father would allow his children to dictate to him.

holiness of God and the coming of His Kingdom or His will; and second (verses 11-13), that which is necessary in this life as we seek it. Paul's prayers focus on the same things amplifying the nature of our needs. It is this aspect of prayer which most attracts us to the privilege of prayer, especially when we look at Jesus teaching, "And whatever you **ask** in My name, that will I do, that the Father may be glorified in the Son. If you **ask** Me anything in My name, I will do it" (John 14:13-14).

These promises often taken in isolation have been the subject of countless sermons and discussions on prayer. However,

Living Inside Out

just as our needs lead us to prayer, awareness of our own sin, unbelief, pride, guilt, our uncertainty about our standing before the Father keeps us from prayer. It is this dichotomy which serves to balance the scriptural perspective on supplication. God never gives us the supposed privilege of dictating to Him. Prayer in its essence is submission to the will of the Father. All the promises associated with prayer must be attached to the requirements. It would be as foolish to think that we could dictate to the Heavenly Father as it would be to assume that any loving earthly father would allow his children to dictate to him. As human fathers we labor to teach our children good manners, wise decision making, humility in requests, and obedience of heart out of which we may bless our children. God, in the same way delights to give to His believing, obedient children the kingdom. He is patient with his foolish and rebellious children but tells clearly that when we ask amiss or simply to consume upon our lusts we do not receive from the Father (James 4:3).

All petitions according to Jesus must be in accord with the Father's will. This presupposes an understanding of the Father's will. Paul asks this very thing for the Colossians (1:9). Having perceived the will of God we ask accordingly. This is beautifully illustrated in the prophet Daniel who had been reading the prophet Jeremiah. In Chapter 9, he says: "I Daniel observed in the books the number of the **years** which was *revealed as* the word of the LORD to Jeremiah the prophet for the completion of the desolations of Jerusalem, *namely,* **seventy years**. So, I gave my attention to the Lord God to seek *Him by* prayer and supplications, with fasting, sackcloth, and ashes. And I prayed to the LORD my God and confessed and said, "Alas, O Lord, the great and awesome God, who keeps His covenant and lovingkindness for those who love Him and keep His commandments, we have sinned, committed iniquity, acted wickedly, and rebelled, even turning aside from Thy commandments and ordinances. Moreover, we have not listened to Thy servants the prophets, who spoke in Thy name to our kings, our princes, our fathers, and all the people of the land" (Daniel 9:2-6).

He continues for another 14 verses confessing his sins and the sins of his people, calling upon God's faithfulness, making his plea for mercy for the Lord's sake, "…because of our sins and the iniquities of our fathers, Jerusalem and Thy people *have become* a reproach to all those around us. So now, our God, listen to the prayer of Thy servant and to his supplications, and for Thy sake, O Lord, let Thy face shine on Thy desolate sanctuary" (Daniel 9:16-17).

Several things should be noted regarding supplication. First, it is according to the will of God. "If we ask anything according to His will, He hears us. And if we know that He hears us *in* whatever we ask, we know that we have the requests which we have asked from Him" (1 John 5:14). Requests contrary to the will of God as revealed in His word may be answered for the sake of instruction. We see this throughout the history of Israel. In their rebellion, the children of Israel asked for meat in the wilderness. God answered by sending quails, yet disaster followed. The scripture says, "God gave them their request and added leanness to their souls" (Psalm 106:15 KJV). Later, in rejecting God's kingship, the people requested a king that they might be like the nations around them. Again, God granted their request but explained to them the dire consequences of having a human king.

In each of these cases, it is noteworthy that God accomplishes His perfect will at all times and in all circumstances.

Living Inside Out

Some have attempted to resolve the difficulty of man's freewill and God's sovereignty by positing a *permissive will of God.* That is a scenario in which God's perfect will is something which is almost never achieved because of man's sinfulness. He is constantly making accommodations to our failures, and we are always left with a compromise.

> if we are transformed by the renewing of our minds, we will be able to discern the will of God that which is good and acceptable and perfect (12:1-2).

On the contrary, the Biblical record assures us that ". . . all the inhabitants of the earth are accounted as nothing, But He does according to His will in the host of heaven and among the inhabitants of the earth" (Daniel 4:35). Paul, in the book of Romans, reminds us that if we are transformed by the renewing of our minds, we will be able to discern the will of God that which is good and acceptable and perfect (12:1-2). Some have suggested that this implies a secondary *permissive will of God* for those who are not transformed by the renewing of their minds. In fact, what it says is those whose minds are not transformed do not discern and approve the perfect will of God but instead are ignorant of it and disprove of that which God ordains.

But God "works all things after the counsel of His will" (Ephesians 1:11). We must then fix it in our minds. As Luther says so well, "We pray not to change the will of God, or to overcome His reluctance, but rather to take hold of His willingness".[288] Prayer must first be according to the will of God and this requirement is variously stated throughout the scriptures. When Jesus said, "Whatever you ask in my name and I will do it,"[289] we should remember that His name is "**The Lord**

Jesus Christ". Therefore, in asking in His name, we submit ourselves to the Lordship of Jesus. We ask according to His will and in His authority. This is authority not to **resist** the Father's will—but to **do** the Father's will. Jesus said, "I do nothing of my own initiative, but whatever I see the Father doing, that I do" (John 8:28 ESV).

He judges according to the Father's will. He **always** does the Father's will. Even as He approaches the cross in His suffering humanity he said, "Not my will but your will be done" (Luke 22:42). He prayed, "If it is possible, let this cup pass from me" (Matthew 26:39). However, knowing the impossibility of redemption apart from His suffering on the cross, He embraces His Father's will. "I delight to do your will Oh God. Your law is within my heart. This is the day the Lord has made. I will rejoice and be glad in it. Bind the sacrifice with cords to the horns of the alter. You are my God, and I will praise you. The stone that the builders rejected has become the chief corner stone. This is the Lord's doing and is marvelous in our eyes" (Ps 40: 8, 118 27, 22-23).

Thirdly, all prayer must be offered in faith. As discussed earlier in the chapter on faith, prayer is a means by which faith is exercised and grows. For prayer to be offered in faith, the request must somehow be attached to a promise of God or to an understanding that the request is in accordance with the will of God. The classic text on faith is James 1:5-8: "But if any of you **lacks wisdom**, let him ask of God, who gives to all men generously and without reproach, and it will be given to him. But let him ask in faith without any doubting, for the one who doubts is like the surf of the sea driven and tossed by the wind. For let not that man expect that he will receive anything from the Lord, *being* a double-minded man, unstable in all his ways."

Notice the essential elements here. There is a promise of wisdom, a promise to give it liberally to all, a command to ask, and the asking must be done in faith. Other times the promise may be more general as in Matthew 6:33 where Jesus tells us to "seek first the kingdom of God and His righteousness and all these things will be added to you." This refers to food and clothing. By faith we extrapolate from these promises what we must do in seeking first the kingdom and what God does in providing our food and clothing.

Corporate Prayer

Praise and Worship-Adding a Song

"Let the redeemed of the LORD say *so*, Whom He has redeemed from the hand of the adversary, and gathered from the lands, From the east and from the west, from the north and from the south" (Psalm 107:2-3). The very nature of our salvation is that we have been gathered "together". We who are strangers to the covenant as aliens have been gathered to the people of Israel. The people of Israel who are scattered have been gathered. It is natural that all the activities of our spirituality are practiced not only individually but corporately.

> It is natural that all the activities of our spirituality are practiced not only individually but corporately.

We study the scriptures alone and read and share them together. We pray alone; we pray together. We suffer or rejoice alone and other times together. Though many of the Psalms are composed in isolation, separation, despair, they often are sung in times as national despair and isolation (see Psalm 137). Likewise Psalms of confession may be intimately personal, yet later be a basis for corporate confession (see Psalm 51- entitled specifically a *Psalm of David*- when Nathan the prophet confronted him after he had sinned with Bathsheba). Hannah's prayer of exaltation in 1Samuel 2:1-10 was so commonly known that Mary uses many of her words and thoughts in the *Magnificat* in Luke 1:46-55.

One of the great blessings of corporate praise or prayer is that when a leader stands before the congregation he models intimacy, teaching the younger brother how to pray. In Monastic communities even today, extensive portions of the Psalms are prayed corporately, multiple times throughout the day. "Monastic communities gather five times a day for prayers, chant the Psalter, as do liturgical congregations who gather for vespers."[290] The Ephesian congregation is specifically exhorted to address one another in "psalms, and hymns, and spiritual songs, singing and making melody to the Lord with all of your heart, giving thanks always for everything to God the Father in the name of the Lord Jesus Christ" (Ephesians 5:19-21). Not only is the scripture to be chanted but sung.

In contemporary congregations today, prayer takes the form of congregational singing, praise, and prayer. Scriptures are more easily remembered and celebrated as they are sung. The first book published in the New World was the Puritan Songbook. This has been the pattern throughout the ages. "Sing to the Lord with thanksgiving; Sing praises to our God on the lyre" (Psalm 147:7). Though the use of musical instruments was set aside for a time after the destruction of the second temple in 70AD, as a sign of mourning for the temple, "vocal music remained an essential component of prayer and scripture reading."[291] An

Living Inside Out

interesting Rabbinic instruction on prayer comes from Rabbi Judah he-Hasid: "Say your prayers in a melody that is most pleasant and sweet to you. You shall pray with proper *kavanah* (spiritual intent), because the melody will draw your heart after the words have come from your mouth. Supplicate in a melody that makes the heart weep. Praise in a melody that makes the heart glad."[292]

Charles Wesley composed 8989 hymns[293], many of which were in the form of prayers. Luther also wrote hymns of praise and was fond of chanting his prayer. Thanksgiving with a song is a sacrifice more pleasing to the Lord than the sacrifice of a bull (Psalm 69:30, 31).

Prayer in the Spirit

The Pentecostal movement of the 20th century has brought with it a new freedom of the spirit, a new focus on hearing the voice of God, and yielding to His supernatural guidance. There was concern in the early days of that movement that the Word of God would be displaced by the subjective guidance of the spirit. But that, for the most part, has not been the case. Many excesses that marked early Pentecostalism have fallen by the wayside. One element of this movement which has persisted is a focus on prayer in the spirit (Eph 6:18), which is interpreted to mean prayer "in tongues," or a "heavenly language" known only to God and revealed to one who has the spirit, and another, the gift of interpretation. In many circles speaking in tongues or "praying in the spirit" remains the definitive mark of the baptism of the spirit and by implication foundational to spirituality. Some Charismatics and Pentecostals understand their time of prayer in this manner as the pinnacle of their devotional

Prayer, Communication With God

time or corporate worship. Though Christians remain divided over the role of "tongues" in defining prayer in the Spirit, they are in agreement that prayer should be led by the Spirit of God and may result in intimate spiritual encounter surpassing words.

Foster refers to this as one aspect of the "prayer of the heart."[294] He includes in this category the *rehma* or the word within the word, *glossolalia,* resting in the spirit, holy laughter, as well as "physical warming of the heart" as described by Richard Role in his book *The Fire of Divine Love.* This even seems to apply to John Wesley's experience at Altersgate, in which he described his heart as "strangely warmed"[295] as Luther's commentary on Romans was read. Interestingly, in that case, Wesley's mind was completely engaged whereas Paul writes, "If I pray in a tongue, my spirit prays but my mind is unfruitful. What is the outcome? I will pray with my spirit, but I will pray with my mind also. I will sing with my spirit, but I will sing with my mind also" (1Cor 14:14-15).

Within Charismatic circles there are varying degrees of understanding during these experiences of prayer in the spirit. It is also noteworthy that there is a distinction between prayer "with my spirit" (1Cor 14:15) and prayer "in the Holy Spirit." "But you, beloved, building yourselves up on your most holy faith; praying in the Holy Spirit" (Jude 21), which may mean guided by the Holy Spirit. The filling of the Spirit leads to walking in the Spirit as described in Ephesians 5:18 and

Living Inside Out

Galatians 5:16 and 25. In this case, prayer in the Spirit may refer to prayer directed by the Holy Spirit rather than flowing from the human spirit.[296] Prayer is a deeply spiritual activity which must be guided by the heart of God. The Pentecostal and Charismatic movements have at the very least required a reexamination of the humility of heart and dependence upon God required for all true prayer.

Isaiah 12 is a Model for Prayer in the 21st Century: "Then you will say on that day, I will give thanks to Thee, O Lord; For although Thou wast angry with me, Thine anger is turned away, and Thou dost comfort me. Behold, God is my salvation, I will trust and not be afraid; for the Lord God is my strength and song, and He has become my salvation. Therefore, you will joyously draw water from the springs of salvation. And in that day, you will say, give thanks to the Lord, call on His name. Make known His deeds among the peoples; make them remember that His name is exalted. Praise the Lord in song, for He has done excellent things; let this be known throughout the earth. Cry aloud and shout for joy, O inhabitant of Zion, for great in your midst is the Holy One of Israel" (Isa 12:6).

This prophetic text looks forward to a day when God's **anger is turned away** from His people and He comforts them. It has immediate application to those who turn to God in Christ, who can say, "We who were enemies have become sons."[297] **God is my Salvation**. In a very literal sense God is my savior my Jesus. **I will trust and never be afraid**. Prayer is confession and affirmation of Gods revelation. The Lord my God is my strength and my song. He also has become my salvation. Therefore, you shall draw water from the well of salvation-Jesus spoke repeatedly of the water which those who believe would draw[298]. As we pray, we drink of this spiritual well. In

Prayer, Communication With God

that day you will say, give thanks to the Lord, call on His name, make known his deeds among the nations. Prayer will begin with praise, progress to petition, and blossom into proclamation.

CHAPTER 10

LIVING INSIDE OUT, CONCLUSION

Living inside out is living in the realm of the Spirit. It is living under the empowerment, control, and direction of the Spirit of Christ so that what we do proceeds from who we are in Christ. Put in these terms it seems simple enough, but it is complicated by multiple obstacles, not the least of which is our preoccupation with the external world of our senses, the world of seeing and doing. But Paul writes, "If we have our realm of being in the Spirit, let us walk in the Spirit" (Gal. 5:25).

The Christian life is an enigma. We are well-aware that the Holy one who chose us is full of power, life, forgiveness, and love; but we are not. We are tempted to blame the world, ourselves, and even God himself, but ultimately the enigma is intended! We groan, along with all of creation, at the present situation. We are saved but crushed, rich yet poor, believing yet filled with doubt. Day by day, moment by moment, our present life is often lackluster and mediocre at best—and catastrophic

> Living inside out is living in the realm of the Spirit. It is living under the empowerment, control, and direction of the Spirit of Christ so that what we do proceeds from who we are in Christ.

Living Inside Out, Conclusion

at life's worst. Contemporary Christians flock to action movies with a plethora of gifted but imperfect superheroes, soldiers, and even bumbling but loveable elves, dwarves, wizards, and humans—all fighting evil for truth and justice. We flock to these movies, because they depict a fallen world populated by people just like us visited by superhumans we secretly imagine we might really become.

The reality is that God intends that very thing. He has left us with a vision of what can be in Christ as we get better acquainted with the depth of our fallenness in sin. The adventurous Christian life God intended for us is about listening for God's voice in good times and bad, in war and peace, in prosperity and poverty, and about doing what He asks us to do in His timing and His strength. The

> The adventurous Christian life God intended for us is about listening for God's voice in good times and bad, in war and peace, in prosperity and poverty, and about doing what He asks us to do in His timing and His strength.

monsters, dragons, and evil are out there, and more real than even the best-produced movie. God has a plan for us to defeat them, but we are still in the production phase of the movie. Salvation is already but not yet.

It is not enough to act or speak in ways which seem appropriate on the surface. We must act and speak truth from the right motives with the right strength and at the right time. This is the difference between Moses acting on his own and acting in the Spirit. When he saw an Egyptian beating a Hebrew slave he looked around, killed the Egyptian and hid him in the sand. He offered no warning or correction to the soldier, no prayer to

God, showed no true humility or holiness, and ultimately did not act in faith. He was forty years ahead of God.

Later, after his encounter with God at the burning bush, he returned in the Spirit. This time he was on schedule. He continually acknowledged his own weakness and in humility spoke the word God gave him. He did not flee from pharaoh but confronted him and did not seek to kill him but invited him to escape the judgement of God by freeing his slaves! This time his actions

> We are new creatures but still in our old shells, encumbered with old habits.

were marked by love for God and man, humility, holiness, and faith. These are marks of the leading of the Spirit. But even as he led the nation it was through the wilderness and in the face of constant rebellion on the part of a people who did not yet know the ways of God.

We are new creatures but still in our old shells, encumbered with old habits. We are left in a body and a world that seems unwelcoming to our new life and home to our old, trusted flesh. Though the Spirit leads us, the flesh seems at times to dominate us. The battle between the flesh and the spirit is a recurrent theme discussed in Romans and Galatians. David was a man after God's heart, but when he looked and lusted after Bathsheba, he fell into adultery and murder. It is only as we walk in the Spirit that we will not fulfill the desires of the flesh. We must be increasingly careful to be in the spirit no matter how long we have lived and how many victories we have seen.

Living inside out means we focus more and more on the priorities of the Spirit within. Our love must abound in knowledge and all discernment, that we may approve what is excellent. The inner priorities of the Spirit are love, humility, holiness,

Living Inside Out, Conclusion

and faith. These are mutually dependent and produce the other virtues. They smother the flesh and cause it to be ineffectual. These inner virtues are further nourished by the active priorities of devotion to the word of God, fellowship, worship/remembrance, and prayer. Together they result in a growing awareness and demonstration of the Kingdom of God.

We also have a language problem which allows us to speak of things which we do not understand using words we have not defined or worse, mis-defined. This may be the reason so much talk leads to so little life in our world. We live in a world exploding with so called knowledge. We must first be still and hear the voice of God before we will ever be able to speak or act in his Spirit.

Silence was one of the disciplines exercised by the monks of old. It may have been overdone in the past, but it is certainly underutilized today. Words must be understood to mean the same thing to speakers as hearers. As the familiar saying goes, "I know you think you understood what I said, but what you heard was not what I meant." This is especially true of words such as love or faith. We all tend to think we know their meaning because we hear and use the words. They have many modern definitions though, which overshadow their depth of meaning in the scriptures. This is another reason living inside out means not only keeping the internals at the heart but experiencing them in the context of devotion to the scriptures, fellowship, communion, and prayer. Our words are defined in the context of life. How much more our most important values?

Jesus promised that the Holy Spirit would be in us and teach us. He promised that He would be as a river flowing out of our inner being. We become one spirit with God, and we know Him because he lives in us. However, we are still coming to know

Living Inside Out

Him, growing in the knowledge of God, and laboring until Christ is formed in us.

In every age Christians have discovered that there is a difference between knowing about God and knowing Him. Christ is revealed in the scriptures but known in the heart. This is sometimes referred to as spiritual formation, sanctification, a second work of grace, or simply maturing in Christ. In every generation God delights to make himself known in surprising ways, at different times and places, often, it seems, in unlikely individuals. As a result, each generation records its experiences, champions new movements, and rediscovers tools and techniques of earlier generations. But all have some things in common.

> In every generation God delights to make himself known in surprising ways, at different times and places, often, it seems, in unlikely individuals.

When we focus on the inner journey, we quickly learn the importance of the external disciplines. When we immerse ourselves in the externals, we discover the priorities of our heart in tune with God's own heart. As you have read this book, I hope you have felt a deepening hunger to experience these things in community. One of our greatest needs today is to find our place in the plan of God, not just a place to attend, make friends, learn, or even worship and

> When we focus on the inner journey, we quickly learn the importance of the external disciplines. When we immerse ourselves in the externals, we discover the priorities of our heart in tune with God's own heart.

place to attend, make friends, learn, or even worship and

216

Living Inside Out, Conclusion

volunteer, but a place which nourishes our identity as children of the Kingdom. The values of the kingdom define and direct us.

Defining love overshadows all. It redefines people, places, and times. This is a love for God and neighbor which brings every relationship to its greatest potential. It eliminates competition in its self-centered sense and fosters it in its holy sense: "outdo one another in showing honor" (Rom. 12:10 ESV). Discovering

> This heart of love, humility, holiness, and faith directed the life of Christ, the life of Paul, the leadership in the early church and all who follow in the way of the cross. In every generation there are those who follow and those who do not. It is not complicated... just costly.

humility is a humility before God which believes, obeys, and discovers the role God assigns. It may be visible and prominent or hidden and unnoticed, but it is directed by God who leads the humble in His way. Discerning holiness is a holiness which discerns in every situation what is holy and what is not. Jesus was constantly condemned by religious leaders who failed to discern His holiness due to their preoccupation with externals. Today we must be separated from sin in a spirit of love and humility which convicts yet draws people to God. Delivering faith is a triumphant faith by which we reckon ourselves dead to the world but alive to God and overcome the world! This faith works by love, humility, and holiness.

This heart of love, humility, holiness, and faith directed the life of Christ, the life of Paul, the leadership in the early church and all who follow in the way of the cross. In every generation there are those who follow and those who do not. It is not complicated... just costly.

Living Inside Out

The disciplines of devotion to the Word of God, fellowship, the breaking of bread, and prayer nourish the hearts of the saints and empower them for kingdom living. These must be personal and corporate priorities. To the extent that they are missing or neglected the individual and the church will be compromised. When prioritized they will stimulate and nourish love, humility, holiness, and faith.

May your love abound more and more in knowledge and all judgement, that you may approve the things which are excellent and be sincere and without offense until the day of Christ, being filled with all the fruits of righteousness which are by Christ Jesus to the glory and praise of God (Phil 1:9-11).

BIBLIOGRAPHY

Ahlstrom, Sydney E. A Religious History of the American People. New Haven and London: Yale University Press, 1974.

Althaus, Paul. The Theology of Martin Luther. Philadelphia: Fortress Press, 1966.

Augustine, St. The Rule of St. Augustine. Based on the critical text of Luc Verheijen, O.S.A. La regle de saint Augustin Etudes Augustiniennes. Translated by Robert. Russell. Paris, France: Brothers of the Order of Hermits of Saint Augustine, Inc., 1967. http://www.geocities.com/Athens/1534/ruleaug. html (accessed November 11, 2006).

Augustine, St. The City of God. Translated by Marcus Dods. New York, NY: Random House, 1950.

Bacchiocchi, Samuele. The Sabbath Under Crossfire. Barrien Springs, MI: Biblical Perspectives, 1999.

Bahnsen, Greg L., Walter C. Kaiser, Douglas J Moo, Wayne G. Strickland, Willem A. VanGemeren. Five Views on Law and Gospel. Edited by Stanley N. Gundry. Grand Rapids, MI: Zondervan, 1996.

Bainton, Roland H. Early Christianity. New York, NY: D. Van Nostrand Company, 1960.

_____. Christianity. Boston, MA: Houghton Mifflin Company, 1984.

Living Inside Out

_____. The Reformation of the Sixteenth Century. Boston, MA: Beacon Press, 1985.

Barnett, Paul. 1 Corinthians – Focus on the Bible: Holiness and Hope of a Rescued People. Ross-shire Scotland, UK: Christian Focus Publications, 2000.

Bauer, Walter. A Greek-English Lexicon of the New Testament, 2nd ed. from Bauer's 5th ed. Translated, edited, revised and augmented by William F. Arndt, F. Wilber Gingrich, and Frederick W. Danker. Chicago: Chicago Press, 1996.

Beale, G. K. ed., The Right Doctrine from the Wrong Texts / Essays on the Use of the Old Testament in the New. Grand Rapids, MI: Baker Book House.1994.

_____. Commentary on the New Testament Use of the Old Testament (Kindle Edition). Cambridge, MA: Baker Academic and Brazos Press, 2007.

Bede, Venerablis. The History of the English Church and People. New York, NY: Penguin Books, 1988.

Bender, Harold S. The Anabaptist Vision. Scottdale, Pa: Herald Press, 1984.

Benge, Janet and Geoff Benge. Christian Heroes: Then & Now—Adoniram Judson, Bound for Burma. Seattle, WA: Ywam Publishing, 2000.

Bennet, Arthur, ed., The Valley of Vision/A Collection of Puritan Prayers and Devotions. Edinburgh, UK: Banner of Truth, 2007.

Bercot, David W. A Dictionary of Early Christian Beliefs. Peabody, MA: Hendrickson Publishers, 1998.

Bethge, Eberhard. Dietrich Bonhoeffer. NY, NY: Harper and Row, 1977.

Bibliography

Bonhoeffer, Dietrich. Life Together. Translated by John W. Doberstein. New York, NY: Harper and Row, 1954. and unabridged ed. New York: Collier Books Macmillan Publishers, 1963.

Bosch, David J. Transforming Mission: Paradigm Shifts in Theology of Mission. Maryknoll, NY: Orbis Books, 1998.

Bradshaw, Paul F. and Lawrence A. Hoffman, The Making of Jewish and Christian Worship. Notre Dame, IN: University of Notre Dame Press, 1991.

Brickner, David. Christ in the Feast of Tabernacles. Chicago, IL: Moody Publisers, 2006.

Brodrick, James. The Origin of the Jesuits, Chicago, IL: Loyola Press, 1997.

Brooke, Christopher. The Monastic World. New York, NY: Random House, 1974.

Brown, Colin, and Beyeruther and Bietenhard, ed. Dictionary of New Testament Theology. Vol. 1-4. Grand Rapids, MI: Zondervan Publishing, 1986.

Brown, Francis and S.R. Driver, Charles A Briggs. The New Brown-Driver-Briggs- Gesenius Hebrew and English Lexicon. Peabody, MA: Hendrickson Publishers, 1979.

Buchanan, G. W. To the Hebrews. NY, NY: Doubleday, 1972.

Bultmann, Rudolf. Jesus and the Word. Translated by Louise P. Smith and Erminie H. Lantero. New York: Charles Scribner's Sons, 1958.

Calvin, John. Institutes of the Christian Religion, vol. XX and XXI. Translated by Ford Lewis Battles. Philadelphia, PA: Westminster Press, 1960.

_____. Calvin's NT Commentaries, vol.11. Translated by T.H.L. Parker and edited by David F. Torrance. Grand Rapids, MI: Eerdmans, 1965.

_____. Institutes of the Christian Religion, 1536th ed. Trans. Ford Lewis Battles, Grand Rapids: Eerdmans Publishing, 1989.

Caner, Ergun Mehmet, and Emir Fethi Caner. Christian Jihad. Grand Rapids: Kregel Publishing, 2004.

Carey, William. An Enquiry into the Obligations of Christians to use Means for the Conversion of the Heathens. White Fish, MT: Kissinger Publishing, 2004.

Carson D. A. ed., From Sabbath to Lord's Day: A Biblical, Historical, and Theological Investigation. Grand Rapids, MI: Zondervan, 1982.

_____. Commentary on John. Grand Rapids, MI: Eerdmans, 1991.

Chafer, Lewis Sperry. Systematic Theology, 8 vol. Dallas, TX: Dallas Seminary Press, 1947.

Chaney, Charles L. The Birth of Missions in America. Pasadena, Ca: Wm Carey Library, 1976.

Christianity Today. http://www.christianitytoday.com (accessed February 10, 2009).

Cohen, Abraham. Everyman's Talmud. NY, NY: Scocken Books, 1995.

Collins, Kenneth. John Wesley: A Theological Journey. Nashville, TN: Abingdon Press, 2003.

Colson, Charles, and Ellen Santilli Vaughn. Kingdoms in Conflict. Grand Rapids, MN: Zondervan, 1989.

Bibliography

_____. Nancy R. Pearcey. A Dangerous Grace. Dallas, TX: Word Publishers, 1994.

Conkin, Paul K. Cane Ridge America's Pentecost. Madison, WI: The University of Wisconsin Press, 1989.

Crenshaw, Curtis I. and Grover E. Gunn, III. Dispensationalalism Today, Yesterday, and Tomorrow. Memphis, TN: Footstool Publications, 1987.

Cushman, Ralph Spaulding. A Pocket Prayer Book and Devotional Guide. Nashville, TN: Upper Room Publishing, 1969.

Daube, David. The New Testament and Rabbinic Judaism. Peabody, MA: Hendrickson Publishers, 1956.

Dieter, Melvin, Anthony A. Hoekema, Stanley M Horton, J. Robertson McQuilkin, and John F. Walvoord. Five Views on Sanctification. Edited by Stanley N. Gundry. Grand Rapids, MI: Zondervan, 1987.

Di Sante, Carmine. Jewish Prayer: The Origins of Christian Liturgy. Mahwah, N.J: Paulist Press, 1991.

Dix, Gregory, and Henry Chadwick, eds. The Treatise on The Apostolic Tradition of St Hippolytus of Rome. Ridgefield, CT: Morehouse Publishing1992.

Donin, Rabbi Hayim Halevy. To Pray as a Jew/ A guide to the Prayer Book and the Synagogue Service. Grand Rapids, MI: Basic Books/ Harper Collins, 1994.

Dowley, Tim, ed. Introduction to the History of Christianity. Minneapolis, MN: Fortress Press, 1995.

Duffy, Eamon. The Stripping of the Altars. New Haven, CT: Yale University Press, 1994.

Ebrahimoff, Reuben. The Haftorahman /The Haftarah for The Second Day of Shavuot 5762. (accessed October 21, 2008).

Edwards, A. Jonathan, and David Brainerd. The Life and Diary of David Brainerd, Missionary to the Indians. Diggory Press, 2008.

_____. Jonathan Edwards on Revival. Carlisle, Pa: The Banner of Truth Publishing, 1995.

Elias, Joseph. The Haggada: Passover Haggadah/with Translation and a New Commentary Based on Talmudic, Midrashic and Rabbinic Sources. Brooklyn, New York: Mesorah Publications, Ltd., 1994.

Elwell, Walter A.ed. Evangelical Dictionary of Theology. Grand Rapids, MN: Baker Book House, 1994.

Epstein, Rabbi Dr I.ed. The Babylonian Talmud, Seder Nashim 4Vol. London, England: Soncina Press 1936.

Erickson, Millard J. Christian Theology. Grand Rapids, MI.: Baker Book House, 1985.

Estep, William R. The Anabaptist Story. Grand Rapids, MI: Eerdmans Publishing, 1977.

Eusebius. The Ecclesiastical History of Eusebius Pamphilus Bishop of Cesarea, In Palestine. Translated by Christian Fredrick Cruse. Grand Rapids, Mich.: Baker Book House, 1988.

Fee, Gordon. The First Epistle to the Corinthians: The New International Commentary on the New Testament. Grand Rapids, MI: Eerdmans Publishing, 1987.

Feinberg, John S. ed. Continuity and Discontinuity: Perspectives on the Relationship Between the Testaments. Wheaton, IL: Crossway, 1987.

Bibliography

Fisher, Eugene. "The Jewish Roots of Christian Liturgy." Mahwah, N.J: Paulist Press, 1990.The Fourth Watch. http://www.gotjesus.us/4thWatch//home.htm (accessed October 21, 2008).

Foster, Richard J., and James B. Smith, ed. Devotional Classics/ Selected Readings for Individuals and Groups. San Francisco: Harper Collins Publishers, 1993.

_____. Celebration of Discipline: the Path to Spiritual Growth. San Francisco, Ca: Harper Collins Publishers, 1998.

_____. Prayer: Finding the Heart's True Home. San Francisco, CA: Harper Collins Publishers, 1992.

Foxe, John. The New Foxe's Book of Martyrs. ed. Howard J. Chadwick. Gainesville, Fl: Bridge-Logos Publishers, 2001.

Francis of Assisi, St, A Detailed Biography, Catholic Encyclopedia. http://www.franciscanfriarstor.com/ stfrancis/stf_detailed%20biography%20of%2 0st.%20 francis.htm (accessed October 25 2008).

Fry, Timothy, O.S.B. ed. The Rule of St. Benedict in English. Collegeville, MN: The Liturgical Press, 1982.

Gaebelein, Frank E. ed. The Expositor's Bible Commentary, 12 vol. Grand Rapids, MI: Zondervan, 1992.

Gaffin, Richard B. Calvin and the Sabbath. Thesis submitted to Westminster Theological Seminary, Chestnut Hill, PA: 1962.

Galli, Mark, and Ted Olsen eds. 131 Christians Everyone Should Know. Nashville, TN: Holman Press, 2007.

Gibbs, A. P. Worship: A Christian's Highest Occupation. Kansas City, KS: Walterick Publishers.

Gonzalez-Balado, Jose'Luis, and Janet N. Playfoot, ed. Mother Teresa: My Life for the Poor. NY, NY: Ballantine Books, 1987.

_____. One Heart Full of Love. Ann Arbor, MI: Servant Books, 1988.

Goodman, Philip. The Passover Anthology. Philadelphia, Pa: The Jewish Publication Society, 1993.

Graham, Billy. Just As I Am: The Autobiography of Billy Graham. San Francisco: Zondervan, 1997.

Gruber, Dan. The Church and the Jews: The Biblical Relationship. Hanover, NH: Elijah Publishing, 1997.

Guyon, Madame Jeanne, Experiencing the Depths of Jesus Christ. Goleta. Ca: Christian Books 1975.

Hagner, Donald A. The New International Greek Testament Commentary: The First Epistle to The Corinthians. Edited by I. Howard Marshall, and Anthony C. Thiselton. Grand Rapids, MI: Eerdmans, 2000.

Harnack, Aldolf. Monasticism: Its Ideals and History. London: Williams and Norgate, 1901.

Harris, Laird R., Gleason L. Archer, Jr. and Bruce K. Waltke eds. Theological Wordbook of the Old Testament. 2 vol. Chicago: Moody Press, 1992.

Hedrick, Dr. Gary, and Rabbi Loren, ed. Replacement Theology Its Origins and

Error. http://www.shema.com/Combating%20Replacement%20Theology/crt-004.php (accessed 3 March 3, 2010).

Henderson, Michael D. A Model for Making Disciples. Nappanee, IN: Evangel Publishing House, 1997.

Bibliography

Hendricks, Howard G. Don't Fake it...Say it with Love. Wheaton, Ill.: Victor Books, 1973.

Hernandez, Wil. Henri Nouwen: A Spirituality of Imperfection. Mahwah, N.J: Paulist Press, 2006.

Hodge, Charles. Geneva Series of Commentaries: 1st and 2nd Corinthians. Carlisle, PA.: Banner of Truth, 1974.

_____. Systematic Theology. 3 vol. Grand Rapids, MI: Eerdmans Publishers, 1981.

Hoyt, Herman A., Myron S Augsburger, Arthur F. Holmes, and Harold O. J. Brown. War: Four Christian Views. Edited by Robert Clouse. Downers Grove, Ill: InterVarsity Press, 1991.

Hudson, Christopher, Alan Sharrer, and Lindsay Vanker, eds. Day by Day with the Early Church Fathers. Peabody, MA: Hendrickson Publishers, 1999.

Hyatt, Eddie L. 2000 Years of Charismatic Christianity. Lake Mary, Flordia: Chrisma House, 2002.

Jesus Film Project. http://www.jesusfilm.org/ (accessed February 2, 2009).

"John Calvin: Did You Know?" Christian History Magazine. Issue 12. October 11, 1986, http://www.christianitytoday. com/ch/1986/issue12/1206.html (accessed April 03, 2009).

Josephus, Flavius. The Words of Josephus. Translated by William Whiston. Peabody, MA: Hendrickson Publishers, 1987.

Juster, Dan. Jewish Roots: A Foundation of Biblical Theology. Shippensburgh, Pa: Destiny Image Publishers, 1995.

Kaiser, Walter C. Revive Us Again: Biblical Insights for Encouraging Spiritual Renewal. Nashville, Tenn.: Broadman and Holman, 1999.

Living Inside Out

Kempis, Thomas à . The Imitation of Christ. New Kensington, Pa.: Whitaker House, 1981.

Kirvan, John, ed. Let Nothing Disturb You: Thirty Days with Teresa of Avila. Notre Dame, Indiana: Ave Maria Press, 2008.

Kittel, Gerhard and G. Friedrich, ed. Theological Dictionary of the New Testament, abridged in one vol. Translated and abridged by Geoffrey Bromiley. Grand Rapids, MI: Eerdmans, 1985.

Laniak, Tim. Shepherds After My Own Heart: Pastoral Traditions and Leadership in the Bible. Downer's Grove, IL: InterVarsity Press, 2006.

Ladd, George Eldon. The Gospel of the Kingdom: Popular Expositions on the Kingdom of God. Grand Rapids, MI: Eerdmans Publishing, 1990.

Latourette, Kenneth Scott. A History of Christianity: Beginnings to 1500, 2 vol. Peabody, MA: Prince Press, 1997.

Leith, John, ed. Creeds of the Churches. Louisville, KY: John Knox Press, 1982.

Lewis, Arthur James. Zinzendorf: The Ecumenical Pioneer – A Study in the Moravian Contribution to Christian Mission and Unity. Norwich, London: SCM Press, 1962.

Lightfoot, J.B and J.R. Harmer. The Apostolic Fathers. Grand Rapids, MI: Baker Book House, 1987.

Littleproud, J. R. The Christian Assembly. Glendale, CA: Church Press, 1962.

Loisy, Alfred. The Gospel and the Church. Philadelphia: Fortress Press, 1976.

Bibliography

Lovelace, Richard F. Dynamics of Spiritual Life: An Evangelical Theology of Renewal. Downers Grove, Ill: InterVarsity Press, 1979.

Lull, Timothy F., ed. Martin Luther's Basic Theological Writings. Second ed. Minneapolis: Fortress Press, 2005.

Luther Martin, Early Theological Works: Heidelberg Disputation. Edited by James Atkinson. Westminster: John Knox Press, 2006.

_____. Table Talk. Translated by William Hazlitt. Philadelphia, PA: The Lutheran Publication Society, 2004.

_____. Three Treatisis. Edited by Helmut T. Lehmann. Minneapolis, MN: Fortress Press, 1966.

Marsden, George M. Johathan Edwards: A Life. New Haven, CT: Yale University Press, 2003.

Marsh, Charles. The Beloved Community. New York, NY: Perseus Book Group, 2005.

McGrath, Alister E. Luther's Theology of the Cross. Oxford: Blackwell, 1985.

_____. Christian Theology: An Introduction. 2nd ed. Crowley Road, Oxford: Blackwell Publishers, 1997.

Metzger, Bruce. The Canon of the New Testament. Oxford, NY: Oxford University Press, 1997.

Moravian Covenant for Christian Living; formerly known as The Brotherly Agreement of the Moravian Church. Bethlehem, PA: Interprovincial Board of Communication, 2001.

"Moravians and John Wesley." Christian History Magazine, issue 1 (January, 01, 1982), http://www.christianitytoday. com/ch/1982/issue1/128.html?start=1 (accessed February 10, 2009).

Living Inside Out

Mott, John R. The Evangelization of the World in This Generation. London, England: Student Volunteer Movement, 1902.

Murray, Andrew. Vital Christianity. Christian Focus Publications.

Navigators, The. http://www.navigators.org/us/aboutus (See also) http://www.navigators.org/us/resources/illustrations/items (accessed February 3, 2009).

Nee, Watchman. Sit, Walk, Stand .Wheaton, IL: Tyndale House, 1977.

Noll, Mark A, Nathan O Hatch, George M. Marsden, David F. Wells, and John D Woodbridge, eds. Eerdmans' Handbook to Christianity in America .Grand Rapids, MI.: Eerdmans Publishing. 1983.

_____. The Scandal of Evangelical Mind. Grand Rapids, MI: Eerdmans, 1994.

_____. The Rise of Evangelicalism: The Age of Edwards, Whitefield, and the Wesleys. Downer's Grove, IL: InterVarsity Press, 2004.

Niebuhr, Richard H. Christ and Culture. New York, NY: Harper & Row, 1975.

Nowen, Henri J.M. The Genesee Diary: Report for a Trappist Monastery. Garden City, NY: Image Books. 1981.

_____. The Way of the Heart: Desert Spirituality and Contemporary Ministry. New York, NY: Harper One, 2001.

Orr, William F. and James A Walker. Anchor Bible, 1Corinthians. Garden City, NY: Double Day Publisher. 1976

Passion (The) of the Christ, directed by Mel Gibson 2003. http://www.passionofthechrist.com/splash.htm (accessed October 26, 2008),

Bibliography

Peers, Allison, tr. ed. The Autobiography of Teresa of Avila. http://www.catholicfirst.com/thefaith/catholicclassics/stteresa/life/teresaofavila4.cfm#CHAPTER%20XI. (accessed 25 October 2008).

Pentecost, J. Dwight. Things to Come. Grand Rapids, MI: Zondervan 1974.

Pierson, Arthur T. George Mueller of Bristol and His Witness to a Prayer-Hearing God http://www.whatsaiththescripture.com/Voice/George.Mueller.of.Bristol/George. Mueller.of.Bristol.html (accessed October 25, 2008).

Phillips, Bill. Body for Life. NY, NY: Harper Collins Publishing, 1999.

Pink, Arthur W. The Sovereignty of God. Grand Rapids, MI: Baker Book House, 1991.

Piper, John. Let The Nations Be Glad: The Supremacy of God in Missions. Grand Rapids: Baker Books, 1996.

_____. Amazing Grace in the Life of William Wilberforce. Wheaton, IL: Crossway Books, 2006.

_____. The Future of Justification: A Response to N. T. Wright. Wheaton, IL: Crossway Books, 2007.

Potter, G.R. Huldrych Zwingli. Cambridge: Cambridge University Press, 1977.

Ratzlaff, Dale. Sabbath in Christ. Glendale, AZ: Life Assurance Ministries, 1996.

Raphael, Chaim. A Feast of History: The Drama of Passover Through the Ages. Washington DC: B'nai B'rith Books, 1993.

Living Inside Out

Reformation Ink. "Martin Luther." (1483-1546). http://home-page.mac.com/shanerosenthal/reformationink/mlconversion.htm. (accessed November 11, 2009).

Richardson, Cyril C. ed. Early Christian Fathers. Vol.1. New York, NY: Simon and Schuster, 1996.

Roberts, Alexander and James Donaldson, eds. The Ante-Nicene Fathers. 10 volumes. Grand Rapids, MI: Eerdmans, 1978-1983.

Rock of Ages, 1776. http://www.cyberhymnal.org/htm/r/o/rockages.htm (accessed March 23, 2010).

Rosell, Garth. The Church From the Reformation (Semlink Notebook) S. Hamilton, MA: Gordon-Conwell Theological Seminary, 2000.

Rosen, Moishe and Ceil Rosen. Christ in the Passover, Chicago, IL: Moody Press, 1979.

Rubin, Miri. Corpus Christi: The Eucharist in Late Medieval Culture. Cambridge, England: Cambridge University Press, 1992.

Ryken, Leland. Worldly Saints: The Puritans as They Really Were. Grand Rapids, MI: Zondervan Publishing, 1990.

Schaff, Philip and Henry Wace, eds. The Nicene and Post-Nicene Fathers. Second Series. 14 Volumes Grand Rapids, MI: Eerdmans, 1978-1988.

Schmidt, Leigh Eric. Holy Fairs; Scotland and the Making of Revivalism. Grand Rapids MI: Eerdmans Publishing, 2001.

Schattschneider, Allen W. Through Five Hundred Years: A Popular History of the Moravian Church. Bethlehem, PA: The Moravian Church in America, 1996.

Bibliography

Shaw, Mark. 10 Great Ideas from Church History: A Decision-Maker's Guide to Shaping Your Church. Downers Grove, IL: InterVarsity Press, 1997.

Shelly, Bruce L. Church History in Plain Language, Updated 2nd ed. Nashville: Thomas Nelson Publishers, 1995.

Sider, Ronald J. Rich Christians in an Age of Hunger. Nashville, TN: Thomas Nelson Publisher, 2005.

Simons, Menno and J. C. Wenger. The Complete Writings of Menno Simons. C.1496-1561. Translated by Leonard Verduin. Edited by J. C. Wenger. Scottdale, PA: Herald Press, 1986.

Skinner, Betty Lee. Daws. Grand Rapids, MI: Zondervan Publishing, 1974.

Smith, John E. and Harry Stout, ed., Jonathan Edwards Reader. New Haven: Yale University Press, 1995.

Soulen, Richard N. Handbook of Biblical Criticism. 2nd ed. Atlanta, GA: John Knox Press, 1981.

Spangler, Ann. Praying the Names of God. Grand Rapids, MI: Zondervan, 2004.

Spener, Philip Jacob and Theodore G. Tappert, ed., Pia Desideria. Eugene, OR: Wipf and Stock Publishers, 2002.

Stern, David H. Messianic Jewish Manifesto. Clarksville, MD: Jewish New Testament Publications, 1991.

Stott, John R.W. Christian Mission in the Modern World: What the Church Should be Doing Now. Downers Grove, IL: InterVarsity Press, 1975.

Sweet, Leonard ed. The Church in Emerging Culture: Five Perspectives. Grand Rapids, MI: Zondervan, 2003.

Synan, Vinson. The Century of the Holy Spirit. Nashville, TN: Thomas Nelson Publishers, 2001.

Taylor, Dr. and Mrs. Howard. Hudson Taylor's Spiritual Secret. Chicago, IL: Moody 1989.

Teresa, Mother. The Love of Christ: Spiritual Counsels Mother Teresa of Calcutta. Edited by Georges Gorree and Jean Barbier. San Francisco, CA: Harper and Row Publishers, 1982.

Teresian Carmel in Austria, St. Teresa of Avila. http://www.karmel.at/eng/teresa.htm. (accessed November 28, 2006).

Thieme, R.B. The Faith-Rest Life, Houston, TX: Berachah Tapes and Publications1961.

Thomas, Major W. Ian .The Saving Life of Christ. Grand Rapids MI: Zondervan, 1961.

Van Den Berg, Johannes. Constrained by Jesus' Love: An Enquiry into the Motives of the Missionary Awakening in Great Britain in the Period Between 1698 and 1815. Kampen: Kok, 1956.

Verheyen, Boniface O.S.B. of St. Benedict's Abbey. The Holy Rule of St. Benedict. 1949 ed. Atchison, Kansas. http://www.kansasmonks.org/RuleOfStBenedict.html (accessed November 28, 2008).

Wagner, Clarence H. Lessons from the Land of the Bible: Revealing more of God's Word. Jerusalem Israel: Bridges for Peace, 2000.

Walk Through the Bible: Our History http://www.walkthru.org/site/PageServer?pagename=aboutHistory (accessed 3 February 3, 2009).

Bibliography

Wells, David. God in the Wasteland. Grand Rapids, MI.: Eerdmans, 1994.

Wesley, John. A Plain Account of Christian Perfection. Peabody, MA: Hendrickson Publishers, 2007.

Westminster Confession of Faith, Glasgow, Scotland: Free Presbyterian Publications, 1985.

Westerholm, Stephen. Israel's Law and the Church's Faith. Grand Rapids, MI: Eerdmans 1988.

Willard, Dallas. The Divine Conspiracy: Rediscovering Our Hidden Life in God. SanFrancisco, CA: Harper Collins Publishers, 1997.

_____. Hearing God. Downers Grove IL: InterVarsity Press, 1999.

Williams, George H. and Angel M. Mergal ed. Spiritual and Anabaptist Writers. Philadelphia, PA.: The Westminster Press, 1977.

Wilson, Marvin R. Our Father Abraham. Grand Rapids, MI: Eerdmans, 1989.

Woodbridge, John D. Great Leaders of the Christian Church. Chicago, IL: Moody Press, 1988.

Wright, N. T. Who was Jesus? Grand Rapids, MI: Eerdmans, 1993.

_____. Justification: God's Plan and Paul's Vision. Downer Grove, IL: InterVarsity Press, 2009.

Xavier, Francis and M. Joseph Costelloe. The Letters and Instructions of Francis Xavier. St Louis, MO: Institute of Jesuit Sources, 1992.

Zimmerman, Martha. Celebrating Biblical Feasts in Your Home or Church. Minneapolis, MN: Bethany House, 2004.

Living Inside Out

Zinzendorf. Missiopedia. "Count Nicholas Ludwig von Zinzendorf: The start of Herrnhut." http://www.mission-manual.org/wiki/Zinzendorf. (accessed October 20,

ENDNOTES

[1] Scripture references cited from New American Standard Bible (NASB) unless otherwise noted.

[2] Rabbi Dr I Epstein, ed., The Babylonian Talmud, Seder Nashim, vol. 3, trans. Dr. A Cohen, (London, England: Soncina Press 1936), Sotha 21. "But as for him whose mind is lowly (humble), scripture ascribes it to him as though he had offered every one of the sacrifices; as it is said, the sacrifices of God are a broken spirit. (Ps 51:19) More than that, his prayer is not despised; as it continues a broken and a contrite heart O God Thou wilt not despise. b Sotah 5b.

[3] For he is not a Jew who is one outwardly, nor is circumcision that which is outward in the flesh. But he is a Jew who is one inwardly; and circumcision is that which is of the heart, by the Spirit, not by the letter." (Rom 2:27-28) "But now we have been released from the Law, having died to that by which we were bound, so that we serve in newness of the Spirit and not in oldness of the letter." (Rom 7:6)... Who also made us adequate {as} servants of a new covenant, not of the letter but of the Spirit; for the letter kills, but the Spirit gives life."(2Cor 3:6)

[4] Paul and James (1Cor 13, James 2) both address another faith which I will take up later in the text.

Living Inside Out

5   R.E.O. White, "Humility" in Evangelical Dictionary of Theology edited by Walter A. Elwell (Grand Rapids, Michigan: Baker Books, 1984), 537.

6   This is the summation of the 5th chapter of Galatians, which is concerned with the walk empowered by the Spirit. Compare the ninefold Fruit of the Spirit and this tenth summary command with the 10 commandments of the Old Covenant.

7   Colin Brown, Beyeruther and Bietenhard ed., Dictionary of New Testament Theology, vol. 1. (Grand Rapids, MI: Zondervan Publishing, 1986), 639.

8   Dietrich Bonhoeffer, Life Together. (New York, NY: Harper and Row, 1954), 17-39.

9   Dietrich Bonhoeffer, The Cost of Discipleship (New York: Collier Books Macmillan Publishers, 1963), 285.

10   The words "In memory of the Passover Lamb" are still spoken over the afikomen in the Sephardic Seder. Cecil and Moshe Rosen, Christ in the Passover (Chicago, IL. Moody Publishers, 2006), 108.

11   W. Harold Mare, "1Corinthinans," in Expositors Bible Commentary vol. 10, edited by Gaebelein (Grand Rapids, MI: Zondervan, 1976), 217. 12 1Cor 2:26. 13 1Cor 11:26; Exod 12:26-27; 13:8-10. 14 Marvin R Wilson, Our Father Abraham (Grand Rapids, MI: Eerdmans, 1989), 74-84. 15 Gen 18:18; 22:18; 50:20; Ps 115.

12   1Cor 2:26.

13   1Cor 11:26; Exod 12:26-27; 13:8-10.

14   Marvin R Wilson, Our Father Abraham (Grand Rapids, MI: Eerdmans, 1989), 74-84.

Endnotes

15 Gen 18:18; 22:18; 50:20; Ps 115.

16 Acts 2:42.

17 Andrew Bowling, "Heart" Vol 1 of Theological Wordbook of the Old Testament, Ed. R. Laird Harris, Gleason L. Archer Jr., and Bruce K. Waltke, (Chicago Moody Press, 1992), 466.

18 Author's Note: This illustration originated with a mentor, Jim McCotter, who shared it with me when I was still in my late teens. Though I have modified it slightly, the basic content remains unchanged. It has become a pivotal concept in my life. I have shared it hundreds of times probably with thousands of people, and it always rekindles the vision we shared so long ago. In contemplating this illustration, it is helpful to write your own name in the center of the cross.

19 Mark Shaw, *10 Great Ideas from Church History: A Decision-Maker's Guide to Shaping Your Church*. (Downer's Grove, IL: InterVarsity Press, 1997), 50-51. John Calvin agrees. Shaw writes, "the essence of Calvinism is captured not in the doctrine of election or predestination but in Calvin's declaration of God's ownership of our lives."

20 The Passion of the Christ directed by Mel Gibson 2003, http://www.passionofthechrist.com/splash.htm (accessed October 24, 2008).

21 George Eldon Ladd, *The Gospel of the Kingdom* (Grand Rapids, MI: Eerdmans, 1959), 14-15.

22 Mark Shaw p51

23 Donald A Hagner, I. Howard Marshall, Anthony C. Thiselton eds., *The New International Greek Testament*

Commentary: The First Epistle to the Corinthians (Grand Rapids, MI: Eerdmans, 2000), v-xiii.

See also: William F. Orr and James a. Walker, *Anchor Bible, 1Corinthians* (Garden City, NY: Double Day Publisher, 1976), x-xv.

[24] Gordon Fee, *The First Epistle to the Corinthians: The New International Commentary on the New Testament* (Grand Rapids, MI: Eerdmans Publishing, 1987), 21-23. See also: Gerhard Kittel, *Theological Dictionary of the New Testament*, vol. 4, trans. Geoffrey W. Bomiley (Grand Rapids, MI: Eerdmans, 1974), 669.

[25] The Philippians like the Corinthians were "begotten by Paul" (1Cor 4:15).

[26] John Calvin, *Calvin's NT Commentaries* vol.11. Translated by T.H.L.Parker, David F. Torrance, ed. (Grand Rapids, MI: Eerdmans, 1965), 280. Calvin's comment strikes a nice balance: "By this word he means that it is all one to him whom they choose for imitation, provided they conform themselves to that purity of which he was a pattern. By this means all suspicion of ambition is taken away, for the man who is devoted to himself avoids rivals. At the same time he warns them that all are not to be imitated indiscriminately, as he explains more plainly."

[27] Christopher Hudson, Alan Sharrer, Lindsay Vanker, eds., *Day by Day with the Early Church Fathers*, (Augustine *On The Trinity* 14.17) (Peabody, MA: Hendrickson Publishers, 1999), 189.

[28] Phil 2:12.

[29] Cyril C Richardson,.ed., *Early Christian Fathers* (The So-called Letter to Diognetus) vol.1, (New York, NY: Simon and Schuster, 1996), 221.

Endnotes

30 Richardson, ed., *Early Christian Fathers* (The So-called Letter to Diognetus), 216-217. In the same letter other distinctives of the Christian life are enumerated: "For Christians cannot be distinguished from the rest of the human race by country or language or customs. They do not live in cities of their own; they do not use a peculiar form of speech; they do not follow an eccentric manner of life. This doctrine of theirs has not been discovered by the ingenuity or deep thought of inquisitive men, nor do they put forward a merely human teaching, as some people do. Yet, although they live in Greek and barbarian cities alike, as each man's lot has been cast, and follow the customs of the country in clothing and food and other matters of daily living, at the same time they give proof of the remarkable and admittedly extraordinary constitution of their own commonwealth. They live in their own countries, but only as aliens. They have a share in everything as citizens and endure everything as foreigners. Every foreign land is their fatherland, and yet for them every fatherland is a foreign land. They marry, like everyone else, and they beget children, but they do not cast out their offspring. They share their board with each other, but not their marriage bed. It is true that they are "in the flesh," but they do not live "according to the flesh." They obey the established laws, but in their own lives they go far beyond what the laws require. They love all men, and by all men are persecuted. They are unknown, and still they are condemned; they are put to death, and yet they are brought to life. They are poor, and yet they make many rich; they are completely destitute, and yet they enjoy complete abundance. They are dishonored, and in their very dishonor are glorified; they are defamed and are vindicated. They are reviled, and yet they bless; when they are affronted, they still pay due respect. When they do good, they are punished as evildoers; undergoing punishment, they rejoice because they are brought to

Living Inside Out

life. They are treated by the Jews as foreigners and enemies and are hunted down by the Greeks; and all the time those who hate them find it impossible to justify their enmity."

[31] J.B Lightfoot and J.R. Harmer. *The Apostolic Fathers (Ignatius, "Letter to the Romans" 3:2)* (Grand Rapids, MI: Baker Book House, 1987).

[32] Alexander Roberts, James Donaldson, eds., *The Ante-Nicene Fathers (Clement of Alexandria 2.412 ANF)* (Grand Rapids, MI: Eerdmans, 1978-1983.

[33] Thomas à Kempas, *The Imitation of Christ*, (Mineola, NY: Dover Press, 2003), 73, 83-84.

[34] Kenneth Scott Latourete, *A History of Christianity: Beginnings to 1500*, vol.1-2 (Peabody, MA.: Prince Press, 1997), 648-649.

[35] Latourete, *A History of Christianity: Beginnings to 1500*, 648. Another branch of the *Devotio Moderna* whose members took no vow but lived and worked in community seeking to follow the instructions of the Apostle Paul. Interestingly, J. I. Packer refers to Puritanism as "a kind of monasticism outside the cloister" in his forward to Leland Ryken's *Worldly Saints*: Leland.Ryken, *Wordly Saints: The Puritans as They Really Were* (Grand Rapids, MI: Zondervan Publishing, 1990).

[36] Thomas à Kempas, *The Imitation of Christ*. "He who follows Me, walks not in darkness," says the Lord. By these words of Christ, we are advised to imitate His life and habits, if we wish to be truly enlightened and free from all blindness of heart. Let our chief effort therefore be to study the life of Jesus Christ. The teaching of Christ is more excellent than all the advice of the saints, and he who has His spirit will find in it a hidden manna.

Endnotes

Now, there are many who hear the Gospel often but care little for it because they have not the spirit of Christ. Yet whoever wishes to understand fully the words of Christ must try to pattern his whole life on that of Christ. This is the greatest wisdom -- to seek the kingdom of heaven through contempt of the world. It is vanity, therefore, to seek and trust in riches that perish. It is vanity also to court honor and to be puffed up with pride. It is vanity to follow the lusts of the body and to desire things for which severe punishment later must come. It is vanity to wish for long life and to care little about a well-spent life. It is vanity to be concerned with the present only and not to make provision for things to come. It is vanity to love what passes quickly and not to look ahead where eternal joy abides. Often recall the proverb: "The eye is not satisfied with seeing nor the ear filled with hearing." Try, moreover, to turn your heart from the love of things visible and bring yourself to things invisible. For they who follow their own evil passions stain their consciences and lose the grace of God."11-12.

[37] Dietrich Bonhoeffer, *The Cost of Discipleship*, 99.

[38] Saint Augustine, The City of God, Book 14, Paragraph 28, Page 477

[39] R.E.O. White, "Humility" in *Evangelical Dictionary of Theology* edited by Walter A. Elwell (Grand Rapids, Michigan: Baker Books, 1984), 537. "With Barnabas it was part of 'inward fasting' with Chrysostom, the 'foundation of our philosophy;' Augustine said, 'If you ask me what the first precept of the Christian religion is, I will answer, first, second and third, Humility.' A Kempis and Bernard held humility necessary to imitation of Christ. Luther condemned, "Instead of being humble, seek to excel in humility...Unless a man is always humble, distrustful of himself, always fears his own understanding,

Living Inside Out

passions…will…he will be unable to stand for long without offence. Truth will pass him by.' Humility is 'aptness for grace,' the essence of faith. For Calvin, humility alone exalts God as sovereign; it is part of self-denial… Puritans cultivated humility as an antidote to self-righteousness, by constant self-examination." Jonathan Edwards thought humility an essential test of religious affection.

[40] Leonard J. Coppes, `anaw. Humble, meek #1652 in vol. 2 of Theological *Wordbook of the Old Testament*, eds. Harris, Laird R., Gleason L. Archer, Jr. and Bruce K. Waltke (Chicago: Moody Press, 1992) 682-683. `anaw. Humble, meek. This adjective stresses the moral and spiritual condition of the godly as the goal of affliction implying that this state is joined with a suffering life rather than with one of worldly happiness and abundance. `anaw expresses the intended outcome of affliction: humility. Moses' description of himself (Num 12:3) as such a man is no proud boast, but merely a report of his position: absolute dependence on God (cf. Paul's statement in Acts 20:19).

Of all men he was most properly related to God. Throughout the rest of scripture such an attitude and position is lauded as blessed and to be desired. This is the goal which God intended when he afflicted his people and toward which they are to endure affliction. The humble consider and experience God as their deliverer (Ps 10:17; 76:9) receiving grace (undeserved favor) from him (Prov 3:34). They rejoice when God is praised, seek God (Ps 69:32), and keep his ordinances (Zeph 2:3). They wait on God (Ps 37:11) and are guided by him (Ps 25:9). As such they are commended as being better than the proud (Pro 16:19). They are contrasted with the wicked (Ps 37:II) and the scorners (Prov 3:34). Isa 61:1 states that it is to such that the anointed of the Lord is to preach

Endnotes

the good news of salvation (the parallel here is "the broken hearted"). They are conscious of divine approval and are confident that in the eschaton God will save them (Ps 76:9; 147:6; 149:4).

It is interesting that the unleavened bread of Passover is called the bread of affliction (Deut 16:3) inasmuch as it constitutes a material reminder of sin which is the ultimate (sometimes immediate) cause of affliction (Ps 25:18), the bondage of sin (especially that hardship in Egypt), and God's deliverance (Lam 3:19). `anawa. Humility, gentleness. This word sets forth the dual qualities gained by man in the school of affliction. Applied to the Messiah it connotes his gentleness in submission to his own nature (Ps 45:4 [H 5]). `ani. Poor, weak, afflicted, humble. The `ani is primarily a person suffering some kind of disability or distress. (Gray, G. B., *Isaiah*, ICC, I, P. 310). The `ani, although frequently in synonymous parallelism with `ebyon and dal, differs from both in that it connotes some kind of disability or distress. In Deut. 24:14-15 the hired servant is described as `ebyon and `dal. Israel is told not to oppress their hired servant by withholding the wages due him because he is `ani.

Furthermore, if he is oppressed he may call on God his defender. We see that financially the `ani lives from day to day, and that socially he is defenseless and subject to oppression, Consequently, this word is used frequently in connection with `ebyon expressing the difficulty accompanying a lack of material possessions. The people are commanded to give alms to the `ani under sanction of God's blessing (Deut 15:11). God instructs his people to grant loans to the `ani of Israel even when they have only their outer garment as collateral or pledge (see `abat) and not to further afflict them by keeping that garment overnight because the `ani would need it to keep warm (Exod 22:25-26), for it was his only outer garment. In Lev 19:10 the `ani is classed with the stranger as having a right to

245

Living Inside Out

the gleanings of the field. `ani is distinguished from dal (the poor) in Prov 22:22, "Rob not the poor (*dal*) for he is poor (*dal*), neither oppress the afflicted (`ani) in the gate. "God is set forth as the protector and deliverer of the afflicted, and he enjoins his people to be the same. So the one who complies is considered godly (Ezek 18:17), while those who do not are considered ungodly (Job 24:9; Prov 14:21; Isa. 58:7).

[41]   D. A. Carson, "Matthew" in T*he Expositors Bible Commentary*, vol. 8, ed. Frank E. Gaebelein (Grand Rapids, MI: Zondervan, 1984), 131.

[42]   Ronald J Sider, *Rich Christians in an Age of Hunger* (Nashville, TN: Thomas Nelson Publisher), 2005.

[43]   Bruce L Shelley, *Church History in Plain Language*, 2nd edition (Nashville, TN: Thomas Nelson Pub. 1995), 205-214. They were often accompanied by extremes but consistently confronted the errors of self-indulgence associated with pride and self-interest. Numerous prominent movements of voluntary poverty arose in the 12th and 13th centuries including Waldenses, Cathari, Dominicans, and Franciscans, some of which were frankly heretical, others evolved in direct response to heresies while acknowledging the legitimacy of the call to poverty.

[44]   Scripture alone - a statement of commitment to the scriptures alone as an authority as opposed to scripture plus... tradition, councils, popes etc. For background and discussion of contemporary positions as well with extensive bibliography see: Alister E. McGrath, *ChristianTheology: An Introduction*, 2nd. ed. (Oxford: Blackwell Publishers, 1997), 181-235. Also see: Charles Hodge, *Systematic Theology* (Grand Rapids, MI: Eerdmans Publishers, 1981), 61-188.

Endnotes

45   J. H. Mere D'Aubigne, *Life and Times of Martin Luther* (Chicago, IL: Moody Press, 1950), 433.

46   Calvin did not like to waste a minute of his time. Even on his deathbed, his friends pleaded with him to refrain from his labors. He replied: *"What! Would you have the Lord find me idle when he comes?"* During the course of his ministry in Geneva, lasting nearly twentyfive years, Calvin lectured to theological students and preached an average of five sermons a week. This was in addition to writing a commentary on nearly every book of the Bible as well as numerous treaties on theological topics. His correspondence fills eleven volumes. "John Calvin: Did You Know?" *Christian History Magazine* issue 12, October 11, 1986, http://www.christianitytoday.com/ch/1986/issue12/1206.html (accessed November 03, 2009).

47   See John Pipers excellent discussion of this text in chapter 8 of *The Pleasures of God.* John Piper, *The Pleasures of God* (Portland, Oregon: Multnomah Press, 1991)

48   R.E.O. White, "Humility" in *Evangelical Dictionary of Theology* edited by Walter A. Elwell (Grand Rapids, Michigan: Baker Books, 1984), 537.

49   Compare 1 Kings. 9:4, Job 4:6-7, Psa 78:72.

50   James 4:6, 1Pet 5:5.

51   Richard F. Lovelace, *Dynamics of Spiritual Life: An Evangelical Theology of Renewal* (Downers Grove, IL: InterVarsity Press, 1979), 11-21.

52   Lovelace, *Dynamics of Spiritual Life*, 14.

Living Inside Out

53 Leland Ryken, *Wordly Saints: The Puritans as They Really Were* (Grand Rapids, MI: Zondervan Publishing, 1990), 213-221. This could also be translated, "a Reformed church always being reformed," that is, the reforming work is always God's work, not a human work. The Puritans would struggle with this balance in the New World.

54 Lovelace, 52.

55 Lovelace, 34. See also Philip Jacob Spener, and Theodore G. Tappert, ed., *Pia Desideria* (Eugene, OR: Wipf and Stock Publishers, 2002), and A. W. Boehm, "Preface" to Johann Arndt's *True Christianity*, 2nd ed. , (London: D. Brown and J. Dowing, 1720), xxii. Cited by Lovelace, *Dynamics of Spiritual Life*, 14-15.

56 Ergun Mehmet Caner and Emir Fethi Caner, *Christian Jihad* (Grand Rapids, MI: Kregel Publications, 2004), 19.

57 Menno Simons and C Wenger, *Reply to Gellius Faber in The Complete Writings of Menno Simons* (Scottsdale PA: Herald Press, 1956), 670-671. "After [the tragedy at Munster] had transpired, the blood of these people, although misled, fell so hot on my heart that I could not stand it, nor find rest in my soul .I reflected upon my unclean, carnal life, also upon the hypocritical doctrine and idolatry which I still practiced daily in the appearance of godliness, but without any relish. I saw that these zealous children, although in error, willingly gave their lives and their estates for their doctrine and faith. And I was one of those who had disclosed to some of them the abominations of the papal system. But I myself was continuing in my comfortable life and acknowledged abominations simply in order that I might enjoy physical comfort and escape the cross of the Christ. Pondering these things, my conscience tormented me so that I could

Endnotes

no longer endure it. I thought to myself-I, miserable man, what am I doing? If I continue in this way and do not live agreeable to the Word of the Lord according to the knowledge of the truth which I have obtained; if I do not censure to the best of my little talent, the hypocrisy, the impenitent, carnal life, the erroneous baptism, the Lord's supper in the false service of God, which the learned ones teach; if I through bodily fear do not lay bare the foundations of the truth, nor use all of my powers to direct the wandering flock who would gladly do their duty if they knew it, to the true pastures of Christ-oh how shall their shed blood, shed in the mist of transgression, rise against me at the judgment of the Almighty and pronounce sentence to my poor, miserable soul! My heart trembled within me. I prayed to God with sighs and tears that he would give to me, a sorrowing sinner, the gift of His grace, create in me a clean heart, and graciously through the merit of the Crimson blood of Christ forgive my unclean walk and frivolous easy life and bestow upon me wisdom, Spirit, courage, and a manly spirit so I might preach His exalted and adorable name and holy word in purity, and make known His truth to His glory."

[58]   Menno Simons, *Reply to Gellius Faber in The Complete Writings of Menno Simons*, 674.

[59]   Simons, 111-112.

[60]   For he is not a Jew who is one outwardly, nor is circumcision that which is outward in the flesh. But he is a Jew who is one inwardly; and circumcision is that which is of the heart, by the Spirit, not by the letter (Rom 2:27-28); "But now we have been released from the Law, having died to that by which we were bound, so that we serve in newness of the Spirit and not in oldness of the letter" (Rom 7:6); who also made us adequate {as} servants of

Living Inside Out

a new covenant, not of the letter but of the Spirit; for the letter kills, but the Spirit gives life (2Cor 3:6).

[61] "Those who desire to make a good showing in the flesh try to compel you to be circumcised, simply so that they will not be persecuted for the cross of Christ. For those who are circumcised do not even keep the Law themselves, but they desire to have you circumcised so that they may boast in your flesh. But may it never be that I would boast, except in the cross of our Lord Jesus Christ, through which the world has been crucified to me, and I to the world. For neither is circumcision anything, nor uncircumcision, but **a new creation**; and those who will **walk by this rule**, peace and mercy {be} upon them, and upon **the Israel of God**" (Gal 6:12-16).

[62] Marvin Wilson, *Our Father Abraham* (Grand Rapids, MI: Eerdmans, 1989), 1-80.

[63] The church faced a time of general disarray in society prior to and following the fall of the Roman Empire. Monastic orders abounded, and with them a series of "rules." These were, in a sense rules of order, designed to bring order to the monastery and to the individual. The One who joined the monasteries took vows which always included obedience. Our English word obedience is from the Latin *obedere* meaning to listen. This captures the meaning of the Hebrew which uses hearing for obedience. For some the rules were a form of discipline for spirituality, for others they were a natural outworking of the inner workings of true faith. Also: The following is from the first chapter of Augustine's Rule: "Before all else, dear brothers, love God and then your neighbor, because these are the chief commandments given to us. The following are the precepts we order you living in the monastery to observe. The main purpose for you having come together is to live harmoniously in your house, intent

Endnotes

upon God in oneness of mind and heart. Call nothing your own, but let everything be yours in common. Food and clothing shall be distributed to each of you by your superior, not equally to all, for all do not enjoy equal health, but rather according to each one's need. For so you read in the Acts of the Apostles that they had all things in common and distribution was made to each one according to each one's need (4:3235).

Let all of you then live together in oneness of mind and heart, mutually honoring God in yourselves, whose temples you have become." Robert Russell, O.S.A.trans., *The Rule of St. Augustine*, based on the critical text of Luc Verheijen, O.S.A, *La regle de saint Augustin Etudes Augustiniennes* (Paris France: Brothers of the Order of Hermits of Saint Augustine, Inc., 1967).

http://www.geocities.com/Athens/1534/ruleaug.html (accessed November 11, 2006).

[64] C. T. Marshall, "Monasticism" in *Evangelical Dictionary of Theology*, 720-729. Probably the most famous of all the Rules was that of Benedict. "To the old promises of poverty, chastity, and obedience to Christ the Benedictines added stability. Monks could no longer drift about from monastery to monastery but were bound to one for life. The essence of Benedict's rule is its sensible approach to Christian living. It forbade excess and provided practical advice for every aspect of monastery life. It gave an elaborate description of the role of each person in the community from the abbot, who represented Christ in the community, to the lowliest postulant. For this reason the Benedictine Rule became the standard in Western Europe. Because of their devotion to the rule, monks came to be known as the "regular" clergy, from the Latin regula, "rule." The Rule opens with a prologue in which St Benedict sets forth the main principles of the religious life: "The renunciation of one's own will and

Living Inside Out

arming oneself "with the strong and noble weapons of obedience" under the banner of "the true King, Christ the Lord." Now, brethren, that we have asked the Lord who it is that shall dwell in His tabernacle, we have heard the conditions for dwelling there; and if we fulfill the duties of tenants, we shall be heirs of the kingdom of heaven. Our hearts and our bodies must, therefore, be ready to do battle under the biddings of holy obedience; and let us ask the Lord that He supply by the help of His grace what is impossible to us by nature....We are, therefore, about to found a school of the Lord's service, in which we hope to introduce nothing harsh or burdensome. But even if, to correct vices or to preserve charity, sound reason dictateth anything that turneth out somewhat stringent, do not at once fly in dismay from the way of salvation, the beginning of which cannot but be narrow. But as we advance in the religious life and faith, we shall run the way of God's commandments with expanded hearts and unspeakable sweetness of love; so that never departing from His guidance and persevering in the monastery in His doctrine till death, we may by patience share in the sufferings of Christ, and be found worthy to be coheirs *with Him of His kingdom*." Timothy Fry, O.S.B.ed., *The Rule of St. Benedict* in English (Collegeville, MN: The Liturgical Press, 1982). Prologue 3,

[65] He concludes the rule by reminding his followers of their true freedom: "The Lord grant that you may observe all these precepts in a spirit of charity as lovers of spiritual beauty, giving forth the good odor of Christ in the holiness of your lives: not as slaves living under the law but as men living in freedom under grace." *The Rule of St. Augustine*, translated by Robert Russell, O.S.A., http://www.geocities.com/Athens/1534/ruleaug.html (accessed November 11, 2006).

Endnotes

66   Loyola is often seen as the embodiment of the Catholic or Counter-Reformation. In 1540 he founded the Society of Jesus (Jesuits) which were to become a new 'spiritual elite' at the disposal of the pope to use in whatever way he thought appropriate for spreading the 'true Church'. Absolute, unquestioning, military-style obedience became the hallmark of the new society. The famous Jesuit dictum was that every member of the society would obey the pope and the general of the order as unquestioningly 'as a corpse'....The constitution required a forth vow in addition to the traditional vows of poverty, chastity, and obedience: a special oath of absolute obedience to the pope." Robert D. Linder, "The Catholic Reformation," in *Introduction to the History of Christianity* edited by Tim Dowley, 418.

67   Robert G. Clouse, "Flowering: The Western Church," *Introduction to the History of Christianity*, 267-271. The Benedictine Rule would eventually gain ascendancy and define our popular image of monasticism. The Benedictine monasteries of the eighth to tenth centuries became cultural and educational centers with large libraries and collections of manuscripts not only of scripture but of ancient Latin prose and poetry which would have been lost except for these monasteries. Under Boniface in the eighth century the monastery became a center of evangelism among pagan Germans. Over the next two hundred years the monasteries gained favor with the nobility and merchant class eventually moving from a focus on study to manual labor producing high quality goods. Their economic activities including sheep-farming, stone, metal and wood working, baking, and other means of trade made some wealthy orders. The Cistercians were remarkably successful by 1300 with over 600 monasteries. They were soon accused of greed by their brethren. See also Michael A. Smith, "Christian Ascetics

Living Inside Out

and Monk" in *Introduction to the History of Christianity*, 217–221.

[68] Ronald Finucane, *"Medieval Monasticism in the West"* in *Introduction to the History of Christianity*, 315. See also: J.P.Donnley, "The Society of Jesus," in. *Evangelical Dictionary of Theology* edited by Walter A.Elwell (Grand Rapids, MN: Baker Book House, 1994), 1030.

[69] C. T. Marshall, "Monasticism" in *Evangelical Dictionary of Theology* edited by Walter A. Elwell, (Grand Rapids, MN: Baker Book House, 1994), 728-729.

[70] G. M. Burge, "Obedience" in *Evangelical Dictionary of Theology* edited by Walter A. Elwell, 784-785. "The whole of biblical theology centers on the notion of divine revelation and the receptive response of man: God speaks his word; man hears and is required to obey. The connection between hearing and obeying is therefore essential. Hearing is always viewed as a process of the mind. When divine revelation is its subject, man must respond with obedience. This connection is borne out in particular by the language of obedience in the Bible. In the OT *sama* conveys the meaning of both "to hear" and "to obey." Israel must hear Yahweh's voice and act in obedient response. In the Torah the theme of responsive obedience is underscored (Exod 19:5, 8; 24:7; Deut 28:1; 30:11-14). Abraham was blessed because he heard and obeyed the Lord's voice (Gen 22:18). This theme lies behind the prophetic injunction, "Thus says the Lord." The prophetic word reveals both who God is and what he is calling Israel to do. Disobedience, then, is any hearing which is not attentive, and this too is the story of Israel: "They have ears, but do not hear" (Ps 115:6; cf. Jer 3:13; Isa 6:9-10). 785. In the LXX *sama* is regularly translated by words in the akouein word group, and this again expresses the inner relation between hearing and

Endnotes

response. Emphatic forms hypakouein and hypakoe (lit. "to hear beneath") convey the meaning "obey/obedience" (in the NT the verb appears 21 times; the noun 15 times, esp. in Paul). The NT, to be sure, brings out this OT background in full when Jesus demands that he "who has ears to hear, let him hear" (Matt 11:15; 13:9, 15-16; Mark 4:9, 23; 8:18; Luke 14:35). This kind of constructive response to divine revelation is illustrated well in the parable about the man who built his house on the rock. The story follows the exhortation of Christ: "Why do you call me 'Lord, Lord,' and not do what I tell you?" (Luke 6:46-49). In Matthew this same parable concludes the Sermon on the Mount (Matt 7:21-27), clearly indicating the seriousness of personal response to Jesus' ethical injunctions.

71 For discussion of the place of God's law in the Christian life see: Greg L Bahnsen, Walter C. Kaiser, Douglas J Moo, Wayne G. Strickland, Willem A. VanGemeren, *Five Views on Law and Gospel* edited by Stanley N. Gundry (Grand Rapids, MI: Zondervan, 1996). See also John Piper, *The Future of Justification: A Response to N. T. Wright* (Wheaton, IL: Crossway Books, 2007). And N. T. Wright, *Justification: God's Plan and Paul's Vision* (Downer Grove, IL: InterVarsity Press, 2009). Also see: Stephen Westerholm, *Israel's Law and the Church's Faith* (Grand Rapids, MI: Eerdmans 1988).

72 In the Sermon on the Mount, Jesus refers to "sayings of old" from 5:21-48, such as 'Love your neighbor and hate your enemy" (Matt 5:43). However, that phrase is not found anywhere in the Old Testament, though hatred for one's enemies was an accepted part of the Jewish ethic at the time. Jesus specific statement that anyone who "breaks one of the least of these commandments and teaches others to do the same will be called least in the kingdom of heaven", must refer not to the subtle

Living Inside Out

additions such as the one above but to the least of the law and the prophets. "Do not think that I've come to abolish the law of the prophets. I've not come to abolish but to fulfill" (Matt 5:17).

[73] G. M. Burge, "Obedience" in *Evangelical Dictionary of Theology* edited by Walter A. Elwell, 784. Quoting R. Bultmann's work, *Jesus and the Word*. "Bultmann points out that Jesus' call has radicalized an obedience already well known in Judaism. First century Judaism had emphasized cultic and ceremonial rules to such an extent (365 prohibitions, 278 positive commands) that any notion of virtue was almost unknown. Jesus presses beyond the casuistic rules and expects a true obedience, not blind obedience: "You tithe mint and dill and cummin, and have neglected the weightier matters of the law, justice and mercy and faith" (Matt 23:23). Man, in effect, must exceed the demands of the law (Matt 5:20) and perceive for himself what God commands. That is, single-minded obedience grasps the spirit of God's intentions (cf. Mark 10:2-9 on how Jesus applies this to one law) and exceeds God's desires, not with the measured efforts of a servant (Luke 17:7-10), but as people who enjoy a vital and responsive relationship with him. Bultmann sums up: "Radical obedience exists only when a man inwardly assents to what is required of him... when the whole man stands behind what he does; or better, when the whole man is in what he does, when he is not doing something obediently, but is essentially obedient."

[74] G. M. Burge "Obedience" in *Evangelical Dictionary of Theology*, 784. "Paul regards obedience as being one of the constituent parts of faith. Initially Christ stands as the model of obedience (Phil 2:5-8), and through his obedience, which is contrasted with Adam's disobedience, "many will be made righteous" (Rom 5:19; cf. Heb

Endnotes

5:8-9 for the parallel thought). Paul in fact views his task as bringing about the "obedience of faith" among the nations (Rom 1:5; 16:26). For him, every thought should be made "captive to obey Christ" so that the Christian's obedience might be complete (2Cor 10:5-6). This means that Paul too despairs of any faith that is either simply cognitive (a Hellenistic weakness) or mechanistically legal (a Jewish fault). Obedience is of the essence of authentic saving faith and should provide evidence of a responsive relation the Christian shares with his God (cf. James 1:22-25; 2:14-20; I Pet 1:22; I John 3:18)."

[75] R. L. Raymond, "Obedience of Christ" in *Evangelical Dictionary of Theology*, 785. The New Testament speaks explicitly of the obedience of Christ only three times: "Through the obedience of the one man the many will be made righteous" (Rom 5:19); "He humbled himself and become obedient to death" (Phil 2:8); and "He learned obedience from what he suffered" (Heb 5:8). But the concept which these verses contain is clearly alluded to in many other places, e.g., (**1**) the several contexts in which Christ is called "servant" (Isa 42:1; 52:13; 53:11; Phil 2:7; cf. Matt. 20:28; Mark 10:45); (**2**) the numerous passages where he declares his purpose in coming to earth is to do his Father's will (Ps 40:7; John 5:30; 8:28-29; 10:18; 12:49; 14:31; Heb 10:7); (**3**) the oft-made assertion by Himself to both friends and enemies alike of his sinless and righteous life (Matt 27:4, 19-23; Mark 12:14; Luke 23:4, 14-15; John 8:46; 18:38; 19:4-6; 2Cor 5:21; Heb 4:15; 7:26); and (**4**) the passages which affirm his submission to authority (Matt 3:15; Luke 2:51-52; 4:16).

[76] David J. Bosch, *Transforming Mission: Paradigm Shifts in Theology of Mission*. (Maryknoll, NY: Orbis Books, 1998), 69-83.

[77] David J. Bosch, *Transforming Mission*, 59.

Living Inside Out

[78] Bosch, *Transforming Mission*, 57.

[79] **"Walk Thru the Bible"** has taught more people life-changing truths than any other Bible seminar organization, hosting more than 2 million participants in its live Bible seminars since 1976. These **seminars** blend seamlessly with the ministry of the local church. How are we to teach a written Word in a visual age? How are we to present sixty-six books to a world that would rather watch sixty-six channels? For a difficult challenge, God raised up an ingenious answer and placed it in the hearts of six full-time teachers in 1976. Drawing from a concept developed in his Master's thesis, a young seminary student named Bruce Wilkinson created the "Walk Thru the Bible Seminar," where in just one day, just about anyone can learn the geography, characters, and key concepts of every book of the Old Testament in chronological order. Today the ministry has grown from the original six teachers to tens of thousands. And it has expanded from seminars to include monthly devotionals, video series, and more. In fact, Walk Thru the Bible is now the largest conductor of live seminars on earth, religious or secular. And through our international outreach, we have created the largest faculty of Bible teachers ever assembled the." *Walk Thru Bible*, http://www.walkthru.org/site/PageServer?pagename=aboutHistory (accessed February 3, 2009).

[80] John Wesley, *A Plain Account of Christian Perfection* (Peabody, Ma: Hendrickson Publishers, 2007), 55-56. He who loves his neighbor has fulfilled the law.[…] Love therefore is the fulfillment of the law (Rom 13:8b, 10). "Now mistakes, and whatever infirmities necessarily flow from the corruptible state of the body, are no way contrary to love; nor therefore, in the Scripture sense, sin. To explain myself a little farther on this head: 1. Not only

Endnotes

sin, properly so called (that is , a voluntary transgression of a known law), but sin, improperly so called (that is, an involuntary transgression of a divine law, known or unknown), needs the atoning blood. 2. I believe there is no such perfection in this life as excludes these involuntary transgressions which I apprehend to be naturally consequent on the ignorance and mistakes inseparable from morality 3. Therefore *sinless perfection* is a phrase I never use, lest I should seem to contradict myself. 4. I believe, a person filled with the love of God is still liable to these involuntary transgressions. Such transgressions you may call sins, if you please: I do not, for the reasons above mentioned.

Scripture perfection is, pure love filling the heart, and governing all the words and actions. If your idea includes anything more or anything else, it is not scriptural; and then no wonder, that a scripturally perfect Christian does not come up to it."

[81] Melvin Dieter, Anthony A. Hoekema, Stanley M Horton, J. Robertson McQuilkin, and John F. Walvoord. *Five Views on Sanctification* edited by Stanley N. Gundry (Grand Rapids, MI: Zondervan, 1987), 17.

[82] John Wesley, *A Plain Account of Christian Perfection* (Peabody Ma: Hendrickson Publishers, 2007), 51.

[83] Penned in 1776. Music score written by Tom Hastings in 1830, http://www.cyberhymnal.org/htm/r/o/rockages.htm (accessed March 23, 2010).

[84] Vinson Synan, *The Century of the Holy Spirit* (Nashville, TN: Thomas Nelson Publishers, 2001) is the best resource for a balanced theological presentation on the history of the Pentecostal and Charismatic Renewal movements. Synan has written over ten books on related subjects.

85 Synan, *The Century of the Holy Spirit*, 29. "The cessation of the charismata became part of the classical theology of the Western church. Augustion and Chrysostom were quoted by countless theologians and commentators in the centuries that followed."

86 For an excellent view of Charasmata traced from the early church to the present, see Eddie L. Hyatt, 2000 Years of *Charismatic Christianity* (Lake Mary, Flordia: Chrisma House,2002).

87 Charles H Spurgeon, "Spurgeon's Sermons" in Vinson Synan, *The Century of the Holy Spirit*, 129-130.

88 Vinson Synan, *The Century of the Holy Spirit* (Nashville, TN: Thomas Nelson Publishers, 2001). 32-33. Also see: *Christian History Magazine*, Issue 45, January 1, 1995.

89 Vinson Synan, *The Century of the Holy Spirit*, 34.

90 Synan, *The Century of the Holy Spirit*, 58. The Los Angeles Times reported it with headlines: *"Weird Babble of Tongues; New Sect of Fanatics is Breaking Loose. Wild Scene Last Night on Azusa Street. Gurgle of Wordless Talk by a Sister"*, quoting *The Los Angeles Times*, April 19, 1906.

91 Melvin Dieter, Anthony A. Hoekema, Stanley M Horton, J. Robertson McQuilkin, and John F. Walvoord. *Five Views on Sanctification Five Views on Sanctification*, 72.

92 Timothy Smith, *"Called unto Holiness,"* (Kansas City, MO: Nazarene Publishing House, 1962), 25. "The conflict spread to America when Dwight L. Moody; R.A. Toney, first president of Moody Bible Institute, Chicago; Adoniram J Gordon, father of Gordon College, Boston; A. B. Simpson, founder of the Christian and Missionary Alliance; and the evangelist J. Wilbur Chapman began to

Endnotes

propagate the Keswick version of the second blessing."
Synan, 20.

[93] Synan, 29.

[94] Reformation Ink, *Martin Luther* (1483-1546) http://home-page.mac.com/shanerosenthal/reformationink/mlconversion.htm (accessed November 11, 2009). The selection is taken from the *Preface to the Complete Edition of Luther's Latin Writings*. It was written by Luther in Wittenberg, 1545. This English edition is available in Luther's Works Volume 34, *Career of the Reformer IV* (St. Louis: Concordia Publishing House, 1960), 336-337. In the first few lines of this selection, Luther writes, "during that year;" the immediate context indicates he is referring to the year of Tetzel's death (July, 1519). This puts the date for Luther's conversion, in his own view, two years after the posting of the ninety-five theses. "Though I lived as a monk without reproach, I felt that I was a sinner before God with an extremely disturbed conscience. I could not believe that he was placated by my satisfaction. I did not love, yes, I hated the righteous God who punishes sinners, and secretly, if not blasphemously, certainly murmuring greatly, I was angry with God, and said, 'As if, indeed, it is not enough, that miserable sinners, eternally lost through original sin, are crushed by every kind of calamity by the law of the Decalogue, without having God add pain to pain by the gospel and also by the gospel threatening us with his righteousness and wrath!' Thus I raged with a fierce and troubled conscience. Nevertheless, I beat importunately upon Paul at that place, most ardently desiring to know what St. Paul wanted. At last, by the mercy of God, meditating day and night, I gave heed to the context of the words, namely, In it the righteousness of God is revealed, as it is written, 'He who through faith is righteous shall live.'

Living Inside Out

There I began to understand that the righteousness of God is that by which the righteous lives by a gift of God, namely by faith. And this is the meaning: the righteousness of God is revealed by the gospel, namely, the passive righteousness with which merciful God justifies us by faith, as it is written, 'He who through faith is righteous shall live. Here I felt that I was altogether born again and had entered paradise itself through open gates. There a totally other face of the entire Scripture showed itself to me. Thereupon I ran through the Scripture from memory. I also fount in other terms an analogy, as, the work of God, that is what God does in us, the power of God, with which he makes us wise, the strength of God, the salvation of God, the glory of God. And I extolled my sweetest word with a love as great as the hatred with which I had before hated the word 'righteousness of God.' Thus that place in Paul was for me truly the gate to paradise. Later I read Augustine's The Spirit and the Letter, where contrary to hope I found that he, too, interpreted God's righteousness in a similar way, as the righteousness with which God clothes us when he justifies us. Although this was heretofore said imperfectly and he did not explain all things concerning imputation clearly, it nevertheless was pleasing that God's righteousness with which we are justified was taught."

[95] Mark 12:32-34; Also in Deut. which serves as a summary of the Mosaic covenant, a heart of love and obedience is repeatedly seen as the whole: Deut 4:26-31; 6:4-9; 10:12-16. Note the responsibility to circumcise the heart and be no longer stubborn. Outward circumcision was merely a sign of the inner reality as Romans 2:29; 11:1, 13, 22; Chapter 29 of Deut anticipates the failure of heart and subsequent judgment. Chapter 30 begins, "when all theses things come upon you" anticipating a return: 2, 6,

Endnotes

8, and concludes with the famous text quoted by Paul in explaining the gospel of faith Romans 10:5-11.

[96] The Psalms are replete with regard to this truth: Ps 18:1-2; 25; 26:2; 36:7; 37; 78; 91;116; 118. Though Paul introduces the theoretical possibility of "faith without love" (1Cor 13:2) I take it to be similar to James "faith without works"- impossible.

[97] For a fuller discussion of Faith and Law see Greg L. Bahnsen, Walter C. Kaiser, Douglas J Moo, Wayne G. Strickland, Willem A. VanGemeren, Five *Views on Law and Gospel* edited by Stanley N. Gundry (Grand Rapids, MI: Zondervan, 1993).

[98] Faith in the scriptures includes both believing a message and trusting a person: One must "believe in the heart that God has raised Him from the dead" (Romans 10:9). There is content to Christian faith. It is not just a matter of believing in God, or having a positive attitude about life. Christian faith is "content full." It is rooted in the historical Jesus, the historical Israel, and the historical resurrection from the dead. But this history represents the testimony of the living God. Jesus claimed not only to be the son of God, but to be a sacrifice for sin. He proclaimed the kingdom throughout his life then established the kingdom through his death and resurrection. Even if we could prove the resurrection from the dead historically apart from the scriptures, we could not prove that Jesus died in order to accomplish our salvation or that he was raised by God for our justification apart from Gods word. These are tenets of faith. A discussion of 19th century Liberalism and the rise of Neo-Orthodoxy is beyond the scope of this chapter. See Millard Erickson, *Christian Theology* (Grand Rapids MI: Baker Book House), 661-681, for fuller discussion see N. T. Wright, *Who Was Jesus?* (Grand Rapids, MI: Eerdmans, 1993).

[99] J. I. Packer, "Faith," in *Evangelical Dictionary of Theology* edited by Walter A. Elwell (Grand Rapids, MN: Baker Book House, 1994), 399-402. Packer comments on the danger of this emphasis "The church grasped from the first that assent to apostolic testimony is the fundamental element in Christian faith; hence the concern of both sides in the Gnostic controversy to show that their tenets were genuinely apostolic. During the patristic period, however, the idea of faith was so narrowed that this assent came to be regarded as the whole of it.... The scholastics refined this view. They reproduced the equation of faith with credence, distinguishing between *fides informis* ("unformed" faith, bare orthodoxy) and fides *caritate formata* (credence "formed" into a working principle by the supernatural addition to it of the distinct grace of love). Both sorts of faith, they held, are meritorious works, though the quality of merit attaching to the first is merely congruent (rendering divine reward fit, though not obligatory), and only the second gains condign merit (making divine reward due as a matter of justice). Roman Catholicism still formally identifies faith with credence, and has added a further refinement by distinguishing between "explicit" faith (belief which knows its object) and "implicit" faith (uncomprehending assent to whatever it may be that the church holds). Only the latter (which is evidently no more than a vote of confidence in the teaching church and may be held with complete ignorance of Christianity) is thought to be required of laymen for salvation. But a mere docile disposition of this sort is poles apart from the biblical concept of saving faith.

The Reformers restored biblical perspectives by insisting that faith is more than orthodoxy, not *fides* merely, but *fiducia*, personal trust and confidence in God's mercy through Christ; that it is not a meritorious work, one facet of human righteousness, but rather an

Endnotes

appropriating instrument, an empty hand outstretched to receive the free gift of God's righteousness in Christ; that faith is God-given, and is itself the animating principle from which love and good works spontaneously spring; and that communion with God means, not an exotic rapture of mystical ecstasy, but just faith's everyday commerce with the Savior. Confessional Protestantism has always maintained these positions."

[100] Bennet, Arthur, ed., *The Valley of Vision* p. 103

[101] Watchman Nee, *Sit, Walk, Stand* (Wheaton, Il: Tyndale House, 1977), 14. These are the words of the martyr Watchman Nee (1903-1972) in his classic devotional commentary on the book of Ephesians. Nee was instrumental in the planting of the indigenous Chinese Church. Arrested in 1952, he proved the power of his words in his last 20 years in a communist prison where he continued to touch many with his faith and insights into the nature of the Christian life.

[102] Watchman Nee, *Sit, Walk, Stand*, 38.

[103] Nee, *Sit, Walk, Stand*, 55.

[104] Dr. and Mrs. Howard Taylor, *Hudson Taylor's Spiritual Secret* (Chicago, IL: Moody 1989).

[105] For if, when we were enemies, we were reconciled to God by the death of his Son, much more, being reconciled, we shall be saved by his life. Rom 5:10. Major W. Ian Thomas, *The Saving Life of Christ* (Grand Rapids MI: Zondervan, 1961).

[106] "The term *sabbatismos* occurs only here in the NT and it seems to have been deliberately substituted for *katapausis*. The substitution could take place because the writer has already connected *katapausis* with God's rest

Living Inside Out

on the seventh day and because that word is used for the Sabbath rest (Exodus 35:2; 2 Maccabees 15:1 LXX). But the use of *sabbatismos* elsewhere in extant Greek literature gives an indication of its more exact shade of meaning. It is used in Plutarch, *De Superstitione* 3 (*Moralia* 166A) of Sabbath observance. There are also four occurrences in post canonical literature that are independent of Hebrews 4:9. They are Justin, *Dial. c. Trph.* 23:3; Epiphanius, *Panar. haer* 30:2:2; *Martyrium Petri et Pauli cap.* 1; *Const. Ap.* 2:36:2. In each of these places the term denotes the observance or celebration of the Sabbath." D. A. Carson, *From Sabbath to Lord's Day* (Grand Rapids, MI: Zondervan, 1982) A.T Lincoln, 213.

See also: Leon Morris, "Hebrews" in T*he Expositors Bible Commentary* vol. 12, edited by Frank E. Gaebelein, 42. Leon Morris notes, "The term Sabbath Rest (*Sabbatismos*) is not attested before this passage and looks like the author's own coinage. He did not have a word for the kind of rest he had in mind so he made one up." (*but see above*) Morris comments that Buchanan has a long note on rest in which he surveys a number of opinions and rejects all spiritualizing interpretations. He (Buchanan) thinks that many scholars read their own ideas into rest. And he thinks it is impossible for the word to be used in a non-national, non-material sense. "They were probably expecting a rest that was basically of the same nature as the Israelites had anticipated all along." But surely this is precisely what the author is rejecting. He knew that Israel had been in its own land for centuries. There had been quite long periods of peace and independence, yet the promise of rest still remained unfulfilled. Jesus spoke of quite another kind of rest, rest for the souls of men (Matt 11:28-30). This is nearer to what the author means."

Endnotes

[107] Dale Ratzlaff, *Sabbath in Christ* (Glendale, AZ: Life Assurance Ministries, 1996), 287.

[108] Leon Morris, "Hebrews" in *The Expositors Bible Commentary* vol. 12, quoting the Mishnah, *Tamid* 7:4, 42.

[109] Geoffrey W. Bromiley, *Theological Dictionary of the New Testament* abridged vol. 1 (Grand Rapids, MI: Eerdmans, 1985), 989.

[110] Bromiley, *Theological Dictionary of the New Testament*, 990.

[111] See John 5:7-9. Also, Bromiley, *Theological Dictionary of the New Testament*, 991.

[112] Mark 2:25-26, Matthew 12:5, 42, John 5:18. D.A. Carson, *Commentary on John*. (Grand Rapids, MI: Eerdmans, 1991), 247. Dale Ratzlaff, *Sabbath in Christ*. (Glendale, AZ: Life Assurance Ministries, 1996), 148-161. D. A.Carson, *From Sabbath to Lord's Day* (Grand Rapids, MI: Zondervan, 1982).

[113] Carson, *From Sabbath to Lord's Day*, 231. Or Ratzlaff, *Sabbath in Christ*, 326. For listing of comments by the church fathers.

[114] D.A. Carson, *From Sabbath to Lord's Day*, 215.

[115] Leon Morris, "Hebrews" in *The Expositors Bible Commentary*, 38. "Those who disobeyed." The verb *apeitheo* means properly, "disobey," but some accept the meaning "disbelieve" (as NIV). This is possible since for the early Christian "the supreme disobedience was a refusal to believe their gospel" Walter Bauers, William Arndt, G. Wilber Gingrich, *A Greek-English Lexicon of the New Testament* (Chicago: Chicago Press, 1996),

82. But here it seems that we should take the meaning "disobey".

[116] David Brickner, *Christ in the Feast of Tabernacles* (Chicago, IL: Moody Publishers, 2006). The Tabernacle or "tent" represents the dwelling place of God. The Feast of Tabernacles celebrated not only the historical experience of God's dwelling with His people in the wilderness (Lev 23:43), but the anticipation of His dwelling again in the midst of the people (Ps 27:5, 2 Macc. 1, 1-2, 10, 18 and Zech 14:16-19). John portrays Jesus as the word of God dwelling (tabernacling) with us (Jn 1:14); Calling out at the Feast of Tabernacles, "I am the light (*Shekinah* and Pillar of Fire) (Jn 8:12); and concludes in 21:3 in lRevelation with the statement, "Behold, the tabernacle of God is with men, and he will dwell with them, and they shall be his people, and God himself shall be with them, *and be* their God."

[117] For a stimulating discussion of this principle as it relates both to bodybuilding and life I recommend Bill Phillips, *Body for Life* (NY, NY: Harper Collins Publishing, 1999), 42.

[118] G.K. Beale, *Commentary on the New Testament Use of the Old Testament*, Kindle Edition (Cambridge, MA; Baker Academic & Brazos Press, 2007).

[119] *Christian History Magazine* showcases almost all of these people.

[120] For a concise review of the different theological positions see Millard J Erickson, *Christian Theology* (Grand Rapids, MI.: Baker Book House, 1991), 519-540. Buswell and Clark defend the dichotomist position which grew in popularity after 381 (Council of Constantinople) becoming almost universal in later centuries;

Endnotes

trichotomism is found in Clement of Alexandria, Origin, Gregory of Nyssa, and Apollinarius-who was condemned as heretical leading to a decline in this position until the 19th century.

[121] Earl S. Kalland, "Deuteronomy" in *The Expositors Bible Commentary*, vol. 3, 64-65.

[122] David Van Biema and Jeff Cu, "Does God Want You to be Rich?" *Time Magazine*, September 18, 2006. A Time Magazine article entitled, *"Does God Want You to be Rich?"* contrasts two faith perspectives in contemporary evangelicalism. Joel Osteen, Pastor of Lakewood Church in Houston, TX. said, "I think God wants us to be prosperous. I think He wants us to be happy. I think He wants us to enjoy our lives. I don't think He wants us to be rich." Joyce Meyer said, "Who would want something where you are miserable, broken, ugly, and you have to muddle through until you get to heaven." Kirbyjon Caldwell has the opinion that, "God wants you to own land. The entire Old Testament is about land. (Ownership of) land represents that God is with you and that God has blessed you." The same article reported that 61 % of American Christians agree with the statement that God wants people to be financially prosperous.

On the other hand, Rick Warren has responded, "This idea that God wants everybody to be wealthy? Baloney! It is creating a false idol. You don't measure your self worth by your net worth." Both sides point to scriptures supporting their view: "You shall remember the Lord your God for it is He who gives you power to get wealth" (Deut 8:17). (See also Eccles 5:19-19; Mal 3:10; Luke 6:38; John 10:10). The other side argues: "It is easier for a camel to go through the eye of a needle than for a rich man to enter the kingdom of God" (Mark 10:25). (See also Matt. 6. 19-21; Mark 10:24-26; Luke 12:33; James

5:1-3). The same poll reports that American Christians are divided on whether God wants people to be poor. Most think wealth is one of His gifts, but half say poverty is one as well. When asked if you agreed or disagreed that material wealth is a sign of God's blessing, only 21% agreed with 73% disagreeing. Those who believe in a gospel of wealth are quick to point out that as faith is a requirement for prosperity, so lack of faith or unbelief is a requirement for poverty. "Ask and it shall be given." (But ask in faith.)

[123] Vinson Synan, *The Century of the Holy Spirit* (Nashville, TN: Thomas Nelson Publishers, 2001), 325-380.

[124] In Him you were also circumcised with the circumcision made without hands, by putting off the body of the sins of the flesh, by the circumcision of Christ, buried with Him in baptism, in which you also were raised with Him through faith in the working of God, who raised Him from the dead. And you, being dead in your trespasses and the uncircumcision of your flesh, He has made alive together with Him, having forgiven you all trespasses, (Col 2:11-13); Therefore put to death your members which are on the earth: fornication, uncleanness, passion, evil desire, and covetousness, which is idolatry. Because of these things the wrath of God is coming upon the sons of disobedience, in which you yourselves once walked when you lived in them. But now you yourselves are to put off all these: anger, wrath, malice, blasphemy, filthy language out of your mouth.(Col 3:6-8). In this context Paul argues that neither Jewish ritual nor Greek philosophy can achieve what God has already done and what we appropriate by faith. Both circumcision and baptism are initiating signs of their respective covenants pointing to spiritual realities which are to be appropriated by faith. The signs apart from faith are of no value. But both point

Endnotes

us to cutting/putting off the old and walking in newness of love, humility, obedience, and faith. (Deut 10:12-16; 30:6; Jer 4:1-4; 9:23-26; Col 2:6-3:17).

125 Bonhoeffer, D. *The Cost of Discipleship* p 80

126 Some MSS read few things are necessary, only one, not the number of dishes to be served but the priority of listening to Jesus.

127 Alister McGrath, *Christian Theology: An Introduction*, 2nd ed. (Oxford: Blackwell Publishers, 1997), 71, 72. *Sola Scriptura* (scripture alone) along with *Sola Fide* (faith alone) and the priesthood of all believers was said to be the watchword of the Reformation.

128 Mark Galli, 131 *Christians Everyone Should Know* (Nashville, TN: Holman Press, 2007), 213. John Wycliffe as a student at Oxford and later its leading philosopher and theologian was concerned with this corruption and the neglect of the scriptures: more time was spent discussing commentaries on the scriptures than the scriptures. In his inaugural lecture following completion of his Th.D., Wycliffe declared that to understand the scriptures one must first have an inner inclination toward spiritual truth, second, philosophical training, and thirdly, be living in faithful obedience. He continued that to be a priest, bishop or Pope one would need the same qualifications; and he suggested that corrupt church leaders should be stripped of their office. His understanding of the scriptures led to deepening conflict: Christ, in scripture, had called his disciples to poverty, not the wealth of Rome; private confession was, "not used by the Apostles"; the granting of indulgences "blasphemes the wisdom of God"- another reference to the authoritative scriptures. Brought to trial twice (1377 and 1378) and accused on 18 counts he argued, "I have followed the Sacred Scriptures

Living Inside Out

and the holy doctors". Further, the pope and the church were second in authority to the scriptures. Because of his popularity in England and the Great Schism of 1378 at which time two rival popes were elected, Wycliffe was merely placed under "house arrest" and continued his work. He began translating the Bible from the Latin Vulgate into English. It seems amazing in our day that this would incur the wrath of the Church. But it did. "By this translation, the scriptures have become vulgar, and they are more available to the lay, and even to women who can read, than they were to learned scholars, who have a high intelligence. So the pearl of the gospel is scattered and trodden underfoot by swine."

[129] Alister McGrath, *Christian Theology*, 212.

[130] Mark Galli, ed., 131 *Christians Everyone Should Know* (Nashville, TN: Holman Press, 2007), 369-371. A pastor and professor at the university in Prague, Hus was fascinated by the writings of Wycliffe, especially the teaching that the scripture is the ultimate authority. Just as Wycliffe, Huss condemned corruption in the clergy and defined the church as the body of Christ under the headship of Christ alone, not the pope. Like Wycliffe he was supported by his countrymen and his followers banned together in the *Unitas Fratrem, the United Brethren a precursor of the Moravian Ch*urch. Traveling under the Emperor's safe conduct and lauded along the way, he attended the Council of Constance in 1415, expecting to discuss the scriptures but was arrested, condemned and burned as a heretic without any true hearing. The same council ordered the bones of Wycliffe exhumed and burned.

[131] Galli, ed., 131 *Christians Everyone Should Know*, 369.

Endnotes

132 R.W.F. Wooten, "Translating the Bible," *Introduction to the History of Christianity* edited by Tim Dowley (Minneapolis, MN: Fortress Press, 1995), 654.

133 Richard N. Soulen, *Handbook of Biblical Criticism*, 2nd ed. (Atlanta, GA: John Knox Press, 1981), 190. *Tanak*, The Hebrew abbreviation for the Old Testament derived from the initial letters of the names of its three dividions; Torah (Pentateuch), *Nebiim* (early and later prophets), *Ketubim* (writings or *Hagiographa*-sacred writings which comprise the third division, the remainder of the OT).

134 Paul's writings were considered to be on the same level as the authoritative Scriptures 2 Peter 3:16. For a full discussion see Bruce Metzger, *The Canon of the NT* (Oxford, NY: Oxford University Press, 1997).

135 Something prescribed, a statute or due, so prescribed portion or allowance of food, see Gen 47:22, Prov 30:8, 31:13, Ezek 16:27. Francis Brown, S.R. Driver, Charles A Briggs,eds. *The New Brown-Driver-Briggs-Gesenius Hebrew and English Lexicon.* (Peabody, MA: Hendrickson Publishers. 1979), 349.

136 Richard N. Soulen, *Handbook of Biblical Criticism*, 2nd edition, (Atlanta, GA: John Knox Press, 1981), 87, 25, 186, 196.

137 David J. Bosch, *Transforming Mission: Paradigm Shifts in Theology of Mission* (Maryknoll, NY: 1998), 195.

138 David J. Bosch, *Transforming Mission*, 197. In its Jewish context the people of God related to Him as a deliverer. "The Hebrew concept *yasha*, to save, primarily means to save people from danger and catastrophe or to free captives; the Greek concept *soteria* tended to refer to being rescued from one's bodily existence, being relieved from

Living Inside Out

the burden of a material existence." See also page 194. "Increasingly the emphasis was laid on the immortality of the soul which Lactantius labeled 'the greatest good.' The Eucharist became the 'medicine of immortality.' It became more important to re flect on what God is in Himself than to consider the relationship in which people stand to God. See also page 195 God's revelation was no longer understood as God's self communication in events but as the communication of the truths about the being of God in three hypostases and the one person of Christ in two natures. The various church counsels were intent on producing definitive statements of faith.... A comparison between the Sermon on the Mount and the Nicene Creed confirms this point. The entire tenor of the Sermon is ethical. It is devoid of metaphysical speculation. The later, in contrast is structured within a metaphysical framework, makes a number of doctrinal statements, and says nothing about the believer's conduct.

[139]   Michael S. Smith, "Christian Ascetics and Monks," in *Introduction to the History of Christianity* (Minneapolis, MN: Fortress Press, 1995), 212-224. The monastery became the center of culture, civilization, and the repository of truth. Not all monasteries emphasized the same commitment to the scriptures: for some the primary focus of spirituality was prayer, manual labor, simple separation from outside activities, or even silence. But for others the focus of preserving the scriptures, copying them, studying, and chanting them became preeminent.

[140]   Bruce A. Demarst, "Interpreting the Bible," in *Introduction to the History of Christianity*, 304.

[141]   Bosch J. *Transforming Mission*, 242.

[142]   John H. Yoder and Alan Kreider, "The Anabaptists," in *Introduction to the History of Christianity*, 403.

Endnotes

[143] 2 Thessalonians 2:15, 3:6-12.

[144] John H. Yoder and Alan Kreider, "The Anabaptists," in *Introduction to the History of Christianity*, 404.

[145] Sydney E Ahlstrom, *A Religious History of the American People* (New Haven and London: Yale University Press, 1974), 182, 212 – 213. Regarding Rhode Island Ahlstrom notes "it is the first commonwealth to make religious liberty, (not simply a degree of toleration) a cardinal principal of its corporate existence and to maintain the separation of church and state on these grounds."
Pennsylvania "was to become a crossroads of the nature... a world center of Quaker influence... a Presbyterian stronghold... a dominant force in the organization and expansion of the Baptists. The Protestant Episcopal church in the United States would be constituted in Philadelphia... its toleration would allow the Roman Catholic church to lay deep foundations on which later immigration would build. The German Reform church had its strength in this state. "Moravians, Mennonites, Amish, Schwenkfelders, Dunkers, and other German groups including Rosicrucians would flourish there. From its western edge the Restoration movement of Thomas and Alexander Campbell would be launched. In Philadelphia, too the African Methodist Episcopal Church –The first independent Negro organization had its origins. As the chief residence of Benjamin Franklin the seat of the American Philosophical Society, and the birth place of both the declaration of Independence and the Constitution, Philadelphia also served as a symbol to the Enlightenment's vast contribution to American religion. Finally, it was in this province that all of these groups experienced the difficulties and discovered the possibilities for fruitful coexistence that American democracy was

Living Inside Out

to offer. Within the borders of no other state was so much American church history anticipated or enacted."

[146] Bosch, *Transforming Mission*, 246. "Whereas the Reformers no longer consider the 'Great Commission' as binding, (cf Warneck 1906:14,17f; Littell 1972: 114-116), no Biblical texts appear more frequently in the Anabaptist confessions of faith and court testimonies than the Mattean and Markan versions of the 'Great Commission,' along with Psalm 24:1. They were among the first to make the commission mandatory for all believers."

[147] John H. Yoder and Alan Kreider, "The Anabaptists," in *Introduction to the History of Christianity*, 404.

[148] R. F. W. Wooten, "Translating the Bible," in I*ntroduction to the History of Christianity*, 654.

[149] William Carey, *An Enquiry into the Obligations of Christians to use Means for the Conversion of the Heathens* (White Fish, MT: Kissinger Publishing, LLC, 2004). Original document was published in 1792.

[150] R. F. W. Wooten, "Translating the Bible," in *Introduction to the History of Christianity* Dowley, 656.

[151] *The Jesus Film Project*, http://www.jesusfilm.org/ (accessed 2 February 2009). Every four seconds, some-where in the world, another person indicates a decision to follow Christ after viewing the "JESUS" film. Every four seconds... that's 21,600 people per day, 648,000 per month and more than 7.8 million per year! That's like the population of the entire city of Seattle, WA, coming to Christ every 27.5 days. And yet, if you are like most people, you may have never even heard of it. Called by some "one of the best-kept secrets in Christian missions," a number of mission experts have acclaimed the film as one of the greatest evangelistic tools of all time. Since

Endnotes

1979 the "JESUS" film has been viewed by over 6 billion people across the globe, and has resulted in more than 225 million men, women and children indicating decisions to follow Jesus.

[152] *The Passion of the Christ* directed by Mel Gibson 2003, http://www.passionofthechrist.com/splash.htm (accessed October 26, 2008).

[153] *The Navigators*, http://www.navigators.org/us/aboutus (accessed February 3 2009). "Navigators have invested our lives in people for over 75 years, coming alongside them one to one to study the Bible, develop a deepening prayer life, and memorize and apply Scripture. An inter- denominational, nonprofit organization, The Navigators is dedicated to helping people navigate spiritually, *to know Christ and to make Him known* as they look to Him and His Word to chart their lives. Our ultimate goal is to equip them to fulfill 2 Timothy 2:2. To teach what they have learned to others."

[154] "The Hand Illustration," http://www.navigators.org/us/resources/images/The%20Word%20Hand.pdf (accessed February 3, 2009).

[155] "The Wheel Illustration," http://www.navigators.org/us/resources/illustrations/items/The%20Wheel%20-%20Overview%20of%20the%20Wheel (accessed February 3, 2009).

[156] "Topical Memory System," http://www.navigators.org/us/resources/illustrations/items/Topical%20Memory%20System (accessed February 3, 2009). This chart has a good overview of the Bible Memory system.

[157] Betty Lee Skinner, *Daws* (Grand Rapids, MO: Zondervan Publishing,1974), 384.

Living Inside Out

[158] Skinner, *Daws*, 379.

[159] Ibid,379, 385.

[160] See also Jeremiah 44:10.

[161] Dietrich Bonhoeffer, *Life Together* (New York, NY: Harper and Row, 1954), 77.

[162] Bonhoeffer, *Life Together*, 94-95. "He who would learn to serve must first learn to think little of himself. Let no man 'think of himself more highly than he ought to think' (Rom 12:3). 'This is the highest and most profitable lesson, truly to know, and to despise, ourselves. To have no opinion of ourselves, and to think always well and highly of others, is great wisdom and perfection' (Thomas a Kempis). 'Be not wise in your own conceits.'" (Romans 12:16)

[163] Charles Colson, *A Dangerous Grace*. (Nashville, TN: Zondervan Publishers, 1994), 30.

[164] Colin Brown, Beyeruther and Bietenhard, ed., *Dictionary of New Testament Theology*, vol. 1. (Grand Rapids, MI: Zondervan Publishing, 1986), 639.

[165] Rom 15:26; 2Cor 8:4; 9:13; Gal 6:6; Phil 4; 15; 1Tim 6:17; Heb 13:16.

[166] Michael A. Smith, "Spreading the Good News," in *Introduction to the History of Christianity* edited by Tim Dowley (Minneapolis, MN: Fortress Press, 1995), 78- 80.

[167] David J. Bosch, *Transforming Mission: Paradigm Shifts in Theology of Mission* (Maryknoll, NY: Orbis Books, 1998), 230- 236.

Endnotes

168 Philip Jacob Spener, and Theodore G. Tappert, ed., *Pia Desideria*. (Eugene, OR: Wipf and Stock Publishers, 2002).

169 "The Moravians and John Wesley." *Christian History Magazine*, Issue 1, January 1, 1982, http://www.christianitytoday.com/ch/1982/issue1/128.html?start=1 (accessed February 10, 2009).

170 Mark Shaw, *10 Great Ideas from Church History* (Downer's Grove, Ill.: InterVarsity Press, 1997), 138.

171 Shaw, 141.

172 Ibid., 143.

173 Mark A Noll, Nathan O Hatch, George M. Marsden, David F. Wells, John D Woodbridge, eds. *Eerdmans' Handbook to Christianity in America*. (Grand Rapids, MI.: Eerdman's Publishing. 1983), 188.

174 A. F. Walls, "Societies for Mission," in. *Introduction to the History of Christianity* edited by Dowley, 571.

175 A. F. Walls, "Societies for Mission, 573.

176 Dietrich Bonhoeffer, *the Cost of Discipleship. revised* and unabridged ed. (New York: Collier Books Macmillan Publishers, 1963) 284.

177 Shaw, *Ten Great Ideas from Church History*, 195.

178 Eberhard Bethge, *Dietrich Bonhoeffer* (New York, NY: Harper and Row, 1977), 20.

179 Bonhoeffer fled to England where he carried on a correspondence with the churches in the nation culminating in the Barmen Declaration. Drafted by Karl Barth, it challenged the right of the church to submit itself to political

authorities in contradiction to the scriptures. "We repudiate the false teaching that the church can turn over her message and ordinances at will or according to some dominant ideological and political convictions." John Leith, ed, *Creeds of the Churches*, 3rd ed. (Louisville, KY: John Knox Press,1982).521. This document confronted the Fuhrer Principle which had given Hitler sweeping powers within the church which had in turn endorsed the ideal of Aryan Supremacy and Anti-Semitism, actually excluding Jewish Christians from their churches.

[180] Eberhard Bethge, *Dietrich Bonhoeffer*, 385.

[181] Bonhoeffer, *The Cost of Discipleship* (New York: Collier Books Macmillan Publishers, 1963). Bonhoeffer, Life Together (New York, NY: Harper and Row, 1954).

[182] Shaw, *10 Great Ideas from Church History*, 200-207.

[183] Bonhoeffer, *Life Together*, 31-33.

[184] Bonhoeffer, *Life Together*, 32.

[185] Bonhoeffer, Dietrich, *The Cost of Discipleship*, 47.

[186] Bonhoeffer, *The Cost of Discipleship*, 285.

[187] Bonhoeffer, *Life Together*, 122.

[188] The best introduction to this subject is Moishe Rosen, *Christ in the Passover*, (Chicago, Il: Moody Press, 1979).

[189] Chaim Raphael, *A Feast of History: The Drama of Passover Through the Ages* (Washington DC: B'nai B'rith Books, 1993), 11-32.

[190] Exodus 12:13, 23; cf. Isaiah 31:5.

[191] An excellent overview of the theology of the Old Testament in terms of themes is provided by Walter

Kaiser, "Theology of the Old Testament," in *The Expositor's Bible Commentary*, vol. 1 edited by Frank E. Gaebelein (Grand Rapids, MI: Zondervan, 1992), 285-305.

[192] Multiple commentaries on the Haggadah provide backgrounds to this Seder: Rabbi Joseph Elias, *The Haggadah/Passover Haggadah with Translation and New Commentary Based on Talmudic, Midrashic and Rabbinic Sources* (Brooklyn, NY: Mesorah Publications, 1994). Philip Goodman, *The Passover Anthology* (Philadelphia, Pa: The Jewish Publication Society, 1993).

[193] Joseph Elias, *The Haggada: Passover Haggadah*, 162-163. This is the Afikomen or dessert which some sages saw as representative of the sacrificial lamb itself.

[194] Moishe and Ceil Rosen, *Christ in the Passover* (Chicago, Il: Moody Press, 1979), 61-72.

[195] Mark 14:25.

[196] Rabbi Dr I. Epstein, ed.. *The Babylonian Talmud*. (London, England: Soncina Press 1936). The Tosefta, The Mishnah, and The Talmud all include major divisions discussing these themes as central to the Passover:

[197] W. Harold Mare, "1 Corinthians," in *The Expositor's Bible Commentary*, vol. 10 edited by Frank E. Gaebelein (Grand Rapids, MI: Zondervan, 1992), 218-219.

[198] 1 Corinthians 11:26; Exodus 12:26-27; 13:8-10.

[199] Marvin R Wilson, *Our Father Abraham* (Grand Rapids, MI: Eerdmans, 1989), 74-84.

[200] Genesis 12:1-3; 18:18; 22:18; 50:20; Psalm115.

Living Inside Out

[201] Wilson, *Our Father Abraham*, 24-27. See also Acts 15, Galatians; Philippians 3.

[202] David J.Bosch, *Transforming Mission: Paradigm Shifts in Theology of Mission*, 56-83.

[203] Wagner, Clarence H, *Lessons from the Land of the Bible: Revealing more of God's Word* (Jerusalem, Israel. Jerusalem, Israel: Bridges for Peace, 2003), 155. When Hadrian expelled all Jews from Jerusalem in 135AD, allowing them to return only one day each year on *TishaB'Av* to mourn the temples destruction, this pro-hibition extended to Jewish Christians. It is at this time we see the first Greek name in the leadership of the Jerusalem church.

[204] Wilson, *Our Father Abraham*, 62-84. (This work has a nice overview of these issues).

[205] Dan Gruber, *The Church and the Jews: The Biblical Relationship* (Hanover, NH: Elijah Publishing, 1997), 20. Origen is often seen as the father of the allegor-ical method of interpretation. He is probably one if the greatest scholars of the early church and certainly the most prolific author of the second century. Though devoted to the authority of the scriptures his method of interpretation ultimately shifts authority from the texts itself to the interpreter. He produced what is referred to as the Hexapla which is a parallel text with the Hebrew side by side with the Greek translations of Aquila, Symmachus, and Theodotion as well as the Septuagint. He then produced volumes of commentaries expounding three levels of meaning of any Biblical text: first the lit-eral meaning, secondly a moral application to the soul, and finally an allegorical or spiritual meaning revealing deep mysteries of the Christian faith. Though admired by most of the Greek fathers of the third and fourth centuries

Endnotes

for his scholarship, critical investigation of scripture, and vast learning, his system produced numerous errors and some of the doctrines he believed and taught were considered heretical. As a matter of fact, during his life time he was excommunicated by two church counsels held in Alexandria in 231 and 232. Even today some of his teachings would be considered heretical enough to place him outside the believing church. Nevertheless, his writings had a profound impact on the church as a whole.

206 Gruber, *The Church and the Jews: The Biblical Relationship*, 21.

207 Origen as quoted by Gruber, 21.

208 Gruber, 22.

209 Clarence H. Wagner, *Lessons from the Land of the Bible: Revealing more of God's Word*, quoting Justin Martyr (Jerusalem Israel: Bridges for Peace, 2000), 156.

210 "Justin Martyr," in *A Dictionary of Early Christian Belief* edited by David W Bercot (Peabody, MA: Hendrickson Publishers, 1998). 1.263.

211 "Irenaeus 1.493," in *The Ante-Nicene Fathers* edited by Alexander Roberts and James Donaldson (Grand Rapids, MI: Eerdmans, 1978-1983).1.493.

212 Roberts and Donaldson, eds., *The Ante-Nicene Fathers*, 1:464

213 Wilson, *Our Father Abraham*, 95. In 135AD Also: When Hadrian crushed the Bar Kochba revolt he expelled not only Jews, but the Jewish Christians from Jerusalem. We find the first Greek name in leadership of the Jerusalem church at this time. It was Hadrian, to who changed the name of Israel, Judea, Samaria, and Galilee to Syria

Living Inside Out

Palestina (Palestine) linking the land to the arch enemies of the Jewish people, the Philistines, in an attempt to erase any ongoing right to the land. This tactic continues today. Clarence H. Wagner, *Lessons from the Land of the Bible*, 155. Also: Under Roman law Judaism was a legal religion *(religio licita)* since it predated Rome but Christianity, postdating Rome was considered an illegal religion *(religio ilicita)*. Early Christian apologists attempting to avoid persecution sought to cast Christianity as an extension to Judaism however Rome resisted this as did the Jewish community. Later when Christianity became the religion of the state, it passed laws against the Jews in retribution. Wagner, *Lessons from the Land of the Bible* ,156. Under Roman law Judaism was a legal religion *(religio licita)* since it predated Rome but Christianity, postdating Rome was considered an illegal religion *(religio ilicita)*. Early Christian apologists attempting to avoid persecution sought to cast Christianity as an extension to Judaism however Rome resisted this as did the Jewish community. Later when Christianity became the religion of the state, it passed laws against the Jews in retribution. Wagner, 156.

[214]   Ibid., 95.

[215]   Dr. Gary Hedrick, Rabbi Loren, ed. *Replacement Theology Its Origins and Errors* http://www.shema. com/Combating%20Replacement%20Theology/crt-004.php (accessed March 3, 2010). "One defender of Replacement Theology writes: "The Jewish nation no longer has a place as the special people of God; that place has been taken by the Christian community which fulfills God's purpose for Israel" (Bruce Waltke, "Kingdom Promises as Spiritual," in *Continuity and Discontinuity: Perspectives on the Relationship Between the Testaments*, ed. John S. Feinberg (Wheaton, Illinois: Crossway, 1987),

Endnotes

275. This is how one evangelical theologian summarized the essence of supersessionism in a paper he presented at the Evangelical Theological Society annual meeting a few years ago: "The issue is whether national Israel as an administrative structure is still in the plan of God" (*"A Future for Israel in Covenant Theology: The Untold Story"* by R. Todd Mangum, Instructor in Historical and Systematic Theology at Biblical Theological Seminary in Hatfield, Pennsylvania [November 16, 2000], 20. Theological Basis: Replacement Theology is closely associated with Reformed (or Covenant) Theology, the brand of theology historically linked to John Calvin (1509-1564) and the Protestant Reformation. Reformed/ Covenant Theology, in turn, is closely associated with amillennialism, an eschatological view with a spiritualized (rather than literal-historical) interpretation of the prophetic Scriptures. The natural affinity these views (that is, Replacement Theology and amillennialism) seem to have for each other is understandable because Replacement Theology relies so heavily on a non literal and allegorical interpretation of the biblical promises to Israel. Although many of the early Reformers and Puritans - including even Calvin himself - wrote about the nation of Israel one day being restored by the grace of God and experiencing a national regeneration, that is an increasingly marginalized, minority view in Reformed Christianity today (which is ironic, since we have seen the amazing rebirth of the nation of Israel, just as the Word of God predicted!). And even among those who allow for an end-time work of the Spirit of God among the Jewish people, there is still a reluctance to acknowledge that God is not finished with His people Israel as a nation, or to acknowledge the prospect of a future Kingdom on the Earth. This view stands in contrast to the teachings of Dispensational Premillennialism, which affirms the continuing role that Israel plays (in tandem

Living Inside Out

with the Church) in the outworking of God's plan of redemption."

[216] Gruber, *The Church and the Jews: The Biblical Relationship* (Hanover, NH.: Elijah Publishing, 1997), 30-41.

[217] Gruber, 41.

[218] Colin Buchanan, "The Sacraments Are Developed," in *Introduction to the History of Christianity*, 265-266. Though the doctrine of transubstantiation was not fully developed until the Forth Lateran Council (1215), sacramentalism was well on its way by the sixth century. Ratramnus in the ninth century was one of the last writers to describe the elements at the Eucharist as symbols but his book was condemned in 1050. He opposed the Paschasius who took the realist doctrine a step further towards transubstantiation which was finally adopted as orthodox at the Fourth Leteran Council. This taught that the underlying permanent reality of the bread and wine are changed at consecration into Christ's body and blood (Luke 22:14-16). In the early 12th century Hugo of St Victor listed 30 sacraments in keeping with Augustine's earlier writings. Shortly thereafter, Peter Lombard produced a tightly organized scheme of seven sacraments which were adopted as Orthodox... the doctrine of transubstantiation itself led to the baring of lay people from the wine lest the spilling of transubstantiated wine should occur and cause scandal. Theories were developed that through the offerings of Christ Himself under the forms of bread and wine in the sacrifice of the Mass, atonement was made for both living and dead. This in turn led to the later medieval proliferation of Masses for the dead."

[219] Alister E McGrath, *Christian Theology: An Introduction* (Crowley Road, Oxford: Blackwell Publishers, 1997),

Endnotes

495.The English term sacrament is from the Latin sacramentum translating the Greek *mysterion*. The mystery of God's saving work in Christ was tied to the visible signs of baptism and the Lord's Supper from the beginning but during the third and fourth centuries, this linkage is developed in North Africa in the writing of Tertullian, Cyprian, and Augustine. The New Testament Greek uses mystery in the singular, Tertullian translated sacrament both as the singular mystery and in the plural referring to individual signs (sacraments) associated with salvation. The normal Latin meaning included the concept of a sacred oath linking the sign to the pledge

[220] McGrath, *Christian Theology*, 503.

[221] McGrath, 500.

[222] Ibid., 499. "In his reforming treatise of 1520, *The Babylonian Captivity of the Church*, Luther launched a major attack on the Catholic understanding of sacraments. Taking advantage of the latest humanist philological scholarship, he asserted that the Vulgate use of term sacramentum was largely unjustified on the basis of the Greek text. See also: Martin Luther, *Three Treatises*, Helmut T. Lehman, ed. (Minneapolis, MN: Fortress Press, 1966), 113ff.

[223] Michael Smith, "Worship and the Christian Year," in *Introduction to the History of Christianity*, 152. Christian worship in the second and third century was almost entirely in Greek though in a few places local languages such as Syriac, Coptic or Latin were probably beginning to be used. In general services in this period were extempore, the local Bishop being free to pray or preach as the spirit led within certain fairly broad guidelines. There were a few fixed formulas in use including the dialogue lift up your hearts *{sursum corda}* The hymn beginning

Living Inside Out

holy, holy, holy or *{sanctus}* based on Isaiah 6 and the "words of institution" commemorating the Last Supper at the communion service."

[224] J.I. Packer, "the Faith of the Protestants," in *Introduction to the History of Christianity*, 374. J. I Packer, in summarizing Luther's beliefs regarding sacraments notes, "Luther affirmed the final authority of a self interpreted Bible and rejected non scriptural beliefs. He taught a spiritual doctrine of the church. He depicted it as a serving Priesthood of believer as against the Medieval ideal of the church as a hierarchical institution under the Bishop of Rome administering salvation through sacraments. Luther taught the infants were regenerated in baptism through infant faith. He reaffirmed the 'real presence" of Christ's body *in, with, and under* the Eucharistic bread. Calvin and the Reformed theologians generally rejected these ideas holding that Christ's body is *in heaven* and not here and that Christ encounters his people at the Communion table, not by bodily presence in the elements but by the Spirits presence and power in their hearts."

[225] Three recent works do begin to address this issue: Carmine Di Sante, *Jewish Prayer: The Origins of Christian Liturgy* (Mahwah, N.J: Paulist Press, 1991); Eugene Fisher, *The Jewish Roots of Christian Liturgy* (Mahwah, N.J: Paulist Press, 1990); and Paul F. Bradshaw and Lawrence A. Hoffman, *The Making of Jewish and Christian Worship* (Notre Dame, In: University of Notre Dame Press, 1991).

[226] *The Complete Writings of Menno Simons*, C.1496-1561, Leonard Verduin , tr. J. C. Wenger, ed. (Scottdale, Pa: Herald Press, 1986) ,143 "Hence the paschal lamb was called the Lord's Pesach, that is, Passover, The sign stood for the reality, for the lamb was not the Passover, although it was called that, but it only signified the

Endnotes

Passover, as was said. So in the Holy Supper the bred is called the body, and the wine the blood of the Lord: the sign signifies the reality."

[227] Dan Gruber. *The Church and the Jews: The Biblical Relationship* (Hanover, NH: Elijah Publishing, 1997), 270-305.

[228] A. Lindt, "John Calvin," in *Introduction to the History of Christianity*, 381.

[229] G.R Potter, *Huldrych Zwingli* (Cambridge: Cambridge University Press, 1977), 208-209.

[230] Miri Rubin, *Corpus Christi: The Euchrist in Late Midevil Culture* (Cambridge, England: Cambridge University Press, 1992). Eamon Duffy, *The Stripping of the Altars* (New Haven, Ct: Yale University Press, 1994), 100. Both works provide excellent overviews of the excesses in this era. Also: Martin Luther, *Table Talk*, translated by William Hazlitt (Philadelphia, PA: The Lutheran Publication Society, 2004) described this as the "abominable idolatry of elevating the sacrament on high to show it to the people, which has no approbation of the Fathers, and was introduced only to confirm the errors touching the worship thereof, as though bread and wine lost their substance and retained only the form, smell, and taste. This the papist called transubstantiation, and darkened the right use of the sacrament; whereas, even in Popedom at Milan at Ambrose's time to the present day, they never held or observed in the Mass either Cannon or elevation or the Dominus vobiscum." (The Lord be with you). He adds, "The operative cause of the sacrament is the Word and institution of Christ, who ordained it. The substance is bread and wine, prefiguring the true body and blood of Christ, which is spiritually received by faith." Luther, *Table Talk*, 228.

Living Inside Out

[231] Thomas å. Kempis, *The Imitation of Christ* (New Kensington, Pa.: Whitaker House, 1981), 221-222.

[232] Thomas å. Kempis, *The Imitation of Christ* , 233. O Lord Jesus, how greats are the pleasure of the devout soul that feasts with Thee in Thy banquet. Where there is set no other food to be eaten but Thyself, the only beloved and most to be desired above all the desires of the heart. Ibid., 241. Two things I have perceived to be exceedingly necessary to me in this life without which this miserable life would be intolerable to me. When I am detained in the prison of this body, I acknowledge myself to stand in need of food and light. Thou has given therefore unto me in my weakness Thy sacred companionship for the refreshment of my soul and body (John 6:51). And Thou has set 'as a lamp unto my feet (Psalm 119:105) Thy word. Without these two I shall not be able to live. The word of God is the light of my soul and Thyself the bread of life. These also may be called the two tables set on this side and on that in the treasure house of the church. å. Kempis, 242-243. All of this is written in the context of commentary on Holy Communion. Commenting on mysticism within the Catholic Reformation which was not particularly welcomed by the Church of Rome, Robert Linder writes, "Mysticism makes the institutional church nervous because carried to its logical conclusion it does away with the priesthood and the sacraments. They mystic emphasizes personal religion and his or her direct relationship to God. The ultimate goal of the mystic is to lose himself or herself in the essence of God." Robert Linder, "The Catholic Reformation," in *Introduction to the History of Christianity*, 423.

[233] The last is often referred to as the Thirty Years War from 1618 to 1648 which represented religious struggles with political overtones. The Peace of Westphalia was

Endnotes

hammered out in a series of conferences between 1643 and 1648 in the province of Westphalia in Germany.

[234] John E. Smith and Harry Stout, ed., *Jonathan Edwards Reader* (New Haven: Yale University Press, 1995), 59, 63. *Johnathan Edwards on Revival* (Carlisle, Pa: The Banner of Truth Publishing, 1995), 9, 13. George M Marsden, *Johathan Edwards: A Life* (New Haven, Conn.: Yale University Press, 2003).

[235] Leigh Eric Schmidt, *Holy Fairs; Scotland and the Making of Revivalism* (Grand Rapids MI: Eerdmans Publishing, 2001).

[236] Schmidt, *Holy Fairs; Scotland and the Making of Revivalism*, 19.

[237] Schmidt, 134-135. The Five Articles had included (1) the necessity to receive the Lord's Supper kneeling, (2) permission for private dispensing of the Eucharist to the sick, (3) the acceptance of private baptisms, (4) catechetical instruction of the young that would culminate in confirmation from a bishop, (5) reinstatement of the Holy Days including Good Friday, Pentecost, and Christmas.

[238] Schmidt, *Holy Fair*, 134-135.

[239] Schmidt, 70. Scottish Presbyterians in the New World held similar services and one detailed account from Boothbay, Maine in the 1760s records in John Beath's church; six cups, three large flagons, six large platters, and four large dishes made of "the best hard metal and the most elegant fashion" were procured. The cups were large cups used as common cups for the various tables set up for the communion. The large flagons would be filled with wine, even as the large platters would hold the loaves of bread to be shared. The clothes used as coverings for the tables and the elements had to be the purest

white without wrinkle or blemish. All care was given for these vessels were to represent the purity of Christ and the gospel.

240 Ibid., 146.

241 Schmidt, *Holy Fairs*, 158-166.

242 Schmidt, 172.

243 Ibid., 188.

244 This was the largest recorded sacramental service in Scotland paralleling the Great Awakening. Whitfield attended the August gathering in 1742, where it was estimated that thirty-thousand were in attendance. He later wrote that this communion was the highlight of his career for "such a Passover has not yet been heard of." From Paul K.Conkin, *Cane Ridge America's Pentecost*, (Madison, WI: The University of Wisconsin Press, 1989), 22.

245 Paul K.Conkin, *Cane Ridge America's Pentecost*, 3. Cane Ridge has a special epochal position in American religious history. From August 6-12, 1801, in the first summer of a new century thousand of people   gathered in and around the small Cane Ridge meeting house in Bourbon County in central Kentucky to prepare for and the to celebrate the Lord's Supper, Never before in Americana had so many people attended this type of sacramental occasion. Never before had such a diversity of seizures or "physical exercised" affected, or afflicted, so many people. The Cane Ridge sacrament has become a legendary event, the clearest approximation to an American Pentecost, prelude to a Christian century. It arguably remains the most important religious gathering in all of American history, both for what it symbolized and for the effects that flowed from it.

Endnotes

246 Paul K.Conkin, *Cane Ridge America's Pentecos*t, 4.

247 Ibid., 9-10. They had recovered a Pauline Christianity which Conkin describes this way: Paul himself knew the ecstasy produced by the Spirit, at times established his credentials among Gentile Christians by his ecstatic speech. The gifts of the Spirit were also necessary for salvation, but like church membership, good deeds or participation in the sacraments, they were logically, not causally, necessary. Each is inseparably linked to faith, but as a corollary of faith and not its cause. Each is meaningless or impossible apart from love, which is the all-important gift of the Spirit.

248 Paul K.Conkin, *Cane Ridge America's Pentecost*, 91. One eye witness account describes it this way, Assembled in the woods, ministers preaching day and night; the camp illuminated with candles, on trees, at wagons, and at the tent; persons falling down, and carried out of the crowd, by those next to them, and taken to some convenient place, where prayer is made for them; some Psalm or Hymn suitable to the occasion, sung. If they speak, with what they say is attended to, being very solemn and affecting- many are struck under such exhortations. But if they do not recover soon, praying and singing is kept up, alternatively, and sometimes a minister exhorts over them- for generally a large group of people collect, and stand around, paying attention to prayers and joining in singing. Now suppose 20 of these groups around; a minister engaged in preaching to a large congregation , in the middle, some mourning, some rejoicing, and great solemnity on every countenance, and you will form some imperfect ideal of the extraordinary work!

249 Conkin, 102. For good reason all the pre-rational experiences at Cane Ridge and the oversimplified theological understanding frightened some of the Presbyterian

clergy. They represented a venerable religious tradition, one tied to systematic   doctrines. It was a traditional that justified, even exalted, deep feelings or a type of experiential religion, but always in the context of proper understanding. The complementary poles of experience and reason broke apart at Cane Ridge At best, the doctrinal component lost precision and distinctiveness and lapsed into a vague, general, loose, sentimental, or even visceral version of Christianity. Even the ecumenical flavor- Cane Ridge was a meeting ground for doctrine diversity-threatened the Presbyterian tradition. So many present did not properly understand the tradition sacramental service. Most did not even come to participate. They did not care about such established forms. The old religion required learning, the assimilation of beliefs and attitudes, and a relatively homogeneous religious community. In the American West, for the first time, Scotch-Irish Presbyterians were losing such homogeneity.

[250] Conkin, *Cane Ridge America's Pentecost*, 166.

[251] Bosch, *Transforming Mission*, 173. Gentile Christians should never lose sight of the fact that Israel is the Matrix of the Eschatological people of God; they should therefore never surrender the continuity of God's story with Israel. The Christian faith is "an extension, or fresh interpretation, of what it meant to be Jewish in the first century. (Kirk 1986:253). The church is not the new Israel (in the sense that God has switched the covenant from unbelieving Jews to Gentile); it is, rather an enlarged Israel. A Gentile Christian existence may never be detached from Israel. Paul explains this with the aid of a metaphor that defies every horticultural practice; the branches of the wild olive tree are graphed "contrary to nature, into the cultivated olive tree.

Endnotes

[252] Dan Gruber, *The Church and the Jews: The Biblical Relationship*. (Hanover, NH.: Elijah Publishing, 1997).401. "Orpah was a loving daughter-in-law but she ended up staying with he own people. Ruth saw something that Orpah did not see. Naomi said, 'Do not call me Naomi (pleasant) call me mara (bitter) for the Almighty has dealt very bitterly with me. I went out full but the Lord has brought me back empty. Why do you call me Naomi, since the Lord has witnessed against me and the Almighty has afflicted me?'" Ruth 1:19-21. It was obvious that the Lord was against Naomi. Just as it was obvious that the Lord was against Job on the ash heap, and Paul when the viper bit him after the ship wreck: Obvious but not true. Despite what people thought, God was not against Naomi, Job, or Paul. Despite what people think, God is NOT against the Jewish people. Ruth, a gentile saw something that Orpah and Naomi missed. She made the same choice that Abraham made. She left her family, her people, and her land behind. She lost her life in order to find it. "Do not urge me to leave me or turn back from following you; for where you go I will go and where you lodge I will lodge. Your people shall be my people and you're God, my God." Ruth 1:16. Naomi's Gentle daughter-in-law Ruth was to be the means of her greatest blessing. God planned it that way. Ruth embraced the Jewish people and God blessed her eternally.

[253] Harold H. Rowdon, *"The Brethren,"* in *Introduction to the History of Christianity*, edited by Tim Dowley, 526.

[254] J. R. Littleproud, *The Christian Assembly* (Glendale, Ca.: Church Press, 1962), 51-84. Based on the "holy priesthood to offer up spiritual sacrifices acceptable to God through Jesus Christ" (1Peter 2:3); and a "royal

Living Inside Out

priesthood …to proclaim the excellencies of him who called you out of darkness into his marvelous light" (1Peter 2:9).

[255] A. P. Gibbs, *Worship: A Christian's Highest Occupation* (Kansas City Ks.: Walterick Publishers).

[256] Foundational texts for understanding dispensationalism include J. Dwight Pentecost, *Things to Come*, (Grand Rapids, MI: Zondervan 1974). And: Lewis Sperry Chafer, *Systematic Theology*, 8 Vol. (Dallas, TX: Dallas Seminary Press, 1947). For a reformed response consider: Curtis I. Crenshaw and Grover E. Gunn, III, *Dispensationalalism Today, Yesterday, and Tomorrow* (Memphis, TN: Footstool Publications, 1987).

[257] Moishe Rosen, *Christ in the Passover*, (Chicago, Il: Moody Press, 1979).

[258] Dan Juster. *Jewish Roots: A Foundation of Biblical Theology* (Shippensburgh, Pa: Destiny Image Publishers, 1995).

[259] David H. Stern, *Messianic Jewish Manifesto* (Clarksville, MD: Jewish New Testament Publications, Inc, 1991), 8.

[260] Richard J. Foster, *Prayer: Finding the Heart's True Home* (San Francisco, CA: Harper Collins Publishers, 1992), 80.

[261] Talmud of Babylon, Taanit 2a. See also: Rabbi Donin and Hayim Halevy, *To Pray as a Jew: A Guide to the Prayer Book and the Synagogue Service* (Grand Rapids, MI: Basic Books/ Harper Collins, 1994), 10.

[262] Foster, *Prayer: Finding the Heart's True Home*, 1.

[263] Foster, *Prayer: Finding the Heart's True Home*, 13.

Endnotes

264 Madam Guyon, *Experiencing the Depths of Jesus Christ* (Goleta, Ca: Christian Books, 1975), 47.

265 Babylonian Talmud: Taanit 2 A.

266 Richard J. Foster, *Devotional Classics: Selected Readings for Individuals and Groups*, edited by James B. Smith (San Francisco: Harper Collins Publishers, 1993), 68-71.

267 Foster, *Devotional Classics*, 71.

268 Arthur W. Pink, *The Sovereignty of God* (Grand Rapids, MI: Baker Book House, 1991), 169.

269 Pink, *The Sovereignty of God*, 176.

270 Psalm 20, 21, 27, 28.

271 C Ralph Spaulding Cushman, *A Pocket Prayer Book and Devotional Guide* (Nashville, TN: Upper Room Publishing, 1969), 21-22.

272 Psalm 27:4.

273 Westminster Confession of Faith, (Glasgow, Scotland: Free Presbyterian Publications, 1985), 129.

274 Deuteronomy 6:5.

275 Paraphrased by this author from a sermon preached by John McArthur in the 1990's.

276 Matthew 16:18.

277 1Corinthians 13:12.

278 Genesis 22:1-18.

279 Exodus 15:26.

Living Inside Out

280 Exodus 17: 8-16.

281 Ann Spangler, *Praying the Names of God* (Grand Rapids, MI: Zondervan, 2004).

282 Rabbi Hayim and Halevy Donin, *To Pray as a Jew: A Guide to the Prayer Book and the Synagogue Service* (Grand Rapids, MI: Basic Books/ Harper Collins, 1994), 5.

283 Foster, *Prayer, Finding the Heart's True Home*, 81.

284 Rabbi Hayim and Donin, *To Pray as a Jew*, 5.

285 1John 1:9.

286 Philippians 4:6-7.

287 Richard Foster, *Prayer: Finding the Heart's True Home*, 9.

288 Pink, Arthur W. *The Sovereignty of God* (Rapids, MI: Baker Book House, 1991), 169.

289 John 14:13, 14; John 15:7, 16; John 16:23.

290 Foster, *Prayer: Finding the Heart's True Home*, 110.

291 Rabbi Hayim and Donin, *To Pray as a Jew*, 21.

292 Hayim and Donin (Sefer Hasidim:11).

293 Mark Galli and Ted Olsen eds. *131 Christians Everyone Should Know* (Nashville, TN: Holman Press, 2007), 157.

294 Foster, *Prayer: Finding the Heart's True Home*, 137-139.

295 Mark A. Noll, *The Rise of Evangelicalism: The Age of Edwards, Whitefield, and the Wesleys* (Downer's Grove, IL: InterVarsity Press, 2004), 97. John Wesley,

Endnotes

A Plain Account of Christian Perfection (Peabody, Ma: Hendrickson Publishers, 2007), xi.

[296] Frank E. Gaebelein, ed. *The Expositor's Bible Commentary*, vol. 12 (Grand Rapids, MI: Zondervan, 1992), 395.

[297] See Rom 5:10 and Col 1:21.

[298] KJV John 7:38 He that believeth on me, as the scripture hath said, out of his belly shall flow rivers of living **water**. KJV Acts 1:5 For John truly baptized with **water**; but ye shall be baptized with the Holy Ghost not many days hence. KJV Acts 11:16 Then remembered I the word of the Lord, how that he said, John indeed baptized with **water**; but ye shall be baptized with the Holy Ghost. KJV Revelation 21:6 And he said unto me, It is done. I am Alpha and Omega, the beginning and the end. I will give unto him that is athirst of the fountain of the **water** of life freely. KJV Revelation 22:1 And he shewed me a pure river of **water** of life, clear as crystal, proceeding out of the throne of God and of the Lamb. KJV Revelation 22:17 And the Spirit and the bride say, Come. And let him that heareth say, Come. And let him that is athirst come. And whosoever will, let him take the **water** of life freely.

CPSIA information can be obtained
at www.ICGtesting.com
Printed in the USA
BVHW072058130423
662304BV00001B/1